550 words to
Boyd Tonkin
by Jan 19. 04

Ernö Goldfinger

Ernö Goldfinger

The life of an architect

Nigel Warburton

Routledge
Taylor & Francis Group
LONDON AND NEW YORK

First published in 2004
by Routledge
11 New Fetter Lane, London EC4P 4EE

Simultaneously published in the USA and Canada
by Routledge
29 West 35th Street, New York, NY 10001

Routledge is an imprint of the Taylor & Francis Group

Typeset in Charter by Florence Production Ltd, Stoodleigh, Devon
Printed and bound in Great Britain by TJ International, Padstow, Cornwall

British Library Cataloguing in Publication Data
A catalogue record for this book is available from the British Library

Library of Congress Cataloging in Publication Data
Warburton, Nigel, 1962–
Ernö Goldfinger: the life of an architect/Nigel Warburton
p. cm.
Includes bibliographical references and index.
1. Goldfinger, Ernö. 2. Architects – Great Britain – Biography.
3. Modern movement (Architecture) – Great Britain. I. Title.
NA997.G62W37 2003
720′.92–dc21 2003011245

ISBN 0–415–25853–7

For my children Hannah and Joshua

Contents

Acknowledgements

Many people have helped me with my research for this book. I am extremely grateful to them all. I am particularly grateful to Peter Goldfinger for giving me permission to quote extensively from his father's writings and from his mother's letters, and to reproduce photographs, as well as for meeting to discuss his father and commenting in detail on a draft of the book. I am also very grateful to Nick Goldfinger for spending many pleasant hours talking about his grandfather and visiting several of his buildings together and for spotting a number of mistakes in my penultimate draft. I would also like to give special thanks to James Dunnett, for his encouragement and advice throughout my research, for his detailed comments, and for letting me see his notes on conversations he had with Goldfinger between 1979 and 1984. I am deeply indebted to Harriet McKay of the National Trust for giving me regular access to the Willow Road house and its amazing collection of art, furniture, papers, personal letters, photographs, books and magazines, and to Eleanor Gawne, RIBA archivist, for helping me to find my way. Helen Langley, Barbara Pezzini and Rebecca Milner all helped me focus my thoughts about Goldfinger, and I benefited greatly from conversations about their research and from their comments on my final draft. My wife Anna Motz's perceptive reading of the final draft helped me eliminate a number of mistakes and tighten the argument in several places. Peter Hamilton was particularly helpful with the illustrations for the book, both in lending me equipment and in taking new photographs. Special thanks also to Melanie Unwin of the National Sound Archive at the British Library. The Architects' Lives series of audio tapes proved invaluable in my research, and I am extremely grateful to the interviewers and contributors to that project. I have also benefited greatly from reading published work by James Dunnett, Gavin Stamp, Alan Powers and Robert Elwall. The careful cataloguing of the frighteningly diverse collection of Goldfinger's papers in the RIBA collection has made my task much easier than it would otherwise have been.

Others who have helped me in the course of writing this book and to whom I am extremely grateful include John Allen, Edward Barber, Tim Benton, Colomb and Lee Boland (who were particularly helpful with my research on Trellick Tower), Caroline Dawnay (my agent), Herbert Edlis,

Emilie, Frances and Ursula Goldfinger, Michelle Green, Judith Hanson, Stephen Law, Caroline Mallinder, Ekka Morgan, Kevin Morgan, Sara Parkin, Mark Pittaway, the late Lotte Motz, Claudia Sotile, Alan Turner, Emma Wildsmith and Simon Willey. Generally my research was made a great deal easier by the efficiency of staff at the RIBA library in London, at the National Sound Archive in the British Library, at the Bodleian Library in Oxford and at the Open University library in Milton Keynes.

Nigel Warburton, Oxford.

Notes on sources

Written material

The principal collection of Goldfinger papers, drawings and models is currently held by RIBA, though it is in the process of being transferred to the Victoria and Albert Museum. The National Trust 2 Willow Road collection includes numerous photographs, letters, books, magazines and other artifacts. The National Sound Archive's Architects' Lives, housed in the British Library, includes many hours of material relevant to anyone doing research on Goldfinger: the CADENSA online catalogue gives details of the relevant tapes. These are the three main archival sources I have used.

There have been a dedicated issue of *Architectural Design*, three books and a pamphlet about Goldfinger and his work. I have benefited greatly from these. They are:

Architectural Design, *1924–1962 Ernö Goldfinger*, January 1963.
Major Máté, *Goldfinger Ernö*, Budapest: Akadémia Kiadó, 1973 [in Hungarian].
James Dunnett and Gavin Stamp, *Ernö Goldfinger: Works 1*, London: Architectural Association, 1983.
Robert Elwall, *Ernö Goldfinger*, RIBA Drawings Monograph 3, London: Academy Editions, 1996.
Alan Powers, *2 Willow Road Hampstead*, pamphlet, London: The National Trust, 1996.

The RIBA catalogue of the manuscript material also contains a wealth of information about Goldfinger:

Jane Collings with the assistance of Andrea Meyer Ludowisz 'The Ernö Goldfinger Papers: A Descriptive List', unpublished catalogue, the British Architectural Library, Royal Institute of British Architects, 1997.

Illustrations

The photographers whose work illustrates this book include Bill Brandt, Dale and Ewbank, André Kertész, Sam Lambert, Colin Penn, and Man Ray. The author and publisher would like to thank these individuals and organizations for permission to reproduce material.

We have made every effort to contact and acknowledge copyright holders, but if any errors have been made we would be happy to correct tham at a later printing.

I am very grateful to Peter Goldfinger for giving permission to use Goldfinger's own photographs and to the National Trust for providing access to the 2 Willow Road collection.

I am particulary grateful to Peter Hamilton for supplying the photographs that illustrate Chapter Ten.

Ernö Goldfinger's life – key dates

1902	11 September, born in Budapest
1902–08	Brought up in Szazyregen in Southern Carpathians
1912–19	Attends Gymnasium in Budapest
1919	Vienna, attending Schotten Gymnasium
1919–20	Attends the Rosay school in Gstaad, Switzerland
1920–34	Moves to Paris
1922–3	Attends Atelier Jaussely
1922–4	Joins École Nationale Supérieure des Beaux-Arts. Takes part in the formation of the Atelier Perret
1926	Designs Helena Rubinstein salon in London with André Sive
1931	Marries Ursula Blackwell
1933	French delegate to the CIAM conference in Athens. First building: studio for house at Le Touquet
1934	Settles in London
1937	House at Broxted
1939	Moves into 2 Willow Road, Hampstead, the house he designed for his family
1940	His two young children evacuated to Canada
1941–44	Writes on the art of enclosing space. 'Aid to Russia' exhibition. Designs numerous wartime exhibitions
1945	*The County of London Plan Explained* published
1947	*Daily Worker* Building, London
1954	Flats, Regent's Park Road
1956	Albermarle Street office building
1959	Alexander Fleming House
1963	Odeon Cinema, Elephant and Castle
1965	Balfron Tower, Rowlett Street Housing
1973	Trellick Tower, Edenham Street Housing
1977	Retires
1983	Work exhibited at the Architectural Association, London
1987	15 November, dies at home in Hampstead

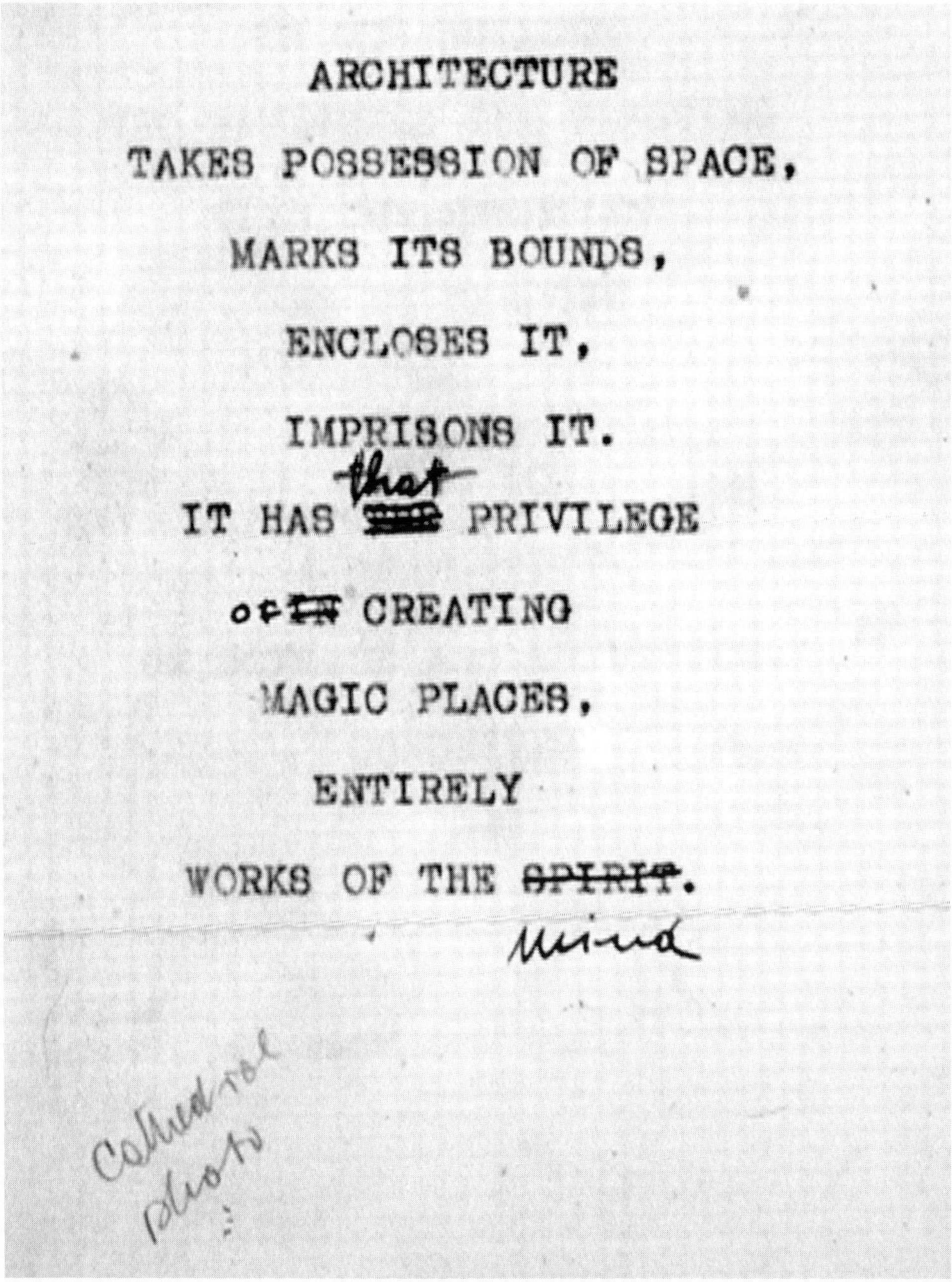

ARCHITECTURE

TAKES POSSESSION OF SPACE,

MARKS ITS BOUNDS,

ENCLOSES IT,

IMPRISONS IT.

IT HAS that PRIVILEGE

of CREATING

MAGIC PLACES,

ENTIRELY

WORKS OF THE ~~SPIRIT~~. mind

Cathedral photo

Page from Goldfinger's translation of Auguste Perret's aphorisms

Introduction

The real Goldfinger

For most people Goldfinger is the name of James Bond's enemy. He is Auric Goldfinger, the eponymous villain in Ian Fleming's novel. Surprisingly, the architect Ernö Goldfinger was the source of the name, if not the character. The question of how Fleming's villain got his name is the one I've been asked most often while researching this book, so I've included my account in this introduction to save journalists and reviewers the need to read any further.

In March 1959, Fleming's book *Goldfinger* was in press. Ernö somehow got to hear about it. Fleming often used the names of friends and acquaintances for characters. In this case John Blackwell, a cousin of Goldfinger's wife Ursula Blackwell, was a friend of Fleming's. They played golf together regularly at the St George's golf club in Sandwich and Fleming would occasionally come to stay with Blackwell. At some point Blackwell had discussed the architect Goldfinger with Fleming, and the name had appealed as suitably villainous.[1] One story is that Fleming, who for a time lived in Hampstead, disliked Goldfinger's terrace of houses in Willow Road and, in schoolboy fashion, saw the use of the name as a way of getting even. There is no evidence to support this account. Whatever the explanation, Ernö Goldfinger was undoubtedly the source of the character's surname and Fleming never denied this.

In the novel, Goldfinger threatens the economic stability of the Western world by accumulating huge quantities of gold and passing them to the Russians. Although obsessed with gold to the point of painting women from head to toe with it, Goldfinger's motivation is not pure avarice: he is idealistic. He is working for SMERSH, a fictional agency furthering Soviet aims by devious means. James Bond, predictably, thwarts Goldfinger's attempt to steal the gold from Fort Knox and by the end of the novel has even managed to convert the lesbian Pussy Galore to heterosexuality.

A character called John Blackwell, 'a pleasant-spoken Import and Export merchant' living in Mexico with a sister who was a heroin addict in England, makes a brief appearance in chapter one of the book. The real golf professional at the Sandwich club, Albert Whiting also becomes Albert

Blacking. So it would have been difficult for Fleming to maintain that the connection between characters' names and the Blackwells and Goldfingers was coincidental. Furthermore, Fleming had already irritated (and occasionally flattered) several acquaintances by borrowing their names.[2] The character 'Boofy', for example, a villain in *Diamonds are Forever*, got his name from 'Boofy' Gore (later the Earl of Arran), a relative of his wife's by marriage. Boofy had not been amused.[3] Nor was Goldfinger. On hearing that his name was to be taken in vain in this way, his response was 'Shall we sue?'

Goldfinger's solicitors, Davenport, Lyons and Company, sent him a pre-publication copy of the novel with all descriptions of the character marked. Ernö brought it into the office one morning and asked his associate Jacob Blacker whether he agreed that Goldfinger ought to sue: 'Read the book and tell me whether it's true or not!' Blacker came in the next morning and Goldfinger duly asked him what he thought. Blacker's ironic response was that he could only find one substantial difference between him and Fleming's character: 'You're called Ernö and he's called Auric!'[4]

This is how Auric Goldfinger is first described: 'You won't believe it, but he's a Britisher. Domiciled in Nassau. You'd think he'd be a Jew from the name, but he doesn't look it.'[5] There are, though, relatively few resemblances between the character Goldfinger and the architect. This was typical of Fleming's use of names, as his friend Ivar Bryce, whose name Fleming also used, remarked:

> He took immense trouble with names and plots, although the names sometimes came before the plots. He enjoyed using the names of his friends, or even those whom he knew only slightly. [. . .] But it was the names alone which he used, for in most cases the characters bore no resemblance to their real-life originals.[6]

Auric, for example, was no more than five feet tall, whereas Ernö was six feet two. Yet both were naturalised émigrés, and both possessed fast cars. On the other hand, modernist architecture in Britain had often been attacked as a foreign import, as 'Modernismus', and Goldfinger would have been alert to the typecasting of the foreigner, the outsider, as villain. There was also the implicit anti-Semitism in the novel, giving a Jewish-sounding name to a character obsessed with gold. Perhaps Ernö was sensitive about having his name associated with villainy at all; perhaps it was the link with Russia that worried him, given that he was a Marxist and had spent a significant part of the Second World War raising money for the Soviet cause and had later worked on both the *Daily Worker* building and the Communist Party Headquarters in London. During the Cold War this was probably not something that he wanted to remind at least some of his potential clients.[7]

Goldfinger went ahead and instructed his solicitors to take action against the publishers Jonathan Cape who, fearing that they might have to pulp the whole edition, agreed out of court to a number of conditions.[8] These included undertaking to make clear in all advertising for the book that this was a work of fiction; that wherever possible the character would be referred to as 'Auric Goldfinger' rather than just 'Goldfinger'; and that in any future printing of the book a note would be inserted to the effect that all the characters were fictitious and no reference was intended to any person living or dead (a condition which hasn't been respected in the version of the book currently in print).[9] Most significantly, Jonathan Cape agreed to pay costs. They also delivered six free copies of the book to Willow Road.

Jonathan Cape's concessions to Goldfinger in turn enraged Fleming who wanted the publisher to insert an erratum slip in the book, changing the name throughout to Goldprick (a name originally suggested by Cyril Connolly) and explaining why the name had been changed.[10] It is unlikely, though, that Goldfinger's reputation was damaged by the book's publication. However, the release of *Goldfinger* the film in late 1964 *did* have an impact on his life. For weeks afterwards he was woken in the middle of the night by practical jokers who would call and hiss into the phone in a bad impersonation of Sean Connery, 'Goldfinger? This is Agent 007 . . .'[11] or else start to sing the film's theme tune – an irritation still endured by members of the family who list their name in the telephone directory. The only long-term consequence for Ernö, as he once wryly remarked to an interviewer, was that he never again had to repeat his name when first introduced.[12]

Even his friends acknowledge that the real Goldfinger could be something of a bully – albeit a charming one. But he was no villain. Indeed he is emerging as a hero of modernist architecture despite being described as 'no more than a pimple on the rump of Wren' by Brian Sewell[13] and one of his best-known buildings, Trellick Tower, being disparaged by Roger Scruton as embodying a 'contemptuous conception of life's value'.[14] Though Sewell and Scruton might find support from Prince Charles (in later years Goldfinger kept a caricature of Prince Charles pinned to the wall of his study), most of those who have lived in buildings designed by Goldfinger know that his success as an architect goes far beyond creating external forms which are pleasing (or, to some, repellent) to the eye of architectural historians. Some inhabitants of his buildings still rail against him, but in most cases the blame for the buildings' shortcomings lies with those charged with maintaining and servicing them rather than with the architect. Once vilified as the champion of high-rise living, he is now, for the most part, admired for his integrity and his adherence to his own fundamental values in the teeth of harsh criticism. A repeated victim of town planners' commitment to what I have dubbed the

'Prince Charles Fallacy' – the misguided notion that the only buildings which should be allowed to be built are those that look more or less like the buildings already in the area – Goldfinger never wavered in his commitment to rational design.

When roused, Goldfinger could be a tyrant. He was a larger-than-life eccentric who made a deep impression on everyone who met him. Journalists would report him as literally larger than life: he was on several occasions described as being six feet five inches tall, even though he was six feet two.[15] Inevitably, word about his volatile temper and outbursts spread around the profession. Once those who worked with him overcame their fear, though, most seemed on balance to have gained from the experience: a surprisingly large number of architects pay tribute to his brilliance as a teacher and feel that they learnt most of what they know about the profession in his office.

My motivation for writing this book was my experience of living in two of Goldfinger's buildings – Balfron Tower and the Motz House. In both cases, I was there more or less by chance. Reading about Goldfinger, I became fascinated by the man, his connections, and his vision of architecture.

In writing the book I have assumed, but not laboured, an 'auteur' theory. This is an idea borrowed from 1950s film theory. It is the view that great artists stamp their artistic personality on all their work, major and minor. Even when working within the constraints of the Hollywood film industry, John Ford or Alfred Hitchcock were in control of what happened to such an extent that we can meaningfully talk of their individual style. The usual criticism of such an approach to film is that it underestimates the degree to which camera operators, actors, prevailing market forces, studio policies, and so on, all shaped the finished product. Analogously, in architecture, engineers, planning regulations, budgets, builders and clients' whims might all be considered major factors in the creation of a building, factors which in most cases where the architect is working to a tight brief can predominate, and so work against the notion that an architect has achieved a freely chosen style.

I wouldn't want to defend the idea that major architects necessarily express a personal style in all their work, no matter what it is. In Goldfinger's case, though, the strength and consistency of his personality, his unwillingness to compromise on matters he thought important, together with his pragmatic policy of re-using successful features of earlier designs with only minor modifications, have resulted in a remarkable consistency of approach throughout a lifetime. He really did get his way on most issues, and as a result his buildings are stamped with his architectural personality, even when he was working within severe budgetary constraints. If the style of his buildings seems to change substantially over time, much of this is due to his being given larger projects, such as Alexander Fleming House, and the Balfron and Trellick towers, rather than to a radical shift in his approach to building. Many of the features of his 1960s tower blocks were already present in a drawing he did for the Congrès International d'Architecture Moderne (CIAM) cruise to Athens in 1933, a drawing which pre-dated and anticipated a number of aspects of high-rise living that Le Corbusier used in his famous Unité d'Habitation in Marseilles. It was only some thirty years after presenting his CIAM project that Goldfinger was given the opportunity to build tall apartment buildings.

While I am unapologetic about using an approach that is now considered passé in film studies, I don't want to be considered guilty of defending what might be called the 'fallacy of architectural omnipotence'.[16] (An alternative name might be the 'Goldfinger fallacy', so often was he subject to it in his lifetime, but this name might be taken to imply that he was the perpetrator rather than the victim.) This is the obviously absurd idea unique to opponents of modern architecture that whatever happens in and to a modern building is somehow all the architect's responsibility and fault. In contrast, what happens in an older building has nothing to do with the architect. So, for example, if drug dealers and violent criminals are active in a tower block, those who are tempted by the fallacy of ominipotence will blame the architect; when similar activities take place in a Victorian terrace, the buildings are rarely mentioned. If the council neglects the servicing of a boiler in a large block, and the heating system breaks down, ultimately the architect must be to blame.

Clearly, large social housing projects shape how people live. And any architect with a conscience will do everything possible to design such projects in a way that will increase the likelihood of their inhabitants leading happy lives. But the architect is often powerless to affect the local authority policies on upkeep, amenities, security and policing of large estates. Take the case of drug dealing on the staircases of tower blocks. This can be minimised by having a concierge system, something that Goldfinger always advocated; but it takes a local authority to institute such a feature. Such factors determine the quality of people's lives at least as much as the design of the buildings. The architect, nevertheless, gets blamed for much that is completely outside his or her control. Critics of high-rise living have frequently resorted to this fallacy of architectural omnipotence, and Goldfinger as the architect of tower blocks on the Edenham Estate in Tower Hamlets, and Goldborne Road in Notting Hill has often been targeted in this way, both in his lifetime and posthumously. At times the architects of tower blocks have been decried as the source of all social ills in London. Yet the reasoning of those who make these claims is often risibly fallacious.

While I hope that architectural historians will be interested in this book, I have written it with a more general readership in mind, and have tried not to presuppose knowledge of architects, buildings and theories. I have also tried to avoid turning this into simple hagiography, though, after two years immersing myself in the man and his work, I confess that I think there is something both revealing and true in his immodest declaration:

> There are good and bad architects. I am a good architect.

Notes

1 This is Peter Goldfinger's view. It is consistent with Ernö's own comments, recorded in James Dunnett, Conversations with Ernö Goldfinger, unpublished notes, 29/8/79. In César Garçon's 'Goldfinger' [in French], *City*, no. 17, December 1985, pp.92–6 (a copy of which is in the National Trust 2 Willow Road collection), the author of the article suggests that Ernö met Fleming on a Scottish golf course. This is certainly not true.

2 Andrew Lycett compares Goldfinger the architect with Goldfinger the villain on p.329 of *Ian Fleming*, London: Phoenix, 1995. He claims that Auric liked large cigars while Ernö hated smoking. In fact it was Ernö who smoked cigars (see cover photograph of this book) and Auric who hated smoking.

3 Described in Lycett 1995, p.289.

4 Jacob Blacker on F8112, National Sound Archive, Architect's Lives series of audits tapes, see Note on sources.

5 Ian Fleming, *Goldfinger*, London: Coronet, 1989, [1959], p.21.

6 Ivar Bryce, *You Only Live Once: Memories of Ian Fleming*. London: Weidenfeld & Nicolson, 1984, p.97.

7 As late as 1983 he crossed out a paragraph about the Communist Party Headquarters that James Dunnett had written on a draft essay for the book that accompanied the Architectural Association exhibition in the same year and also the line 'unlike his sometime collaborators he never joined the Communist Party' in Gavin Stamp's draft essay for the same publication. See GolEr 399/1, RIBA catalogue of Goldfinger's papers, see Notes on sources p.189.

8 Letter from Davenport, Lyons, and Co. Solicitors, 3 March 1959 in RIBA, GolEr 268/4.

9 Ian Fleming, 1989 [1959].

10 Described in Lycett, 1995. p.345.

11 Mentioned in an article about Liz Goldfinger's furniture, Miriam Maisel 'Furniture You Can Post' *Oxford Mail*, 15 June 1966.

12 *Martins Bank Magazine* vol. 23, no. 3, autumn 1968 p.3.

13 Brian Sewell, 'Let's Kill Off Ernö's Sad Eyesore', *Evening Standard*, 20 September 1993, p.32.

14 Roger Scruton, *The Classical Vernacular*, London: Carcanet, 1994, p.127.

15 See, for example, Lewis Chester 'High and Mighty' *Guardian Weekend*, 16 July 1994, where he is as described as '6ft 5in tall in his socks'.

16 I am grateful to James Dunnett for drawing my attention to this style of reasoning in relation to Goldfinger's buildings.

Chapter 1

Foundations

Don't teach me![1]

Ernö's earliest memory, suitably architectural and an early lesson in rational design, was of a large glass door, some two metres high, falling off its hinges on top of him. He was just three. Fortunately he emerged unscathed.

Born in Budapest on 11 September 1902, he spent his first six years in Szazyregen, in the Translyvanian valleys of the Southern Carpathians, the birthplace of his mother Regine (née Haiman). His father, Dr Oscar Goldfinger, was a wealthy Jewish lawyer who had practised in Vienna, his grandfather the vice president of a bank. His father's family owned large forests in Poland and his mother's family also had forests and sawmills and a flour mill on the river. Despite this privileged capitalist pedigree (or perhaps because of it) Ernö was a Marxist for all his adult life.

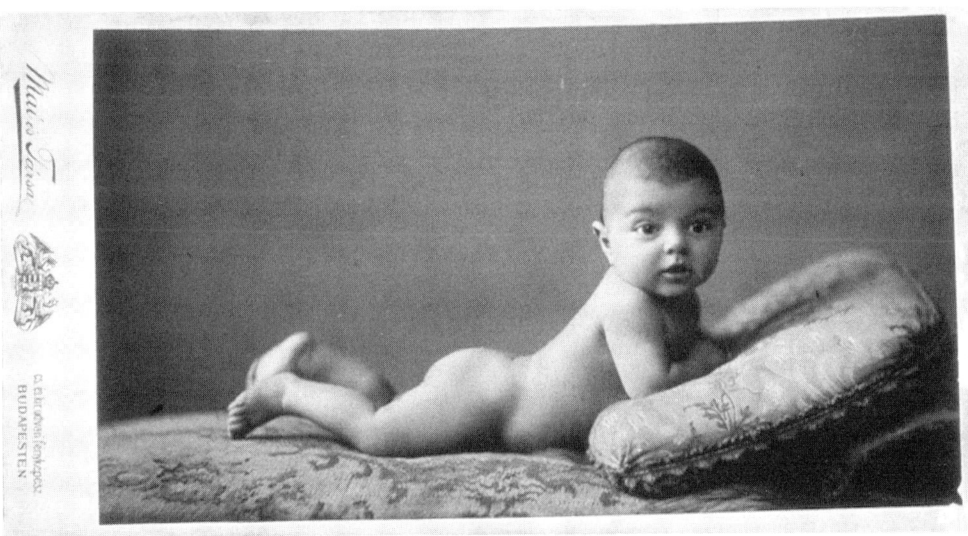

1.1
Young Ernö,
Budapest, 1903

1.2
Ernö with rocking horse c.1904

His first years were lived in a world of horse-drawn carriages, steam engines and paddle steamers. There was no piped water, and lighting was by oil lamps. His family had a coachman, a nanny and servants. His first language was German, but he spoke Hungarian with the coachman – he was officially forbidden to go to the stables, but in fact spent most of his time there. Like many of his compatriots, he never lost his accent, despite spending many more years away from Hungary than living in it.

In 1907, his father's eldest brother presented Ernö with two ponies and a scaled-down pony cart, an event which he remembered well. In a photograph from that year he and his younger brother pose like young royalty on the carriage with his nanny dourly looking on from the doorway. The ponies were indirectly a perk for his father – a small compensation for being brought away from his law practice to help supervise the family forests. Another early memory, from about 1908, was of being taken to the Budapest racecourse to see some of the first aeroplanes, probably the Wright brothers' planes. In the midst of the proceedings, while eating a ham roll, Ernö managed to swallow a tooth. He was whisked away from his grandfather's box in a carriage driven by Lajos the coachman, an event so exciting for the young boy that it erased

1.3
Ernö with his younger brother and nanny, Transylvania

all memory of the aeroplanes.[2] By the time of Ernö's death in 1987, men had walked on the moon, and an unmanned craft had landed on Mars.

In 1908 the Goldfingers returned to Budapest in order to give their three sons, Ernö, George and Paul, a better education.[3] They lived in an apartment near the Houses of Parliament, above the Consulate-General of Japan. Ernö had a private tutor to improve his Hungarian and also attended a primary school. When he got home each afternoon he would explain to his mother whatever he'd learnt that day. 'Don't teach me!' she would chide him – a phrase she found useful in dealing with him throughout her life. The first germs of what many saw as an overbearing didacticism – his 'invisible soapbox'[4] – are present in this childhood scene.

Each summer he'd spend a month in the forests and saw mills in Transylvania, and a month in the Austrian Alps, or at Istria on the Adriatic. The family spent the summer of 1910 on the Lido of Venice, leaving him with clear memories of the Piazza without the Campanile (it had collapsed) – and the evocative smell of the vaporetti.[5] The pattern for travel was set early, and it was one he continued throughout his life. By the time he applied for a job with the BBC Overseas Service in 1941 he could declare a complete command of four languages (German, Hungarian, French, English – the last two with a strong accent), and that he had travelled in most European countries, as well as Turkey, Egypt, Palestine and North Africa.[6]

From 1912 to 1919, Ernö attended the local Gymnasium in Budapest (the name for an elite high school, analogous to a British grammar school). His anglophile parents employed a private English tutor, a Mr P.H. Redmond, who visited twice a week, though at this stage Ernö's English was shaky, and he never quite mastered English spelling. Life did not go smoothly at school for the young Ernö. To move up a class he needed to pass an examination at the end of each year. Failure was deeply shameful. In 1911 the unthinkable happened: Ernö failed geography, an event that haunted him for the rest of his life. Sixty years later, he still felt a deep sense of grievance: 'This imbecile failed me!' As a result he had to spend the summer in his grandmother's house in Transylvania being coached.[7] His situation wasn't helped by the academic brilliance of his brothers, George and Paul, both of whom went on to be professors of physical chemistry. Ernö's main consolation at the time was that he was a better horseman than either of them. Nevertheless, throughout his life his mother taunted him with his brothers' successes. In later years he felt that she had never truly recognised his own achievements. She always saw the merits of his brothers' academic accolades, and he worked hard for her to recognise just how successful he was. This pattern was set early on, and – in her eyes – the successes of George and Paul would always eclipse Ernö's. His powerful drive that some took for arrogance in part stemmed from a small boy's desire for his mother's approval. The glimpse of the young Ernö teaching his mother what he had learnt that day in school in a desperate attempt to convince her that he was as bright as his brothers is illuminating.

When the First World War broke out in August 1914, Ernö was in Transylvania on his maternal grandfather's estate. He had to return to Budapest to say farewell to his father, who immediately went on to Vienna to volunteer for active service. From then on the summer routine changed: still a month in Transylvania, within earshot of guns on the Russian Front.[8] But the second month was spent wherever Goldfinger senior was posted – in Silesia or Poland. For the young Ernö this was a great adventure since he could ride his father's army horses and meet the fellow officers.[9]

In 1916 in Budapest he witnessed the inauspicious coronation of Charles, who proclaimed himself both King of Hungary (known as Károly IV) and Emperor of Austria (known as Karl I). Ernö got a permit to attend from the Boy Scouts and joined the throng. The ceremony involved the newly-crowned king riding a white charger at a gallop up a mound made from soil from the fifty counties of Hungary, pointing his sword to the north, south, east and west. This action was supposed to be imbued with symbolic power, but what Goldfinger saw was a man with a very small head and a crown that wobbled. This felt like a bad omen.[10] Charles was the last of the Habsburg emperors.

In 1916, Ernö's paternal grandfather died. Oscar Goldfinger bought out his brothers and sisters (they were a family of fifteen children) and took over the family saw mills and the forests. He was released from the army and returned to Transylvania to take on this important business. Ernö's uncles and cousins remained on the various front lines. Significantly, his father also bought a house on the southern slopes of Mount Gellert, outside Budapest, overlooking the Danube. The plan was to rebuild it. He commissioned an architect, a M. Agoston, to carry out the job, who, in order to stimulate his clients' interest in architecture, presented them with a copy of Hermann Muthesius's three volume *Das Englische Haus* (*The English House*). Muthesius had been attaché at the Imperial German Embassy in London from 1896 to 1903, and had been commissioned to survey British architecture and design. The book that he produced, published in 1904–5, praised the houses built by the English Arts and Crafts movement. His mother wasn't interested in the book, and his father was far too busy to spend time looking at it, but it stimulated the young Ernö. It did not persuade the Goldfingers to build in the English style, but it became the main focus of Ernö's interest.[11]

He kept these volumes all his life. It was Muthesius's book, at least in retrospect, which sparked Ernö's fascination with architecture, and at some level perhaps connected England in his mind with what was to become his obsession. Visits from a Hungarian architect friend of the family may also have put architecture in his mind as a possible career. The impact of Muthesius's book was long-lasting: as late as 1965 Ernö was still recommending it as 'the most fundamental book on British domestic architecture'.[12]

Ernö had originally considered a career in engineering. He had been thrilled and moved by the sounds and power of machinery in his family's saw mills. Then sculpture seemed a possibility. He never lost his passion for fine art, which may explain the ease with which he mingled with and befriended on equal terms many of the major painters, photographers and sculptors of his day. Soon, though, his focus was exclusively on a career in architecture – as he later put it, houses were more interesting than heads.[13] Architecture combined the scientific and the aesthetic in ways that peculiarly suited his temperament, and indeed combined engineering with sculpture.[14] It was while his father's new house was being built that Ernö saw architects' plans for the first time: 'marvellous plans in yellow and red'. He was hooked.

Ernö was in Budapest in 1918 and witnessed the October revolution at first hand. He took numerous photographs of the demonstrations. The collapse of the Austro-Hungarian empire affected him deeply, though unlike many of his compatriots, he did not suffer food shortages or other deprivations. At the time he didn't understand the full implication of what was happening and when, in 1919, Budapest fell to the communists and his family left for Vienna, he naively wanted to return to his homeland. The family, however, had left for its own security. The political situation was fragile.

During his eight months in Vienna in 1919, Ernö began drawing. His family found him a private tutor, who visited the *pension* where they were staying twice a week. He studied the human figure, though not at that time the nude. At some point his mother threw out his early drawings, which he regretted. Perhaps in reaction or, more likely, out of a sense of his own place in history, from then on he kept and stored almost every sketch, note, diary entry, letter, press cutting, drawing or photograph he ever made or was sent. He eventually passed many of them on to the Royal Institute of British Architecture (RIBA), where they fill more than five hundred boxes in its archives, archives which could provide social historians who are prepared to rummage through them with many insights into the minutiae of an architect's life in the mid-twentieth century, ranging from his correspondence with many of the great architects and artists of his day, to where and how frequently he bought drawing pins and photographic film. Many papers are also still in his house at 2 Willow Road, Hampstead, which is now owned by the National Trust.

In Vienna he attended the Schotten Gymnasium, where he had an inspiring mathematics teacher. Mathematics was one of his favourite subjects and he had a passion and great aptitude for geometry. Already he was developing the combination of skills that would form the basis of his professional life. Between 1919 and 1920 he was sent to a private boarding school in Switzerland – the Rosay school in Gstaad. Here the teaching was in French, but he did not achieve fluency. For the most part he threw himself into physical activities, learning to ski and row. School photographs show him as a tall powerful-looking youth, who was clearly thriving.

In Budapest, Béla Kun's Soviet republic did not receive the support of the people. There was a counter-revolution leading to the 'white' government and eventually to Miklós Horthy's virtual dictatorship of Hungary. The 'white' government introduced the most extreme anti-Semitic laws in Europe – not surpassed until the Nazi laws of the 1930s. As an Austro-Hungarian Jew, Oscar Goldfinger would not have been permitted to keep his commission in the army; however, he had been born in Galicia, which after the Trianon treaty of 1919 became part of Poland. By retaining his Polish nationality, Oscar was able to keep his commission, despite being Jewish. Ernö, as the son of a Pole, was officially Polish himself, a nationality that he maintained until he became a naturalised British citizen in 1947.

In 1920, Goldfinger was ready to begin his studies. He was sent to France by his family in a twentieth-century substitute for the European Grand Tour. The original idea was that he should stay with relatives in Paris and learn some French, but, as he put it later, 'I went for a fortnight and stayed fourteen years.'[15] By this time, the adolescent Ernö had developed into a handsome man with an air of confidence and inner conviction. His thick eyebrows and dark eyes suggested intensity, poetry and passion.

The Paris that he came to in 1920 was very different from the Paris of today. It was surrounded by fortifications and slums; the Boulevard Haussmann hadn't been completed. The quays on the Seine bustled with industrial activity. He was fascinated by the masonry yards around the Quai D'Orsay: the stone from which the Paris buildings were constructed was shipped down the Seine from Burgundy then dragged by teams of horses, sometimes as many as twenty-four pulling together, taking the stones to the building sites. Opposite the Tuileries Gardens were floating swimming baths. Further up the river, by Notre Dame, were the *clochards*, the down-and-outs, meths drinkers photographed by Goldfinger's contemporaries (who became his friends): André Kertész (then still known as Andor) and Bill Brandt. This was not the romantic Paris of weekend breaks: as he later put it 'The romantic idea of loving couples promenading on the quays is of course absolute hooey.'[16]

He began to learn French, staying with his cousin Hélène Bernheim on the rue Libson. Hélène was the same age as Goldfinger's mother. She was related by marriage to Jean Dalsace, and knew Pierre Chareau and Jean Lurçat (the tapestry maker – brother of the architect André Lurçat) and so Goldfinger mingled early on with some of the most significant members of the architectural, artistic and literary avant garde. Jean Dalsace was a well-known gynaecologist, but more significantly for Goldfinger, he was the patron of Pierre Chareau the designer and architect who with Bernard Bijvoët later converted and furnished the famous Maison de Verre (built 1928–32) for him. His family connections were literary as well as artistic and architectural: in his first year in Paris, for example, Ernö met the writer Anatole France.

Soon Ernö began to take steps towards becoming an architect. Finding a teacher didn't prove difficult given his family's connections. Léon Jaussely, a *Prix de Rome* originally from Toulouse, was recommended. He had an atelier near the Beaux-Arts school on the third floor of 15 Rue Debussy: 'I presented myself little-knowing what ordeals that entailed.'[17]

The École Nationale Supérieure des Beaux Arts provided the most prestigious architectural training France could offer. The Beaux-Arts was the main French art school with a tradition stretching back to the seventeenth century. Manet, Renoir and Monet had all studied there. Its architectural programme provided a technical training of a very high standard, albeit in a traditional vein. But the Beaux-Arts also administered the important annual *Grand Prix de Rome*. Entrants to this competition had to design a public building specified by the committee; the winner received a scholarship from the state to study in Rome for four years. More importantly, though, the prize guaranteed professional success and the likelihood of being elected to the architectural academy that judged the *Prix de Rome*.

Goldfinger, who in some ways was a victim of the system, nevertheless described the Beaux-Arts as 'the most democratic school ever.'[18] The theoretical teaching was provided by the Beaux-Arts itself, and took the form of lectures, given by professors from the Sorbonne, and other institutes, including the École Polytechnique, which trained military engineers, and the École Ponts-et-Chaussées, which was the main state school for civil engineers. But the intensive practical work was all carried out in ateliers. There might be between fifteen and twenty of these at any one time and each would house approximately twenty students at various stages in their studies. The students ran these ateliers: they hired their own *chef d'atelier*. Each atelier was a self-governing independent organisation. Students worked on projects in their ateliers, visited frequently by their *chef*, and then sent their work in anonymously for the Beaux-Arts jury to consider. Each student had to submit two projects a year, whether these were accepted or not. Graduation required them to achieve a certain number of *valeurs*, accepted projects, before the age of thirty. Among his fellow pupils in the Atelier Jaussely, van Eesteren and Pinot both went on to distinguished careers. Van Eesteren became the Chief

1.4
Atelier Jaussely, c.1922 – Ernö is third from right holding stove pipe

Architect of Amsterdam, and Pinot became professor of town planning at Dalad University in Indochina.[19]

Jaussely, Goldfinger's first architectural teacher, was also a professor of archaeology at the Beaux-Arts. 'Professor of archaeology' was the title then used for architectural historians. But he didn't teach the history of architecture. His special interest was urbanism, the philosophy of town planning. Jaussely had been responsible for having Raymond Unwin's[20] writings translated into French, by an American student in his atelier. Goldfinger, along with two or three other pupils, was inspired by Jaussely's teaching, which was based on Unwin's philosophy of planning, increasing the quality of life through rational design. At the time, in the Beaux-Arts, this approach to architecture was considered a novelty.

When Goldfinger began his studies in the Atelier Jaussely he was a *nouveau*, a new boy. Sophisticated as Beaux-Arts graduates may seem now at a distance, the ethos of the atelier was much like that of *Tom Brown's schooldays*, as Goldfinger later recalled:

> The *nouveau* is a fag like in English public schools, a fag. All the wrath of the older boys is visited on him.

This wrath took various forms. There was one particularly humiliating form of punishment for any *nouveau* who made a mistake, a punishment which, presumably, at some time Ernö endured. The culprit would be 'undressed and painted various colours and various parts of you stuck together with glue'.[21] When he eventually ran his own office, though there is no record of his resorting to this use of paint and glue, he carried on this tradition of humiliation. He would often stride across the office to tear up an assistant's drawing if it showed the slightest error or deviation from the brief, and he would harangue the unfortunate victim at full and terrifying volume backed up by his imposing physical presence. The source of this bullying may have been his own experience as a bullied *nouveau* in the classic cycle of the victim revisiting his suffering on others.

Interactions between students were not all at this level. There was horseplay in the atelier too. For example, Ernö and his friends played an imaginative practical joke on one unwitting colleague. Each day they dropped casual comments to their victim about how his head looked strangely large. Meanwhile, before he left the workshop each evening, they slipped a layer of paper inside his hat band so that his hat began to feel tighter and tighter, apparently due to this swelling of his head . . .[22]

The annual Bal Des Quat'z Arts was a major event, the equivalent of an Oxbridge May Ball. Students wore fancy dress, and there was intense rivalry between the various ateliers. Photographs, posed by tradition at dawn

1.5
Ernö, Paris, 1920s

outside the Beaux-Arts building, show that Ernö attended the 1921 Bal dressed in a loincloth and fully blacked-up, towering over most of his contemporaries. He was clearly enjoying the social opportunities opened up by his move to Paris.

Goldfinger was studying for the admission, the first level of entry to the Beaux-Arts. He studied geometry, statics, mathematics and, his favourite subject, stereotomy – 'the most fascinating study I have ever undertaken.' Stereotomy is an eighteenth-century French invention: it is the study of the cutting of stone and wood.

Entry to the next level at the Beaux-Arts was by competition. It took Goldfinger two years studying under Jaussely's supervision to gain a place. He had to pass written examinations in history, chemistry, physics and mathematics, and to present a project:

> I failed once, and the second time I got in. Some people failed as many times as twenty times. I had a colleague who was still there from before the 1914 war – in between he was a soldier. But he was still trying to get in.[23]

Goldfinger's entry project for his first attempt at entry in February 1922 was a drawing of a covered loggia. His second, successful, project, presented in June of the same year was of an entrance to a catacomb designed in the Doric style. His choice of style for the drawing was given by the fact that he happened to have a book featuring Greek Doric columns in his pocket. He was also fortunate with the history paper. He'd picked up a copy of the Koran in Munich on his journey from Budapest to Paris. The subject of Muhammad was a gift for him on this paper

For the second class of the Beaux-Arts training, Goldfinger needed eight *valeurs* and eight *mentions*. The system demanded that for each project students produced a sketch, which they deposited at the Beaux-Arts. They then had two months in which to work up the detail at their atelier. Ernö sailed through this stage of the training without failing a single project. He was in the final stage of the Beaux-Arts system, had already achieved two *valeurs*, and had already taped his first white hair into his diary,[24] when he began to feel the full force of the Modern Movement in architecture. At this point, along with a group of his fellow students, he chose the difficult rather than the easy path.

Notes

1 The quotations opening each chapter in this book are all from Goldfinger.

2 Source: card dated 13 January, 'Recollections' RIBA file GolEr/397/.

3 Goldfinger, interviewed for Hungarian television, transcript in National Trust 2 Willow Road collection.

4 A phrase used by Iris Strachan to describe his approach to conversation in an interview for the National Sound Archive's Architects' Lives series, interviewed by Corinne Julius on 10/05/00, tape F8943, side B.

5 From Gavin Stamp, 'Conversation with Ernö Goldfinger' *Thirties Society Journal*, no. 2, 1982, p.19.

6 His CV is in RIBA file GolEr/266/4. Despite the impressive CV he didn't get a job with the BBC, possibly because of his connections with members of the Communist Party.

7 Source: Interview with Peter Dacey, Dan Cruickshank, James Dunnett, for the *Architectural Review*, transcript in RIBA file GolEr 397/3.

8 Stamp, 1982, p.19.

9 Stamp, 1982, p.19.

10 Stamp, 1982, p.19.

11 The author has drawn heavily in this chapter from Monica Pidgeon's 'Ernö Goldfinger in the Twenties', PAV 4/8013, updated.

12 Letter to Professor E.A. Plishcke, 1 March 1965 in GolEr278/1.

13 See *Daily Sketch*, 31 December 1937 in GolEr 393/15.

14 He drew an explicit parallel between architecture and sculpture in a caption for a picture in his article 'Urbanism and Spatial Order', reprinted in Dunnett, (1983) p.51–54: 'The effect of the free-standing building is similar to that of sculpture: the play of light and shade on the plastic shapes.'

15 Interview with Dacey, Cruickshank and Dunnett.

16 Pidgeon, PAV 4/8013.

17 Pidgeon, PAV 4/8013.

18 Pidgeon, PAV 4/8013.

19 Mentioned in interview *Architectural Review*, April 1983, p.47.

20 Unwin (1863–1940) was the British champion of the garden city movement, and designer of Hampstead Garden Suburb. Goldfinger later met Unwin at the Town Planning Congress in Paris in 1928, and subsequently in London in 1935, see letter from Raymond Unwin, 28/2/35, in GolEr 281/4.

21 Pidgeon, PAV 4/8013.

22 Recalled by his grandson, Nick Goldfinger.

23 Pidgeon, PAV 4/8013.

24 This was on 20 October 1922. The notebook is in GolEr 522.

Chapter 2

Lessons in concrete

The idea of perfection haunted Perret and became infectious.

In 1923 Charles-Édouard Jeanneret, better known as Le Corbusier, delivered a bombshell to the Beaux-Arts tradition of architecture by publishing *Vers une architecture*, a book which has been misleadingly translated into English as *Towards a New Architecure*, but which deserves the full force of its original iconoclastic title: *Towards an Architecture*. The book had an enormous influence on Goldfinger. It was created from a series of articles which Le Corbusier had written under the name of Le Corbusier-Saugnier for the *L'Esprit nouveau* (*New Spirit*), a magazine he had founded with the painter Amédée Ozenfant and the poet Paul Dermée in 1920, and which ran for twenty-eight issues until 1925, counting Adolf Loos, Jean Cocteau and Louis Aragon among its contributors. In order to disguise the fact that there were very few contributors to *L'Esprit nouveau* – since most were written by Ozenfant and Jeanneret – Jeanneret first adopted the pseudonym Le Corbusier.[1] *Vers une architecture* was illustrated with photographs of grain elevators, airplanes and cars, set alongside pictures of the Parthenon, which Le Corbusier singled out as a functional building which included the harmonious aesthetic dimension. *Vers une architecture* was a deliberately provocative challenge to complacency, and the outline of a philosophy of architecture for a new technological age. Its message would transform building in the twentieth century and launch Le Corbusier on the trajectory towards becoming the best known architect of the century. The style of the *L'Esprit nouveau* writing has been aptly characterised by Charles Jencks as 'baroque – telegraphic – neo-hysterical'[2]: it reads like a cross between Nietzsche and a futurist manifesto.

Caricatures of *Vers une architecture* pick out the line 'The house is a machine for living in'[3] as evidence of a crude functionalism, as if Le Corbusier were advocating that house design should only be a matter of fulfilling basic human needs, anything else being superfluous excrescence.

This interpretation is in part supported by the rhetoric of the illustrations, with their emphasis on functional modern engineering. Yet this caricature misses the full flavour of Le Corbusier's approach to architecture: his was a more Platonic vision of design. Merely fulfilling the brief would be to produce a work of construction, not a work of architecture:

> The Architect, by his arrangement of forms, realizes an order which is a pure creation of his spirit; by forms and shapes he affects our senses to an acute degree and provokes plastic emotions; by the relationships which he creates he wakes profound echoes in us, he gives us the measure of an order which we feel to be in accordance with that of our world, he determines the various movements of our heart and of our understanding; it is then that we experience the sense of beauty.[4]

This hankering after an abstract world of pure harmony was to be a recurring feature in Le Corbusier's work. He had a vision of the moral force of living spaces which encouraged meditation and recuperation. From a distance, his vision of the function of a living place as one of spiritual meditation in a harmoniously organised enclosed space seems unduly prescriptive, and perhaps overly optimistic, but the paternalistic elements of his philosophy were concealed in the rhetoric. The means of achieving his utopian vision were at hand in new technology. *Vers une architecture* was an impassioned polemic for the new spirit in architecture, for clear thinking about the uses of a combination of engineering and aesthetics for the betterment of humankind. Goldfinger later characterised the book as 'a disjointed muddle of captions and manifestos', but never denied its power.[5] He later acknowledged Le Corbusier's significance:

> The great achievement of Le Corbusier was that he, amongst all innovators of our century, has stated clearly how architecture fits in dialectically into our modern technological environment.[6]

Vers une architecture, written in aphoristic style, was full of exhortations to action. Le Corbusier found inspiration in the clarity of design of a steamship rather than in what he saw as the turgid tradition perpetuated at the Beaux-Arts:

> A seriously-minded architect, looking at it as an architect (i.e. a creator of organisms), will find in a steamship his freedom from an age-long but contemptible enslavement to the past.
>
> He will prefer respect for the forces of nature to a lazy respect for tradition; to the narrowness of commonplace conceptions he will

> prefer the majesty of solutions which spring from a problem that has been clearly stated – solutions needed by this age of mighty effort which has taken so gigantic a step forward.
>
> The house of the earth-man is the expression of a circumscribed world. The steamship is the first stage in the realization of a world organized according to the new spirit.[7]

It is hardly surprising that Le Corbusier's Nietzschean vision of the redemptive power of building, of the architect as the moral saviour of an age corrupted by its unreflective absorption of traditional values in construction, proved irresistible to a number of students at the Beaux-Arts, Goldfinger among them:

> So there I was in the Beaux-Arts, I'd finished my second class and had two *valeurs* in premier class. And here came out this absolutely staggering book, unreadable, but fabulous: *Vers une architecture*.

2.1
Ernö, Paris, 1920s

> So all these things we were doing wasn't really architecture. So said Corbusier. We are going *towards* an architecture, that's all it is. Not a new architecture, not an old architecture, just *towards* architecture: *Vers* une architecture.[8]

Goldfinger and his friends had already come to the conclusion that something about the Beaux-Arts training was not quite right: Corbusier's book crystallised that feeling. Goldfinger encapsulated some of his frustration with the Beaux-Arts system of education in his notebook entry for 1 June 1924, where he argued that an architectural education ought to resemble the sort of protected recapitulation of species development apparent in a human embryo.[9] But far from achieving this, the Beaux-Arts approach treated students like Spartan babies – exposing them on the rocks rather than letting them develop through the various stages protected by their mother's womb. The result was a kind of death.[10] This disenchantment with the teaching method and the sense of a different set of possibilities in architecture emerging in parallel to Beaux-Arts' traditions unsettled Goldfinger.

In 1924, with twelve other students at the Beaux-Arts, he took the logical next step, one which was in principle within the atelier tradition, but was in practice a radical subversion of it. He knew Pierre Jeanneret, Le Corbusier's cousin and collaborator, and he used this connection to gain an audience with the newfound prophet of Modernism at his flat in the rue Jacob.[11] The students invited Le Corbusier to found a Beaux-Arts atelier. Here was a chance to get beyond what they saw as the absurdly reactionary approach to architecture advocated by the powerful Beaux-Arts administration and set up a genuinely modern atelier, with a young and forward-looking *chef* – Le Corbusier was only fifteen years older than Goldfinger. As Goldfinger later put it:

> At the Beaux-Arts everything was dead. All the stirring of modern architecture was ridiculed. The pompous projects for subjects like a 'Governor's Palace in Annam' or a 'French Embassy in Central America', were just so many exercises in the application of the orders. In the country of the Galeries des Machines and of Labrouste, steel or reinforced concrete structures were simply ignored. We felt that something had to be done.[12]

To their disappointment, Le Corbusier declined the invitation. As far as he was concerned, he didn't *teach* architecture, he *made* it.[13] He wasn't prepared to take on these would-be disciples:

> Le Corbusier put us off, he said he wouldn't teach architecture, but he recommended us to go to his master who taught him all he

> knew about concrete, about building, and about architecture. And his name was Auguste Perret.[14]

It would have been out of character had Le Corbusier accepted the invitation: he was a committed opponent of academic training in architecture, and had deliberately remained outside the Beaux-Arts system. In his later book *When the Cathedrals Were White*, he spelt out his reservations about the Beaux-Arts diploma and its cramping effect on the spirit of young architects:

> The studious and painful conquest (I know that from the confidences of many young students) of the diploma demanded by the father or the family (poor people, they imagine that when their child leaves school he will be the beneficiary of exceptional rights in the apportionment of life), the winning of the diploma in four or six years absorbs the precious moments of youth, of generous malleability, of magnificent enthusiasm, of *opening* in the face of multifarious life. The diploma closes everything like a cork. It says: 'It is finished, you have stopped suffering and learning. Henceforth you are free!' The idea of *learning* has become synonymous with *suffering*! Youth is killed. Learning? That is the joy of every day, the ray of sunlight in life. I say that if throughout life we developed the generous faculty of learning, men would discover in it happiness itself – free, unlimited, never-failing happiness, happiness up to their last day. We would make men of a different kind: new men.[15]

Le Corbusier had taken this breakaway group of students seriously enough to recommend that they approach Perret, who was almost as radical a choice as *chef d'atelier* as Le Corbusier would have been. Rather than attend the Beaux-Arts, Le Corbusier had worked in Perret's offices in 1908. He had been inspired by Perret's imaginative use of concrete and his philosophy of architecture which Perret later encapsulated as:

> He who hides any part of the framework deprives himself of the only legitimate and most beautiful ornament of architecture. He who hides a pillar makes a mistake. He who erects a false pillar commits a crime.[16]

In the Beaux-Arts atelier tradition the *chef d'atelier*, or *patron*, was invariably a member of the institute's jury, a *Prix de Rome*, an *ancien de l'atelier* and a member of the institute. Perret (like Le Corbusier) had none of these qualifications. He had been a brilliant student at the Beaux-Arts, but had left early to join the family business, Perret Frères. Without these marks of membership of the inner circle of the Beaux-Arts, Perret's influence on the jury that judged students' drawings was slight. There was serious doubt as to whether any of his students would gain the requisite number of *mentions* for their projects to graduate.

From a practical point of view, approaching Perret was a gamble for the Beaux-Arts students. Without an advocate on the jury, they risked failing to achieve their professional qualifications. This could seriously jeopardise their chances of becoming practising architects. Yet once they had come this far, it would have been a betrayal of their vision of the future of architecture to have capitulated and opted for a traditional *chef d'atelier*.

Besides, Perret was an inspirational figure who had a deep understanding of the potential of reinforced concrete as a building material and a clear vision of the nature and processes of architecture:[17]

> He transformed reinforced concrete from a structural system like the steel frame into an organic element of a new architecture with its laws of monolithic continuity, different from any that came before.[18]

For Goldfinger, he was the modern equivalent of a gothic master builder. He had designed some of the most innovative concrete buildings in Paris, including the Théâtre des Champs Elysées, which he'd completed in 1913. Goldfinger described this building, which combined an austere classicism with new techniques of construction, as 'one of the most beautiful theatres in Europe'.[19] The front of the building has a stark geometrical beauty, though it is not completely devoid of decoration: sculpted panels reflect the ancient Greek inspiration for the design. Throughout, the structural columns form elements of the architecture.[20] More recently Perret had built the chapel of Notre-Dame, Le Raincy (1924), again from reinforced concrete, a building Goldfinger described as 'like the Saint Chapel, but perhaps even more beautiful'.[21] The notion of a chapel with bare concrete pillars and walls, and traditional stained glass windows replaced with a precast concrete grille glazed with coloured glass, was futuristic. This was one of the first buildings to treat exposed concrete as a surface with aesthetic appeal in its own right, an approach later adopted and championed by Goldfinger.

Perret received the young Beaux-Arts architects in his apartment overlooking the park at 25b Rue Franklin, in an eight-storey block he'd built himself in 1903. The building uses a reinforced concrete frame – a technique that Perret, working with his two brothers, pioneered, and although the concrete structural frame was not exposed, the structure of the building was not concealed. The students were even more in awe of him than they had been of Le Corbusier:

> Here was this fabulous old gentleman, all of five foot tall, who looked like a giant of eight foot!

In fact he wore high heels on his shoes to disguise his height. But despite his diminutive stature – and Goldfinger at six feet two must have dwarfed him – Perret's reputation and presence overawed the students:

> . . . we thought he was the greatest architect in France.[22]

When he realised that Le Corbusier had sent them he exclaimed:

> Jeanneret? Jeanneret? Oh! – the young man who used to do those nice watercolour drawings in my *Agence* before the War![23]

Perret treated the students with exceptional generosity. Not only did he accept their invitation to become their *patron*, despite being outside the Beaux-Arts system, but he also put at their disposal, rent-free, a superb atelier. This was in a wing of the Palais du Bois, overlooking the Bois de Boulogne, a building that Perret had recently completed. The Palais du Bois was a pavilion for art exhibitions made from rough timber, which was demountable so that it could be moved from one exhibition to another. It was typical of Perret's approach that when the Palais was eventually dismantled, the boards were taken back to the Perret Frères timber yard and reused as shuttering for concrete.[24] The students didn't quite get their cutting edge modernist *chef d'atelier*, but they did get an original, inventive and charismatic teacher. Moreover, Perret gave his services as *chef d'atelier* free of charge. He was clearly flattered and proud to be sought out by the students for this role.

Goldfinger could not join the atelier immediately – it was not acceptable to desert so senior a Beaux-Arts figure as Jaussely. However, at the point at which Jaussely was about to be superseded as studio master, Goldfinger was able to make the transition.[25] A draft of what appears to be his resignation letter, dated April 1925, with the French corrected in red pencil, was in among his papers.[26]

Goldfinger later described Perret's inspirational teaching, stressing his 'clear thinking and profound knowledge of his métier'.[27] Sloppiness was intolerable:

> The idea of perfection haunted Perret and became infectious.[28]

Berthold Lubetkin, whom Goldfinger introduced to the atelier (though, according to Goldfinger, he hardly ever attended it),[29] recalled the weeks of work needed to design even a simple staircase that Perret would accept. Every element, however minor, had to be positioned rationally; there should be no wastage of material.[30] Teaching was in the informal atelier style with Perret moving from table to table commenting on students' work. He despised and attacked any vagueness in drawing: precision and simple construction were essential. Yet his teaching was not just focused on detail – he was inspirational at every level. He visited twice a week, on Tuesday and Friday afternoons. His teaching ranged from straightforward criticism of the students' drawings to wider discussion of the history of architecture, the Parthenon, mosques at Constantinople, or the techniques of shuttering reinforced concrete.[31]

At this time Perret was quite a distant figure for Goldfinger; in later years they became friends. Goldfinger was influential in Perret's being awarded the RIBA Gold Medal in 1948. He wrote a number of articles about Perret, translated his aphorisms, and even embarked on a book-length study of his mentor which – like most of Goldfinger's projected books – never saw publication. Goldinger revered Perret, encapsulating what he learnt from him as 'Perret for me is logic.'[32] On a more personal level, in the office in his house in Willow Road he kept a low-crowned grey top hat which had belonged to Perret – appropriately in concrete grey. It is still there with Perret's name and address neatly inscribed on a card in the hatband.

The Atelier Perret in the Palais du Bois was formed early in 1924. In Goldfinger's architectural metaphor it 'shook the old school to its foundation'.[33] The Beaux-Arts authorities did not approve of the breakaway atelier, and they did not approve of Perret. But for the students these were exciting times:

> We were a rather happy crowd. There were sculptors among us, engineers. It was a very stimulating atmosphere.[34]

Goldfinger was in charge of the library, and took his role seriously. The library had a collection of Frank Lloyd Wright's drawings in a Dutch magazine, and copies of works by Gropius and Le Corbusier:

> All these were consulted furtively like some filthy pictures, or horror comics read under the cover with a torch after lights out![35]

Goldfinger used his connections with artists to good effect. At his invitation his friends Georges Braque, Amédée Ozenfant and Tsugoharu Foujita all visited the atelier – something that would never have occurred in a conventional Beaux-Arts atelier where the boundaries between art and architecture were rarely blurred.[36]

Perret, and Goldfinger's other teachers at the Beaux-Arts, kept a distance between themselves and the students. In contrast, Walter Gropius, former director of the Bauhaus, who visited Paris from time to time, treated Goldfinger as an equal when they met there in 1925, despite a twenty-year age gap and Gropius's eminence. The rationalism and elegance of Gropius's architecture were a significant influence on Goldfinger. Later he admired him for his moral courage too: Gropius, unlike many of his contemporaries, chose to leave Berlin when Hitler came to power.[37]

While at the Atelier Perret, Goldfinger found time to pursue design work beyond the limitations set by the Beaux-Arts curriculum. For example, with his good friend András Szivessy, who later changed his name to André Sive, he designed chairs, bookcases, tables and cupboards. Furniture design was not an approved part of the Beaux-Arts curriculum,[38] but Sive, who had worked with Bruno Paul, an important innovator in machine-made furniture, inspired Goldfinger to experiment in this area.

Goldfinger met Sive in 1923, and over the next six years worked closely with him, eventually dissolving their partnership in 1929 when Goldfinger got a commission to work on a project in Alexandria,[39] though they remained great friends after this professional separation. In 1925 they took

2.2
Ernö and Sive, 3 Rue de la Cité Universitaire, 1931, Ernö is smoking a pipe

adjacent first floor flats at 98 Boulevard Auguste Blanqui, where they opened their first office. The apartments were joined via the studio. Lubetkin lived on the third floor of the building which was owned by Francine Lecoeur, the wife of their fellow student, Paul Nelson, whom Goldfinger had introduced to the Atelier Perret. Goldfinger and Szivessy's main business was refitting apartments in a modern style. Their first clients, M. and Mme Coutreau, were introduced to them by the artists Robert and Sonia Delaunay. For Coutreau they designed a folding bookshelf on castors. Photographs of the piece *in situ* by André Kertész[40] reveal the main shortcoming of the design very clearly: the castors, carrying the weight of the bookshelf and books, have scored semi-circular tracks in the parquet floor. Other commissions included designs for a film set for Robert and Sonia Delaunay, and furniture and room refittings for Dick Wyndham.

As well as refitting apartments, Goldfinger and Sive were invited to write and illustrate a series of articles for the magazine *L'Organisation ménagère* on such topics as the rational design of kitchens. They also entered several competitions – without success – designing an aeronautical school in Paris and law courts and a science faculty for San Salvador, for instance. Sive, like Goldfinger, was Hungarian by birth. He had come to Paris in 1924 after studying architecture with Peter Behrens in Berlin and later studying in Vienna. He was briefly associated with the Atelier Perret before going into partnership with Goldfinger. He had also worked with Charles Siclis, and had been largely responsible for the design of the Théâtre Pigalle. Working with Sive taught Goldfinger a great deal about drawing – the most important lesson he learnt was knowing when to stop.[41] Most of the Goldfinger/Sive work was upmarket interior design. This involved re-styling the apartments of their wealthy clients, turning them into modern living and working spaces equipped with specially designed furniture and fittings.

After dissolving their partnership – which never made them any profit – Sive had a successful career as a town planner and architect; he was also made a Chevalier of the Légion d'Honneur. He was a hero of the Resistance in the Second World War. They remained close friends, often visiting each other. Goldfinger wrote Sive's obituary in *The Times* after his early death in 1958, where he described him as:

> one of the leading French architects of the modern school and one of the few contemporary French architects and town-planners with an international reputation.[42]

On a personal level, when Sive died, Goldfinger lost not just one of his best friends, but, perhaps as important for him,

. . . the only architect who really understood what I wanted to say.[43]

In 1925,[44] Goldfinger and Sive produced a leather and chrome-plated tubular steel chair with a sprung seat 'so you can throw yourself into it'. The seat would give as you sat down: in one version of the chair there are small rollers easing the movement. The seat back could be fixed at various inclinations and could even be folded flat to turn it into a couch. The chair was based on ergonomic principles and practical considerations. Bolted together, it could easily be dismantled for transport – a real machine for sitting in. Photographs of it appeared in Roger Ginsburger's (1930) book *Junge Französische Architectur* – alongside classic designs by Charlotte Periand and Le Corbusier, though it never went beyond the prototype. Like the work of Le Corbusier and Perriand, this chair was uncompromisingly modern, demonstrating novel yet rational uses of new materials. Other innovative designs that Goldfinger and Sive produced prototypes for included a standard lamp with a chromium base and translucent glass domed shade, and a chromium-plated steel coffee table with a wooden top.[45]

Another important Goldfinger furniture design from the Paris years was the Safari chair and matching footstool, which he first designed in 1928. He designed one version for Lee Miller, the photographer, who was at this time Man Ray's lover. Goldfinger met Miller on her first visit to Paris, when she attended a theatre school with which Goldfinger had links, and they remained friends for many years, Miller subsequently becoming Goldfinger's near neighbour in Hampstead where she lived with Roland Penrose. The Safari chair was a stylish adaptation of a portable chair that had been used on military campaigns and by travellers in the early years of the century – a rot-proof canvas and teak version known as the Indian chair was, for example, available from the London furniture shop, Maples from 1904 onwards. Goldfinger produced his modernist version after seeing the British Army version in London. He eliminated ornamental elements of the wood turning and made it in hide and ash. This low-slung portable chair with tapered legs combined elegance, comfort and practicality. It was slotted together in what Goldfinger described as 'the Arab fashion' with tenons and straps, and so could easily be dismantled and reassembled by hand without a screwdriver. He had taken advice about how to construct this sort of chair from Arabs when he visited Algiers.[46] It was light and readily transportable. Furthermore, the nature of the joints allowed movement in several planes, resulting in a chair that could stand firm on uneven ground – something of a rarity. The pivoted back added to the comfort as did the footstool created in the same style.

The Goldfingers put these transportable chairs to good use on a camping holiday in Gibraltar: holiday snaps show Ursula Goldfinger sitting on

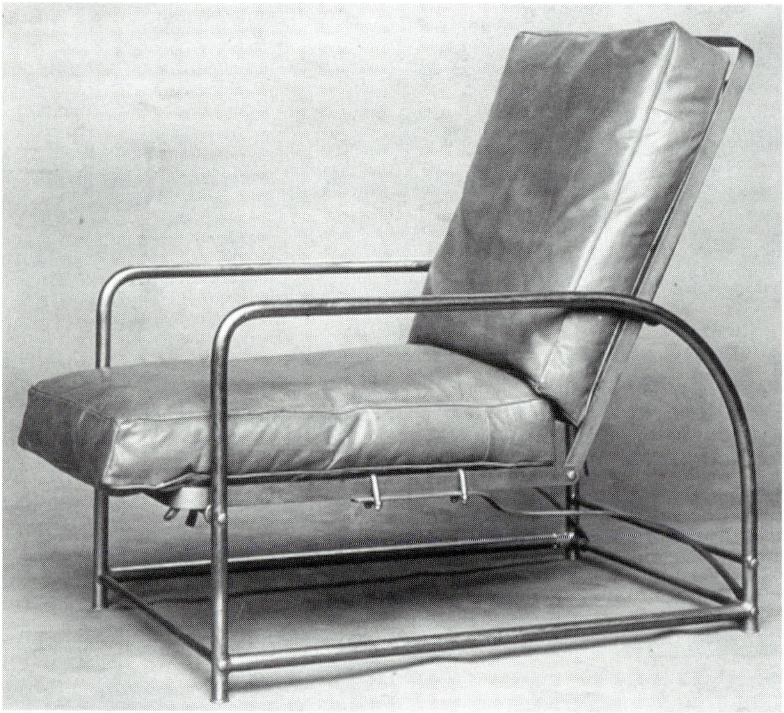

2.3
A chair to throw yourself into

one next to a tent. They also used them as easy chairs in their living room in their house in Willow Road. There are several versions of the design – some with arms, some without, some with high backs, such as those used in his first building at Le Touquet, some with lower ones. He even produced a scaled-down model for children.

Not as starkly machine-like as the chrome and leather sprung chair, the safari chair used traditional construction methods and materials to provide a balanced and simple solution to the perennial problem of practical seating. Goldfinger always favoured low easy chairs, at least until age made it difficult for him to get out of them. He was not alone among modernist furniture designers in adapting the safari chair – Kaare Kinte, the Danish designer, produced a version in 1933. With typical grandiosity and exaggeration, Goldfinger later claimed in conversation to have started the whole twentieth-century Scandivanian furniture movement with his design: Swedes visiting Paris took his ideas home and developed the style.[47]

Goldfinger's variations on this chair, which he produced over a period of more than thirty years, indicate his willingness to build on successful traditions: it would be wrong to see him as relentlessly pursuing the new for its own sake. His motivation was to produce practical streamlined solutions for living.

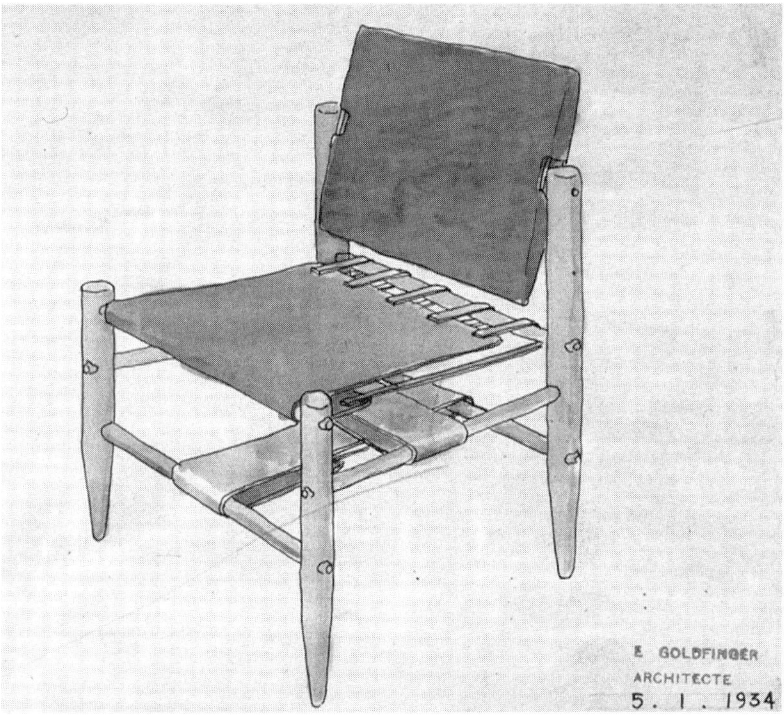

2.4
Safari chair variation drawing, dated 1934

2.5
Safari chair in use. Gibraltar, Ursula

More obviously modernist was his 1931 design for stacking chairs, the 'Entas' chair (*entasser* being French for 'to stack'). This was a dining chair of chrome-plated steel and wood with a pivoted back (a recurring feature in his furniture). The idea of the pivot was to provide greater comfort as the occupant shifted position. These chairs were designed for mass production. They were the chairs Goldfinger used for the dining area in the conversion of the house at Le Touquet, his first major building commission, and later in his own house in Willow Road, Hampstead. As with several of his furniture designs, he later produced a miniature version of the Entas chair scaled to children for the toymakers Paul and Marjorie Abbatt.

Ever systematic, Ernö imposed a four-part system of classification on furniture and fittings. This allowed him to organise his drawings and notes into a reference system with the letters A to D indicating the type of furniture, followed by a number which identified the drawing. The reference letter and number were neatly stencilled on the drawings. Every item was then indexed on reference cards which included small schematic sketches of the piece of furniture in question. His four categories were:

- A Seats and the beds which support the body
- B Tables and work benches
- C Cupboards
- D Other utensils for domestic use such as mirrors, lamps, and coat hooks.

By helping to found the Atelier Perret and by devoting considerable energy to furniture design, Ernö had conspicuously distanced himself from the traditions of the Beaux-Arts. It was obvious from the outset that by changing ateliers he would jeopardise the smooth trajectory of his career. There was a risk that he would never graduate from the Beaux-Arts without an advocate on the panel that judged the drawings he submitted. Yet Perret's practical and inspirational teaching provided the perfect complement to the more traditional Beaux-Arts education. From Goldfinger's point of view he was learning from a master, one of very few contemporary architects who had envisaged the potential of concrete in building.

Realising that he might never graduate as a member of the Atelier Perret, Goldfinger transferred to the Atelier Defrasse in May 1927. Suddenly, his drawings started to be passed and he was able to amass the requisite credits. He was 'diplomable' by 1928, although he did not graduate until 1932. This did not stop him from continuing his education with Perret. Even after the atelier was officially dissolved, he and his peers would visit Perret to hear him praise the new Citroën 'avec traction avant' or rail against the

Corbusian horizontal window: 'une fenêtre, c'est un homme debout'.[48] One important lesson from those visits that had an impact on Goldfinger's taller buildings was Perret's insistence on the cornice finishing off a building 'like the hat on a man's head'.[49]

Notes

1 Ozenfant wrote under six pseudonyms, Jeanneret under three.

2 Charles Jencks *Le Corbusier and the Tragic View of Architecture*, London: Allen Lane, 1973, p.65.

3 Le Corbusier, *Towards a New Architecture*, p.4

4 Le Corbusier, *Towards a New Architecture*, p.1.

5 Ernö Goldfinger writing on Le Corbusier for *Architectural Design*, 17 September 1965, in GolEr 337/21.

6 Ernö Goldfinger writing on Le Corbusier for *Architectural Design*, 17 September 1965, in GolEr 337/21.

7 Le Corbusier, *Towards a New Architecture*, p.103.

8 Pidgeon, PAV 4/8013.

9 Goldfinger's image of recapitulation may have been borrowed from Loos' famous essay 'Ornament and Crime' which opens with the metaphor of recapitulation.

10 GolEr/5224/4 [original in French].

11 Goldfinger had already interviewed Le Corbusier for a Hungarian newspaper in 1923, but the article was never published.

12 Goldfinger, from *The Architectural Review* vol. 115, May 1954, p.341. quoted in Robert Elwall, *Ernö Goldfinger*, RIBA Drawings Monographs no. 3, London: Academy Editions, 1996, p.10.

13 Goldfinger interviewed for Hungarian television, transcript in National Trust 2 Willow Road collection.

14 Pidgeon, PAV 4/8013.

15 Le Corbusier, quoted in Jean Jenger Le Corbusier, *Architect of a New Age*, London: Thames and Hudson, 1996, p.117.

16 Perret, quoted in Goldfinger, 'Auguste Perret', *Architect's Yearbook 7*, 1956, p.45.

17 Reinforced concrete, sometimes known as ferro-concrete, incorporates steel rods or meshes within concrete. This allows the material to be used in beams and other supporting structures where it will be put in tension.

18 Goldfinger, 1956, p.43.

19 Pidgeon, PAV 4/8013.

20 The theatre opened with Vaslav Nijinski performing in the première of Stravinsky's *Rite of Spring*. Perret, who was in some ways conservative, did not approve.

21 Pidgeon, PAV 4/8013.

22 Pidgeon, PAV 4/8013.

23 Quoted in Ernö Goldfinger, 'The Work of Auguste Perret' in *Journal of the American Institute of Architects*, May 1955, pp.195–200 and June 1955, pp.273–6, p.197 in GolEr 389.

24 See Goldfinger, May 1955, pp.195–200 and June 1955, pp.273–276, p.274, in GolEr 389. Goldfinger's approving response to this was 'Economy!'

25 It seems likely that Andre Le Donne and Adrienne Brelet had begun working as students of Perret as early as 1923 and that others joined them in 1924. But it was with the move to the Palais de Bois that the atelier became established. Goldfinger drafted a letter to Jaussely dated 1 April 1925 in which he declared his intention to change ateliers. He crossed out the mention of Perret, describing him simply as 'un autre professeur' in GolEr 530.

26 Unsigned letter, April 1925, in GolEr 530.

27 Goldfinger, 1956, p.45.

28 Goldfinger, lecture on Perret, 1954, notes in GolEr 337/8, p.4.

29 Goldfinger pointed out in conversation with James Dunnett (31/5/80) that Lubetkin was never a member of the Beaux-Arts proper, but of the far less prestigious Ecole Speciale.

30 Paraphrased in Peter Coe and Malcolm Reading, *Lubetkin and Tecton: Architecture and Social Commitment*, London: Arts Council of Great Briatin, 1981, p.40.

31 Quoted in Elwall, 1956, p.27.

32 Quoted by James Dunnett in an essay for a forthcoming exhibition about Perret.

33 Goldfinger, 1956, p.45.

34 Pidgeon, PAV 4/8013.

35 Goldfinger, lecture on Perret, 1954, in GolEr 337/18.

36 Abrams interview with Oskar Nitzchke, another member of the Atelier Perret, April–October 1983 in Abrams, 1985.

37 See Goldfinger's short article about his friendship with Gropius, 'As an Equal', *The Times*, 7 July 1969.

38 Dunnett 'Conversations with Ernö Goldfinger' unpublished, 3/8/82.

39 He designed a library in a building built by Perret, and also a monument in Algiers.

40 Goldfinger claimed that his was the only architectural work that Kertesz ever photographed. 'I had forgotten even this until he wrote to me, and I steamed off the photos from the mounts and found Kertész's round stamp.' James Dunnett 'Conversations with Ernö Goldfinger' (unpublished) 30/9/83.

41 Dunnett Conversations with Ernö Goldfinger (unpublished) 27/2/82.

42 *The Times*, 25 September, 1958, p.15.

43 Goldfinger, letter to Kling, 24/9/58, in response to a telegram informing Goldfinger of Sive's death.

44 Date given in Lowrie bibliography in *Architectural Design*, 1963.

45 These are illustrated in *Architectural Design*, January 1963 (an issue devoted to the work of Goldfinger), p.44.

46 This information comes from Dunnett, 'Conversations with Ernö Goldfinger, unpublished notes, 10/12/83.

47 Dunnett 'Conversations with Ernö Goldfinger' (unpublished) 22/11/80.

48 Goldfinger, lecture on Perret, 1954, p.5 of typescript in GolEr 337/18.

49 Perret, quoted by Ernö Goldfinger May 1955, pp.195–200 and June 1955, pp.273–276, p.198 in GolEr 389. Although today both Trellick Tower and Balfron Tower are 'hatless', they were both built with a cornice, or 'pergola beam' as some architects label it. This was an aesthetic consideration about the profile of these buildings against the sky, and one which was ignored by the local councils that removed them on safety grounds but have as yet failed to replace them.

Chapter 3

In the right place

We don't believe in a decoration applicated arbitarary.

3.1
Outside the *Dôme*, 1926. Ernö is standing.
Photo André Kertész
© Ministère de la culture/France

Although Perret's teaching provided the spine of his architectural training, much of Ernö's education came by less formal routes. For a young man with enthusiasm for art and design, Paris in the 1920s was the most exciting city on Earth. Ernö's contacts gave him the chance to mingle freely with many of the most influential designers and artists of the twentieth century. His friendships with architects such as Pierre Jeanneret and Jean Badovici led to new contacts and friendships. His friend the painter Amédée Ozenfant, co-editor

of *L'Esprit nouveau*, held weekly salons in his recently built studio in the Parc Monsourit, a cube-shaped building designed by Le Corbusier. Here Ernö met and befriended many artists. Acquaintances and friendships were then renewed in the Dôme and the Flore. A photograph by Kertész from 1926 shows Ernö, a cigarette in his mouth, outside the Dôme with the painter Marie Vassilieff, who had been Matisse's pupil, the Hungarian painter Lajos Tihanyi, and a woman called Dora, who was a friend of Berenice Abbott.[1] Ernö knew Alexander Calder (famous for his surreal mobiles) and would call regularly on Braque and Arp. He was a good friend of the poet Paul Eluard, the artist Max Ernst and the model and photographer Lee Miller. He met Lee Miller on her first visit to Paris in 1925 when she attended a theatre school on the rue de Sèvres run by Ladislas Medgyes; in later years she lived around the corner from him in Hampstead.[2] While in Paris he also met Toulouse-Lautrec's nephew Tapies de Celeyran who was studying with Ozenfant. Charlotte Perriand, who designed furniture with Le Corbusier, was a personal friend, and Eileen Gray was an acquaintance. On one of Oskar Kokoschka's visits to Paris, Ernö and he were rivals for the affections of a beautiful Swedish student. With such inspiring company it is hardly surprising that Ernö was happy to extend his student days to well over a decade.

Throughout the 1920s and into the early 1930s, Ernö continued his informal education in the Parisian salons and cafés alongside his official studies. One major inspiration and influence was the remarkable architect and theorist Adolf Loos whom he first met in 1925. Loos, some thirty years Goldfinger's senior, had arrived in Paris the previous year from Vienna, where his friends had included the philosopher Ludwig Wittgenstein[3] and the satirist Karl Krauss who championed Loos' buildings in his paper *Die Fackel*. Loos was an ardent defender of rational simplicity in design an arch-enemy of ornament. His thought and personality had a lasting effect on those around him. Kokoschka, for instance, declared that Loos 'inspired a profound trust in one's feeling and instinct'.[4]

Loos' *sachlich* or 'objective' architecture was derived from his experience of design in America and England. His moment of insight had come in a New York store when he caught sight of a leather cabin trunk with brass fittings, and realised the aesthetic value of practical design. In his pamphlet, 'Ornament and Crime' (1908), he had challenged the assumptions of the prevailing orthodoxy by arguing that obsession with ornament occurs at a primitive stage in the evolution of civilisations, not at a sophisticated one. His polemical conclusion was that 'the evolution of culture marches with the elimination of ornament from useful objects'. Ornament was fit for savages and degenerates, but not for modern humanity. In this and other essays, Loos anticipated many of the conclusions of the Bauhaus designers, and indeed of

Corbusier, who reprinted the article in *L'Esprit nouveau*[5] and declared that he considered Loos' ideas to be ahead of their time.[6] Here was an intellectual justification for a streamlined functional modernist style. The fact that it was based on spurious generalisations about anthropological development did not matter. Loos' ideas were echoed and acknowledged in Corbusier's own writings for *L'Esprit nouveau*, in articles which were later gathered together and published as the book *Decorative Art of Today* (1925). The title of Corbusier's book was deliberately paradoxical since the major thesis of the book was that '*Modern decorative art is not decorated*'.[7] Corbusier wanted 'decorative art' to achieve the degree of perfection and functionality usefulness achieved in industrial tools and machinery:

> Decoration: baubles, charming entertainment for a savage. (And I do not deny that it is an excellent thing to keep an element of the savage alive in us – a small one.) But in the twentieth century our powers of judgement have developed greatly and we have raised our level of consciousness. Our spiritual needs are different, and higher worlds than those of decoration offer us commensurate experience. It seems justified to affirm: *the more cultivated a people becomes, the more decoration disappears.* (Surely it was Loos who put it so neatly.)[8]

Loos himself made buildings which illustrated his theory. Already famous for his 'house without eyebrows' – The Steiner House in Vienna, and for his controversial building on the Michaelerplatz, (1911), he had just completed house in Montparnasse for the Surrealist Tristan Tzara – a building which Goldfinger knew and admired, and had drawn up designs for a streamlined residence for the dancer Josephine Baker. But it was his shop interiors that most impressed Goldfinger.[9]

Neatly dressed and almost completely deaf, Loos would hold court at the Dôme. Goldfinger met him there most evenings for two or three years. He and his fellow architects would gather round and listen attentively: 'we sat at his feet, figuratively speaking'.[10] For the Beaux-Arts students the Dôme was the unofficial university. It was the meeting place for the various émigré artists, designers, writers and architects passing through Paris. Here Ernö and his peers took *café crèmes* or *bock* with the likes of Oskar Kokoschka and Walter Gropius. Julian Trevelyan, the surrealist artist, described it as 'the cauldron in which all the races on this planet were being cooked into one gigantic *bouillabaisse*.'[11] Yet Loos, somewhat surprisingly, argued that the point of coming to Paris was not to learn a new International Style. One evening a young Austrian student came in and went up to Loos, telling him excitedly 'Master, I have a marvellous job. At last Le Corbusier has accepted me to work with him.' To which Loos replied acerbically, 'My dear boy, you know, when you come to Paris you don't come to learn Esperanto, you come to learn French'[12] – thus, incidentally, justifying retrospectively Goldfinger's choice of Perret as teacher. Later, Ernö came to think that Loos had missed the point in his put-down of Le Corbusier, which compared his style to a failed attempt at internationalism: 'It is not Esperanto Le Corbusier taught the world, but the new universal language, which replaced the old.'[13]

Goldfinger tried to arrange a meeting between Perret and Loos, but Perret declined, in part because he identified Loos with Le Corbusier. By this time Perret despised and resented Le Corbusier and his influence.[14] Furthermore, Perret was a French Nationalist. Memories of the First World War were still raw, and in his eyes Loos was an 'Austro-Boche'.[15]

It was Loos who first drew Ernö's attention to the excellence of England's austere Georgian architecture, which was to be a major influence[16] on the design of his own house in Willow Road, Hampstead. Loos was a serious anglophile, though, according to Goldfinger, England and America were somewhat confused in his mind. He told Ernö to visit the Maples department store to see the furniture: 'The great English invention is that you don't have furniture to furnish rooms, but chairs to sit in.'[17] When Loos tried to explain to Ernö that in England they measured in feet and inches rather than metres and centimetres, Ernö wouldn't believe him.

Loos' advocacy of unadorned simplicity in the design of functional objects had a powerful effect on Goldfinger's thought. Indeed, many of Goldfinger's designs echo Loos' own. The force of Loos' character and vision too found echoes in Goldfinger's resolute conviction in the success of his own designs and in his broader conception of the nature of architecture. But in one respect at least Goldfinger defied his mentor's teaching. Loos asserted that architects should not design moveable furniture – that should be left to craftsmen and arranged by the client according to their taste. For him, the architect's role was the creation of permanent fixtures.[18] 'Architects don't design chairs', he told Ernö, 'they sit in them.'[19] Nevertheless, despite designing moveable (and typically demountable) furniture, Goldfinger did in later years adopt something of Loos' attitude. His grandson, Nick Goldfinger, remembers visiting the Lloyds Building in London, being impressed by its design, but ultimately disappointed to see that the directors had chosen to install traditional oak panelling and leather furniture in a resolutely modern building. Goldfinger senior's response was that that was quite right. People should be allowed to use their buildings as they want to use them. Whatever made them feel comfortable. If people wanted oak panelling then they should have oak panelling.[20]

In 1925, Goldfinger accompanied Loos on a visit to the Exposition des Arts Décoratifs in Paris, the exhibition that gave Art Deco its name. For the most part this was, in Lubetkin's words: 'a collection of empty forms without texture, a hotch-potch of goodies without elegance'.[21]

The exhibits that interested Goldfinger – and most of his contemporaries with modernist tendencies – were untypical of the exhibition. These were Le Corbusier's *L'Esprit Nouveau*, Melnikov's Soviet Pavillion and the Japanese Pavilion. Le Corbusier's pavilion now has iconic status in modern architecture.[22] At the time the exhibition organisers tried very hard to block its inclusion. Eventually a young administrator found the last piece of land left on the site for Corbusier – on the cours La Reine in the shadow of the Grand Palais. So worried was Corbusier that he might lose even this marginal space that he sent his draftsmen immediately to occupy the land.[23] Building wasn't completed until several months after the opening of the exhibition. Here he constructed an L-shaped two-storey apartment around a covered courtyard within which a mature tree was growing – it protruded through a circular hole in the roof. This was in many ways a built polemic: the incarnation of the philosophy of *Vers une architecture*.

The apartment was a prototype for an interlocking modular unit of modern housing. It could either be a free-standing unit, or built up into a block, horizontally and vertically. Here was a physical argument that housing could exploit industrial production methods without sacrificing quality of design. Attached to the living area was a rotunda containing a display of some of Le Corbusier's and Jeanneret's plans for a rationally organised Paris with sixty-storey glazed skyscrapers, known as the Voisin Plan (not, as many people have thought, a reference to neighbours – 'Voisin' was the name of an automobile construction company that part-sponsored the project). This aspect of the pavilion didn't impress Goldfinger, mainly because it would have destroyed Haussmann's rational city planning.

Within the apartment was furnished sparsely with Thonet bent wood chairs and simple built-in storage cupboards. Purist paintings by Ozenfant, Léger and Corbusier, and sculptures by Jacques Lipchitz complemented the purist aesthetic of the interior. In place of the ornate glassware on display in other parts of the exhibition, the architect chose to use glass flasks and jugs from chemical laboratories – an idea Ernö later borrowed for his own house. Corbusier's aim was to produce a dwelling using industrial methods and standardised elements. Yet this was not a dwelling for the people – it was targeting a middle-class clientele and included a maid's quarters, as would Ernö's own house in Hampstead.

In the context of the highly ornate Art Deco pavilions in the rest of the exhibition, the *L'Esprit nouveau* building seemed bare and almost clinical. Lubetkin described it as:

> cool, laconic and elegant in its self-assured intellectualised simplicity – tight-lipped, scornful of its surroundings, harbinger of the future – like a sort of pyramid ruling over the arid desert of the Exhibition.[24]

The Soviet Pavilion designed by Konstantin Melnikov was also untypical of the exhibition. This was a different sort of polemic, yet equally provocative. It was propaganda for the USSR which, like Corbusier, was intent on proselytising. Both had a vested interest in appearing different from the mainstream. Melkinov's pavilion, which Lubetkin helped to construct, was to display Soviet industrial goods and to promote the Soviet political worldview. Visitors entered under a huge hammer and sickle. They followed a diagonal walkway with the exhibits on either side. The main open spaces were rhomboidal in form, rather than square or rectangular. Melkinov believed that there was a language of forms producing specific emotions in the spectator and this was the principal means by which an architect affected those who entered a building. The simplicity of the building's construction appealed to Goldfinger. It was made of timber, nailed together and fully demountable. After the exhibition it was rebuilt in the Belleville district of Paris, and Goldfinger provided exhibition materials for it on the life of Karl Marx.

A third exhibit that drew Goldfinger's attention was the Japanese Pavilion, a traditional building. He later described it as 'a revelation'. He spent hours watching it being unpacked – each numbered piece had been carefully wrapped in tissue paper. The logic of the construction was 'true Perret'.[25] But above all, it was the Corbusier pavilion that left the lasting impact and it was probably this that inspired Goldfinger's impassioned heralding of a new age in architecture in his generalised account of the exhibition published in the Budapest German-language newspaper *Pester Lloyd*:

> At the end of the century they built the Eiffel Tower, an exclamation mark in the city of Paris, a sign of hope. Many began to guess that a new epoch was rising on the horizon. Others tried to reconcile the irreconcilable, the true tradition with the false. Yet others wanted to throw off all restraints and took a wrong turning – the art nouveau Secession. A quarter of a century has elapsed, a new style has developed. It is not bound to false traditions. The descendant of a mail coach is an express train, of the horse, an aeroplane, of the messenger, the wireless, of the quill pen, the typewriter; the heirs of the Gothic Renaissance and Empire styles are the steel structures, the ferro-concrete and glass palaces. The grandchildren of Notre Dame are the Eiffel Tower, the hangars of Orly and the skyscrapers of New York.

> We have invented the machines. It seems that we have become their slaves. We shall not become masters again if we behave like ostriches.[26]

The Art Deco fair provided an inspiration and a focus for the radical young students at the Atelier Perret. Before the fair opened, Brelet, Lubetkin, Pinot, Szivessy (Sive) and Goldfinger met in the Sive–Goldfinger office at 36 Rue Abel Hovelacque to set up the optimistically-named Colloboration Internationale d'Architecture – the CIA. This proto-CIAM group was to have formed links with modern architects in other countries, organised exchanges, set up conferences and arranged trips. The Art Deco fair provided the opportunity to establish the contacts needed to create a truly international organisation of modern architects, those who were prepared to break from tradition where the tradition was no longer relevant. Minutes of an early meeting, typewritten in red ink and signed by those attending, reveal that Lubetkin was keen to educate the masses about modern ideas. The CIA's mission should be to inform the people about modern thought and about subconscious thought, deformed as it is by paradoxical appearances and erroneous habits, he thought.[27] In Lubetkin's case at least, this idealism was fuelled by revolutionary Marxism of a kind he never abandoned.[28] The CIA was to set up special educational groups in various countries, consisting of artists – 'in the true sense of the word' – who would spread the enlightening message of the group. These true artists – reminiscent of the philosopher–kings in Plato's *Republic* – are described as:

> Philosophers, synthesisers, people who are aware of the eternal and periodic fundamental laws which rule the world, and are able to create following those laws.[29]

The CIA went so far as to draw up lists of international contacts and to propose the publication of a review, but like so many idealistic movements, it never found its wings. The participants became involved in other projects, and the CIA quietly dissolved.

In 1926, Goldfinger was given a chance to come to London for the first time. As with most of his commissions, this came from a personal contact. Through an American girlfriend, a journalist, Ernö met Helena Rubinstein.[30] She invited Goldfinger and Sive to refit the interior and redesign the exterior of her showroom and beauty treatment rooms at 24 Grafton Street, Mayfair. Rubinstein had an international business in manufacturing cosmetics. She had opened her first salon in Mayfair as early as 1908. She also owned salons in Paris and New York. This was an exciting commission for a young architect – still a student. Ernö was delighted to be able to visit England, and was particularly impressed with the trains and the Georgian buildings. His only sour memory was of having to put pennies into a gas meter in the Grosvenor Hotel.

Rubinstein's Mayfair salon was housed in a Georgian terraced building. Goldfinger and Sive's original design for the shop front included clean lines, with Helena Rubinstein's name in lights repeated four times (naturally, sans serif). Rubinstein thought this in bad taste, and so it was modified to a more discreet single use on the fascia. For the main entrance, the architects used a glass door with a chrome-plated tubular steel handle running the full height of the door. This, Ernö later claimed, was the first time this much-copied solution to shop doors was used. London shop design of the time was traditional and highly ornate. Goldfinger described it as for the most part 'fake Queen Anne, like Fortnum and Mason's' with everything painted in green. In this context, sleek modern design jarred with Londoners' expectations about what a shop should look like.

The interior of the shop reminded Rubinstein of an operating theatre. Certainly the trolley for beauty products, built in tubular steel, would not have looked out of place in a surgery. The walls of the interior were covered in black and plate glass. Goldfinger designed stools (covered in pony skin, and reminiscent on a smaller scale of Corbusier and Perriand's famous chaise longue), cupboards and chairs. He also took care over the lighting, using both indirect lighting from troughs and direct lighting from lamps with

3.2
'The first modern shop in London', Helena Rubinstein salon, London, 1927

silvered shades. He took exception to the later addition of a large centre counter that was not part of his design.[31]

Neither the client nor the shopfitters quite understood or sympathised with the architects' radical vision. The English shopfitters were so used to elaborate ornamentation that they tried adding decorative elements to Sive's drawings, thinking that he had omitted them through incompetence. This elicited Goldfinger's design rationale in broken English:

> We don't believe in a decoration applicated arbitarary. That is to say there is no possibility to hang on a few columns, or false panelling, a few curtins [sic], to hide . . . corners, to do all the plastering & all this innumerous proceedings of so-called classical architecture. The stuff we are doing is simple and plain and gets all its value of the balance of its proportions of the perfect satisfaction it gives in fonction [sic], of the materials . . . in the right place.'[32]

Ernö resented Helena Rubinstein, describing her as 'overbearing' – an adjective others often used to describe him. Yet in retrospect he could see how interesting she was. Though he was still a student at the Beaux-Arts, she invited him to lunch at the Ritz and cooked dinners for him in her flat above the salon at Grafton Street.

Ultimately, Rubinstein wasn't prepared for the austerity of the salon. She refused to pay for the design. They quarrelled over the colour of a carpet, and eventually another designer was employed to finish the job. She had approved Sive's meticulous drawings, yet objected to the finished effect. Ernö took this as an illustration of his dictum that there are basically two kinds of client: those who pretend they can read plans, and those who admit they can't.[33] Later he would come to realise that in a way Rubinstein was right about his design: she had wanted a subdued salon and he had given her a beautiful glazed façade.[34] At the time, however, he was affronted. She had simply failed to appreciate the quality of his design.

With the help of his neighbour Suzanne Blum, who was at the time a law student, but who became famous as the Duchess of Windsor's confidante and one of the top barristers in Paris, he sued for his fee. This was the only client he ever sued, and he recovered the entire amount owed. Blum later employed Ernö to refurbish her Paris office and apartment. He lined her walls with plywood, designed a large table with adjustable chrome legs, and fitted oiled silk curtains. In photographs of the finished interior the telephone and typewriter appear curiously archaic, but the table and chairs could pass as contemporary in a present day office.

The Rubinstein shop, described by Charles Reilly as 'the first modern shop in London',[35] no longer exists – it was destroyed in the Blitz. In many ways we have become accustomed to clean lines in shop-front design. The full impact of the Rubinstein salon only becomes apparent in photographs that include the cars parked outside in the street – these have scarcely evolved from horse-drawn carriages; the shop front, in contrast, is visibly of our age.

In 1927, Goldfinger visited the opening of the Weissenhof Siedlung in Stuttgart with Pierre Chareau, the co-designer of the famous 'Maison De Verre' and with the architect Gevrekiam. The Weissenhof (literally the 'white house estate') was a series of houses designed for workers as a project of the Deutscher Werkbund, an organisation set up to promote good design, and a precursor of the Bauhaus. The Weissenhof houses were by some of the most significant architects of the newly emerging Modern Movement, including Corbusier, Walter Gropius, Jacobus Oud, Mart Stam, and the estate's co-ordinator, Mies van der Rohe. At the opening Ernö met Erich Mendelsohn, who became a friend. He also met Ernst May and Arthur Korn. Already, though still a student, Ernö was mixing easily and more or less as an equal with the architects who had begun to transform twentieth-century design.

The Weissenhof was a full-scale display of the house and small apartment block of the future. The typical house was white, flat-roofed and geometrically simple. This was one of the most influential early displays of what came to be known as the International Style. Far from a morally and politically neutral exhibition, the Weissenhof offered new possibilities for

3.3
At the opening of the Weissenhof Siedlung, Stuttgart, 1927. Ernö with Pierre Chareau and Pierre Barbe

better living conditions for workers as part of a wider social commitment. Finding a better solution to cheap housing was a way of transforming society. Goldfinger shared this vision and political zeal, but it woud be nearly forty years before he would be in a position to make a serious contribution to social housing himself. For the present, though, artistic life in Paris was in its Golden Age and he immersed himself in the cultural and social mêlée.

Notes

1 The identities of the various people are given in Klüver, *Kihi's Paris: Artists and Lovers 1900–1930*, New York: Harry N. Abrams, 1994, p.169.
2 This is mentioned in A. Penrose, *The Lives of Lee Miller*, London: Thames and Hudson, 1985 and also in Klüver, 1994, p.244 (who may have obtained the reference from Penrose's book). James Dunnett remembers Goldfinger mentioning that he met Lee Miller from the train on her first visit to Paris.
3 Wittgenstein later built a house for his sister which bore many signs of Loos' influence. For details of this house, see Paul Wijdeveld, *Ludwig Wittgenstein, Architect*, London: Thames and Hudson, 1994.
4 Quoted in *The Architecture of Adolf Loos*, London: Arts Council, 1985, p.30.
5 *L'Esprit nouveau*, issue no. 2, 1920.
6 This was not the first French publication of 'Ornament and Crime': according to Reyner Banham in D. Sharp, *The Rationalists*, London: Architectural Press, 1978, p.32, it had already appeared translated by George Besson in *Le Cahiers d'aujourd'hui* in 1913, and before that had been reprinted in German in the expressionist magazine *Der Sturm*, 1912.
7 Le Corbusier, *The Decorative Art of Today*, p.xxiii.
8 Le Corbusier, *The Decorative Art of Today*, p.85.
9 Dunnett 'Conversations with Ernö Goldfinger', unpublished, 20/2/82.
10 Pidgeon, PAV 4/8013.
11 J. Trevelyan, *Indigo Days*, London: Macgibbon and Kee, 1957, p.23.
12 In interview, *Architectural Review*, April 1983, p.48.
13 Goldfinger, from his contribution to the Le Corbusier symposium, 1956, in GolEr 337/20.
14 Dunnett, 'Conversations with Ernö Goldfinger', unpublished notes, 29/8/79.
15 Dunnett, 'Conversations with Ernö Goldfinger', unpublished notes, 31/5/80.
16 Recounted in a 1984 Hungarian television interview, *Ernö Goldfinger*, transcript in National Trust 2 Willow Road collection.
17 G. Stamp, 'A Conversation with Ernö Goldfinger', *Thirties Society Journal*, no. 2, 1982.
18 Mentioned in Vellay and Frampton, 1985, p.239.
19 Stamp, 1982, p.19.
20 Author's conversation with Nick Goldfinger, 2002.
21 From Open University A305 radio programme, 'A Commentary on Western Architecture', 27, 1974.
22 For further details, see *Le Corbusier: Architect of the Century*, London: The Arts Council of Great Britain, 1987, pp.212–214.
23 Le Corbusier describes this in J. Peter, *The Oral History of Modern Architecture*, New York: Harry N. Abrams, 1994, p.141.
24 Open University radio programme, 1974
25 Joseph Abram, interview with Goldfinger, London, 3/9/83.
26 Goldfinger, 'Der Neue Baustil' in *Pester Lloyd* (Budapest), 8/8/25, revised translation dated February 1987 in GolEr 338/4.

27 Minutes of the meeting of CIA, 22/3/26 in GolEr491/6.

28 His daughter Louise Kehoe described Lubetkin's political allegiance: 'he turned to communism, rejoicing in the revolution of 1917, and embracing the doctrines of Marx and Lenin as though they held a key to all the mysteries of the universe. He professed himself a communist for the rest of his life, never allowing a word of criticism for the Soviet Union to pass his lips'. In L. Kehoe, *This Dark House: A Memoir*, London. Penguin, 1995, p.12.

29 Minutes of the meeting of CIA, 22/3/26 in GolEr 491/6.

30 This is described in a Hungarian television interview in 1984.

31 The caption to a photograph in *The Architectural Review*, January 1963, states 'The large centre counter was not designed or approved by the architect.'

32 Quoted in R. Elwall, *Ernö Goldfinger*, RIBA Drawings Monographs no. 3 London: Academy Editions, p.33.

33 Quoted, for instance, in Dunnett's 'Conversations with Ernö Goldfinger', unpublished notes, 20/2/82, but repeated elsewhere. Goldfinger added that it was lucky that clients couldn't understand plans as 'otherwise I would never have been able to build what I have built'.

34 Goldfinger acknowledged this in the Hungarian television programme made in 1984. Translated transcript in National Trust Collection 2 Willow Road, Hampstead, p.2.

35 Quoted in Goldfinger's obituary of Sive, *The Times*, 25 September 1958, p.15.

Chapter 4

Connections

Everyone always seems to have known me.

Goldfinger didn't visit Picasso's studio, as he wasn't prepared to kowtow to him,[1] but he did meet almost every other major artist and architect living in Paris in the 1920s and 30s. Many were personal friends. As he later put it in characteristically egoistic form 'Everyone always seems to have known me.'[2] One unexpected connection, though, was with the avant-garde American composer, John Cage, who worked for a month with Goldfinger in the late 1920s. Cage later became infamous with his 1952 composition '4′ 33″', a completely silent piece of music which depended on noises and shuffling from the audience and other environmental sounds for its effect – one of his many unusual and challenging compositions and 'happenings'. But in the late 1920s, Cage wanted to become an architect. He left California for Paris – dropping out of college to travel – and became fascinated with the Gothic buildings he encountered there. He spent six weeks in the Bibliothèque Mazarin studying fifteenth-century building design without a teacher. Then, at a chance encounter at a railway station with a Professor Pijoan whom he'd known from his college in Pomona, he happened to mention his desire to study architecture:

> He gave me literally a swift kick in the pants and then said 'Go tomorrow to Goldfinger. I'll arrange for you to work with him. He's a modern architect.'[3]

This kick in the pants sent him to Goldfinger's office where he expected to learn about modernism. Instead, Goldfinger set him to work copying Greek columns. Throughout his life Goldfinger insisted on the foundational place of drawing skills for both architects and artists. Even the great artists who rejected conventional draughtsmanship and opted for an apparently childlike style learnt to draw skilfully before they dispensed with this way of drawing.

At the time Ernö's main work was still redesigning apartments, turning them into modern spaces, regardless of their original state, and equipping them with streamlined furniture and fittings. His clients included the writer Richard Wyndham, whom he'd met through Lee Miller, and Suzanne Blum, the lawyer who had helped Ernö recover his fee from Helena Rubinstein. Cage was kept busy drawing columns until he was needed to measure up an apartment, then he would produce a drawing of it from which Goldfinger could work.

The turning point came when Cage heard Goldfinger preaching to some girlfriends. 'To be an architect' he declared, 'one must devote one's life solely to architecture.' There was no room for a dilettante. This was perhaps an echo of Perret's teaching, though Goldfinger always maintained that architecture was not a cosy profession that you could take up on a whim. It had to come from within; you had to have it in your guts. These overheard words had a profound effect on Cage. He did not feel ready to make this level of commitment. The next time he got an opportunity to talk with Goldfinger, he revealed that he was pulled in opposing directions, committed to painting and to music as well as to architecture. He decided it was time to move on, later returning to the United States to study composition with Arnold Schoenberg.[4] In later years Ernö could not remember Cage; but Ernö left a strong impression on Cage, who recalled these days in several interviews.

Despite preaching the message that you should live, eat and sleep architecture, Goldfinger found time to enjoy the nightlife of Paris. His landlord passed on complaints from other tenants of late-night parties in his apartment at rue Abel Hovelacque. From the landlord's point of view Goldfinger was at risk of turning the flat into a hotel or a nightclub.[5] Even when socialising though, the subject of discussion was likely to be art, architecture or furniture. Mary McBrady commented in a note after meeting Ernö at a party: 'You interested me a lot with your modernistic raving.'[6] His enthusiasm for architecture and design was infectious. Robert Delaunay dedicated a drawing to him after a long – probably one-sided – conversation about the merits of tubular steel-framed furniture.[7]

Ernö also had a wilder side and a tendency to get into heated arguments and even fights. On one occasion, he had to have a badly split lip sewn up by Dr Dalsace.[8] He quarrelled with taxi drivers over change and with doormen at the Jockey Club, the famous nightclub styled as a Wild West cowboy saloon. According to his contemporary at the Atelier Perret, Oskar Nitzchke, he would say anything to anyone: 'I don't know what he felt he had to prove.'[9] Yet at the same time this young, tall, strong, handsome and supremely confident man was very successful with women. He could be arrogant, rude and even violent, and some of his fellow students disliked him for this. He had, for example, gone on the rampage after one Bal des Quat'z Arts, where there was open hostility between the ateliers, storming off into the night intent on beating up homosexuals. This explosive aspect of his personality erupted loudly with little warning throughout his life, though he appears to have conquered his homophobia, counting several openly homosexual men among his friends.

Ernö's wild spirits even resulted in a challenge to a duel. The source of the insult was his shimmying at a nightclub. Another guest took offence at Goldfinger's antics and the situation was not diffused until lawyers had been brought in to write and exchange elaborate official apologies. Had the duel taken place, Goldfinger might have surprised his challenger as he'd been schooled in fencing by one of the great Italian fencers, Italo Santelli. A duel would probably have been fought with sabres, and would not have been to the death. Although not commonplace, many such duels were fought over matters of honour in Europe in the inter-war period. The publisher George Weidenfeld, for example, fought one in Vienna as late as 1938.[10] Ernö's father, Oscar, had several duelling scars, and had made sure that his son was prepared to defend the family honour if necessary. While his father was recounting a particularly gruesome duelling story at the dinner table, the young Ernö had protested by grabbing a handful of peas and squeezing them through his fingers; but by his twenties, Ernö had developed a more robust attitude to combat.

For recreation, Ernö liked to go horse-riding twice a week in the Bois de Boulogne. On one ride he came across two women whose horses had bolted. He galloped after them and secured their reigns, much to the women's relief. On enquiring their names, he discovered that one of them, a fellow Hungarian, was Madame Njinski, whose husband, in the network of Parisian artistic connections, had danced Stravinsky's *Rites of Spring* on the opening night of the Perret-designed Théâtre des Champs Elysées.

Like many young intellectuals of his generation, Ernö was drawn to Marxism. He became an active member of a revolutionary party, the Association des Écrivains et Artistes Revolutionnaires (AEAR), perhaps the closest he came to joining the Communist Party – the AEAR had direct links with the French Communist Party, though Goldfinger may not have realised this. This organisation had a clear and uncompromising goal:

> To replace present-day society which is anarchical and incapable of using its created resources to the full with a society with a planned economy.[11]

Ernö's involvement included designing a gravestone for an anti-fascist, Albert Perdreaux, who had been killed while preparing for a strike. The design incorporated a large red star and a hammer and sickle. He also designed desks and benches for a projected Workers' University and arranged for clothing packages to be taken to imprisoned comrades. He was given the task of making links with architects in the Soviet Union, and even applied for a visa to visit Russia.[12]

Ernö also found time to act in a film, playing the part of an engine driver. He caused quite a stir in the Dôme when he came in still dressed for the part. Another scene required him to be a parachutist, though he did not actually jump from a plane himself. Ernö may have got this work through his colleague Paul Nelson, who was artistic director on several Hollywood films. Ernö's girlfriend at the time, Margot Monclus, chided him for accepting low wages for his film work. She told him to get in touch with Man Ray to find out how much 'Elizabeth' (i.e. Lee Miller) was paid for her film work. As Margot put it:

> I need a husband who earns plenty of money – or at least defends his own financial interests firmly.[13]

Margot, an elegant woman with exquisite taste in clothes, designed and made knitwear and tapestries, some of it for Eva Schiaparelli. She and Ernö had moved in together and were living as man and wife from 1927 onwards. Margot's business was precarious and she relied heavily on Ernö's financial as well as emotional support. Ernö and Margot were still living together when Ernö met and fell in love with a young English art student seven years his junior, Ursula Blackwell.

Urusla was tall, elegant, quiet, intelligent, witty and, like Ernö, had a rebellious streak. Charlotte Perriand described her as 'a beautiful young girl', yet 'a little distant, friendly, observant' when she first met her with Ernö in the *Deux Magots*.[14] Ursula's family – the Blackwells of Crosse and Blackwell food manufacturers – owned a large estate at Oxhey near Watford. She had been brought up in the hunting, shooting and fishing set, but despised it, though like Ernö she enjoyed riding. She reacted against her family and pursued her passion, going to study art in Paris with her friend Lesley Black, who was still a teenager. (Lesley later married the film director John Huston who proposed to her within fifteen minutes of their meeting, when she was only eighteen; they married in 1937 and divorced in 1945). Together she and Ursula enjoyed the artistic and social whirl of Paris, helped by an extremely generous allowance – so generous that Ursula confessed she found it difficult to spend it all.[15]

Ernö and Ursula told different stories about how they first met in 1931.[16] She remembered him coming up to her with flowers as she got into a taxi. He told her his name was Ernest, anglicising Ernö. As a result Ursula

4.1
Ursula Blackwell and Lesley Black, Paris, c.1931

nearly didn't see him again as she couldn't face going out with someone called Ernest.[17] She liked the name Ernö, though, and delighted in putting the two little dots over the 'o' whenever she wrote his name. He claimed that she started talking to him in a café, asking for a light for a cigarette. A third version is that they met at Ozenfant's studio in Montsouris.[18] Whatever the truth of the first encounter, they began a passionate relationship, and were soon thinking about building a house together in Paris. Ernö persuaded Ursula to study with Ozenfant. Their relationship was, however, made more poignant by Ursula's frequent returns to England, and by Goldfinger's continuing relationship with Margot.

Committing herself to Ernö was no easy decision for Ursula as it represented a significant rejection of her family and their expectations for her. Ernö's letters gave Ursula the strength to resist family pressures:

> It was wonderful to get your letter – I needed it to give me courage. I'm not so brave, really, you know, and it is only your love and my faith in you that can give me the strength to break entirely with this past life of mine.
>
> For me it's already the past life, but even then it's difficult. If only I didn't love these conventional well brought up brothers and

> sisters of mine. If they would only understand. It would be so much easier to just run away to Paris and start with you right away, but their future lives depend rather on mine. They keep asking me what I mean to do, and begging me not to settle definitely in Paris and tie myself with a house etc. etc. – sooner or later I shall have to tell them about you.

When she broke the news of her involvement with Ernö to her brother Anthony, he was shocked that she had allowed herself to become involved with a 'married man' and was afraid of scandal. The fact that Ernö was also a Hungarian Jew and a Marxist was not likely to impress the very English Blackwell family either.

Disentangling Ernö's life from Margot's was far from straightforward. While on holiday in Italy with Lesley Black, Ursula wrote from Assisi revealing how much she was in love with him:

> Ernö, will you still love me when I come back? I've been trying to tell myself the whole time that it would be the best thing for us all if you didn't, but I want you to. I used to be entirely happy when I was with Lesley and now can't concentrate on anything for more than five minutes before my mind has slipped back to you and I'm wondering what you would think of what I'm doing or seeing or I altogether leave Italy and remember all the times we were together. In fact you're a damn nuisance, but I think you're worth it.[19]

As she spent longer away from him, Ursula's mind became firmer. She wasn't prepared to carry on in the same way. Now she knew she loved him, there was no room for Margot in the relationship. She gave Ernö an ultimatum by letter. He had written to her, begging her to return to Paris. Writing from Florence, Ursula told him how much she longed to return to him but that she 'should feel the biggest cad on earth' if she came back while Margot was away – as Ernö had suggested.[20] Ursula had talked to Margot before leaving, and realised that Margot could not bear to break with Ernö. Ursula for her part wasn't prepared to compromise. If Ernö wanted Ursula to return to Paris, he would have to leave Margot:

> Of course we can't go on as we were before I left Paris, it's impossible to be friends with a man when you know you love each other, while there are physical barriers between you. It took me 4 days after I left to realise this and I made up my mind that it is the only possible solution for us, that I should return to Paris and we'll build the house and will have that very complete friendship, and if Margot is big enough to accept that, there is no reason for us to

> want anything else. You love me, for what you think you can make me – 'libre et belle', I know now what I want in life and that is the entirety of it. I was trying to pick out the nice bits before and there are so many I thought these were enough to be happy on for ever. You've shown me already that there's more to it all than that. I'm getting the true 'constructive' idea into my mind, but you can't make me free if we can only console each other during your other 'pick ups'!!![21]

The letter had the desired effect. Ernö broke off his relationship with Margot, though he continued to help Margot financially for some time after they separated. Margot subsequently had a relationship with Goldfinger's contemporary from the Atelier Perret, Oscar Nitzchke,[22] and went on to marry James

4.2
Young lovers – Ursula and Ernö

4.3
Ernö

Butler in 1939, eventually moving to New York. Yet it is clear from her letters to Ernö that many years after their break-up she maintained a tenderness and love for him. Writing at the end of 1937, for instance, she told him:

> You must know that it is impossible for me to tear from my heart what was, even though that has harmed me greatly – and I always have a place within me for you and for everything that touches or concerns you . . .[23]

By mid-1931 Ernö and Ursula, very much in love, were making long-term plans for a life together. Ursula, now back in England, longed to be with him. Her letters are full of optimism and excitement about their future lives together:

> The future is tremendous, limitless. I know my 'but' [goal]. I discovered what it was in Florence one morning – to find pure beauty in reality, with an entire comprehension of reality, that is truth – I have always seen truth fairly clearly but sometimes it hurt and so I gave myself an easy philosophy that wrapped up the sharp edge of truth with a piece of bright-coloured velvet – which gave me a feeling of false security and now you say that sharp edges are beautiful and I believe you – but I must be capable of seeing that

4.4
and Ursula on
holiday

> sharp edge and of using it without chopping others or myself to pieces. Ernö, the whole of the world is ours – we have youth, health, faith, love, you have brains, I have some too, and if we have courage and even more perseverance we should win: it's so very easy to be sidetracked by little things, we mustn't, all the little details of life should lead up to the big ultimate aim. Damn – I won't be petty-minded. I have an awful fear of it.[24]

Ernö wrote to Ursula of his meetings with Hans Arp, Max Ernst, Constantin Brancusi, Ozenfant, and Oscar Kokoschka, but all he really wanted was to see her. Their letters to each other are full of longing, interspersed with optimistic plans for the future. In a letter Ernö sent to Ursula from Paris that year, he spelt out his life's vision and goal:

> I would like to bring a little order into the disorder, clarity into obscurity, straight and pure lines, limpid and clear forms . . . dreams in the place of *abrutissmentent*.[25]

Another love letter from the same year showed him reluctant to commit immediately to building a family home in Paris – something they had begun to plan. Eager as he was to build his first house, particularly for Ursula, he was wary of creating a burden that would chain them for years to a particular place.[26] A few days later he was still contemplating taking up a tentative offer of work in the USSR helping to construct industrial centres in the Urals.[27] If he went, Ursula would accompany him: 'The idea about Russia is good. We must go' she wrote.[28] Their plans were affected by economic factors and the rapidly changing political situation:

> I don't think I dare try to build the house out of income with the pound sterling liable to bust either now or in a year or two.[29]

Instead she would investigate the terms of her inheritance settlement to see if she would be allowed to use capital for the project.

Everything seemed possible – they wanted to travel and they wanted to live together. In the longer term they had decided that Ernö would build a house for them somewhere, but for the present they did not want any ties that would limit their freedom. By mid-September of 1931 Ursula was becoming frustrated by their long separation:

> Next time I run away with a man I shall do it in the correct old-fashioned method, stealing out at midnight and leaving a note on the dressing table. I think it's a more definite and quicker way – this is like a short story that has been eked out into a three volume novel. Very nerve-wracking and unsatisfactory.[30]

Meanwhile, Ernö was re-decorating the flat at 3 Rue de la Cité in preparation for Ursula's return to Paris; Ursula had to make do with shopping in London:

> I've bought the most wonderful things for the flat – all metal, all standard, all British. It makes me quite patriotic. My wastepaper basket, and the clock, and the knives and forks and spoons and salt cellars. I'm longing to show you.[31]

Despite all their plans, though, it wasn't until 1934 that the couple would be living permanently together – until then they were oscillating between England and Paris; sometimes together, often apart.

On 16 February 1932, Goldfinger was eventually awarded his DPLG, his professional qualification. He could now call himself an Architect, Diplômé Par le Gouvernement. Ursula had already begun to investigate Ernö's prospects if they were to move to England. Through her brother she had met a young Cambridge lecturer in history of architecture and quizzed him in a letter (National Trust, 2 Willow Road Collection) about whether there would be openings for modernist architects:

> . . . he said that in two or three years' time he considered that there would be [opportunities] in England as there are very few

modernists here now, at the moment they are really only making modern buildings in the towns, offices, public buildings etc. as it is more expensive to make a flat-roofed concrete small private house, than the old-fashioned brick and tile roofed ones. Apparently Lutyens, the most well-known English architect, made his reputation on small houses and also was advertised in 'Country Life' (an English paper), on the other hand, a young architect has recently made his name by winning a big competition to build a two million pound building.

4.5
Marriage, Paris 1931

In the end, a combination of financial, biological and political events conspired to steer their lives towards England. Ernö and Ursula married on 3 April 1933 in a civil ceremony at the Marie in Paris with Ursula's sister 'Barbie' and their West Highland terrier Pegotty-Anne as the key witnesses. Ursula was several months pregnant. Her grandmother later claimed to have known this all along, though they did not advertise the fact. In a letter to Ernö in the same year, Ursula describes the marriage as 'suspiciously rushed' in the eyes of her family.[32] They had not planned to have a child so soon, but Ursula's pregnancy simply accelerated the process of establishing a home for themselves – and a pattern of life that would allow them to live together – that they had been discussing for the past two years. In the meantime, Goldfinger spent most of his time in Paris, while Ursula returned to England.

Goldfinger was unusual in his combination of artistic temperament with clear and rational thinking with a solid base in science. Throughout his life he saw architecture as a series of problems that he as architect needed to solve by rational means. The extent of his mathematical and scientific confidence and skills is shown by his heliometer, an instrument which he designed to help him solve problems of insolation (exposure to the sun's rays) in his buildings, and of which he was justly proud. He perfected the instrument, with some assistance from the Paris Observatory, in 1932. This ingenious device, built with the help of a mechanic, measures the intensity and penetration of sunlight into buildings and the shadows cast by them at any time of the day, for any season, and in any lattitude. The architect places a scale model of approximately 2′6″ square on to a tilting board. This can be inclined and rotated according to the building's position on the Earth's surface, the season and the time of day.[33] The sun's rays are simulated by a 300 watt lamp with a reflector, positioned across the room, twelve to fifteen feet from the heliometer. The whole operation has to be conducted in a darkened room, like some kind of mystic rite. The pattern of light can be photographed in each position, giving the architect detailed information about where shadows will fall on any day of the year.[34]

Ylla, who was a close friend, photographed Goldfinger, a cigarette in his mouth, sitting behind the heliometer in 1933. The resulting photograph turns the scientific instrument into a surrealist sculpture worthy of Man Ray: the heliometer, superimposed from another negative, appears solarised, and sprouts like a metal tree from his groin while he turns his head from the light. The cigarette in his mouth cuts through the ectoplasmic heliometer.

Ylla's real name was Kamilla Koffler. She had a great deal in common with Ernö. She was tall, of Eastern European origin (her parents

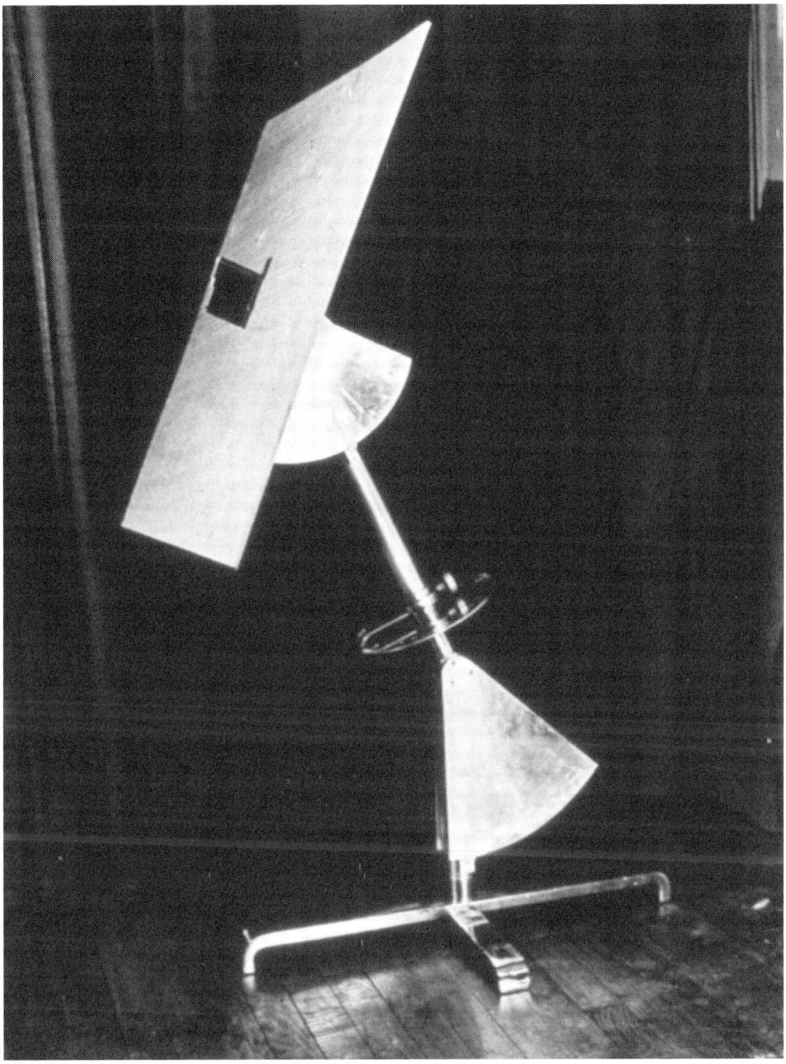

4.6
Ernö's heliometer anticipates the new iMac

were Hungarian and Yugoslav), Jewish, and had come to Paris to be a sculptor. Born in Vienna, she had lived in Hungary, Romania and Yugoslavia, before arriving in Paris aged twenty, in 1932 – indeed many people thought she was Romanian. While working as a sculptor, she made a living by retouching photographs in the studio of the Hungarian photographer Ergy Landau, but, after exhibiting her own photographs of animals, including Georges Braque's dogs, she decided to devote her energies solely to her own photography. As a Jew, she had to flee the Nazis, and managed to escape to New York, where she set up a studio and became famous for animal photography. Her photographs appeared in *The Herald Tribune*, *Picture Post*, *Lilliput* and *Look*; she also published a series of photographic books, all on animals. Later she became more adventurous, photographing animals in the wild, travelling to Africa and India. The Goldfingers kept in touch with her, and she photographed their children a number of times, once at Whipsnade playing with tiger cubs when she visited England – much to the children's amusement, the tiger cubs urinated on their nanny. In 1953 she survived a plane crash into the sea on a journey from Boston – she was pulled from the wreckage and given resuscitation for over half an hour before starting to breathe on her own again. Her mother and another passenger were killed in the crash. She couldn't cheat death a second time. In 1955, while photographing a bullock cart race in India she suffered a terrible accident. She fell from the hood of a jeep, and went into a coma, dying soon after.

Ernö had a very busy year in 1933. Not only was he trying to cope at a distance with marriage and incipient fatherhood and all the readjustments this entailed, but he was also elected as the secretary of the French section of the Congrès International d'Architecture Moderne (CIAM). This upset Le Corbusier and Siegfried Gideon, who wanted to exercise control of CIAM through its central council the Comité International pour la Réalisation des Problèmes de l'Architecture (CIRPAC). They had wanted to put their own preferred candidate in this honorary position, but the French members voted Goldfinger in as their representative. The French section met regularly in Paris at Zervos' flat, but Le Corbusier didn't deign to attend.

It was also in 1933 that Ernö began work on his first building. He took on a commission for conversions to an existing house at Cucq near Le Touquet for a Monsieur Lahousse, a wool merchant whom he'd met through Tapies de Celeyran (a nephew of Toulouse-Lautrec, and a fellow pupil of Ursula's at the Ozenfant school).[35] The commission also involved designing a free-standing studio block in the garden. The studio that Goldfinger built from brick and concrete is two storeys high with a monopitch roof. The ground floor is taken up with a double garage. The first floor, reached by an external spiral staircase is a studio opening onto a terrace. Next to the studio Goldfinger built a pond fed into by a narrow canal with its own system of lock gates for the children to play with. He fitted out the interior of the converted house with his own furniture designs, including a high-backed version of the safari chair, a children's bunk bed in nautical style with a rope ladder, and a dining table of polished stone supported by brick columns which went through the floor to their own foundations. He also created a demountable bed, using the same construction principles as the safari chair. For the walls he used mainly cork sheet, with cork tiling for the floors. The curtains were made of oiled silk. As with all his domestic commissions, Goldfinger devoted far more energy and time to this house than could possibly be reflected in the fees charged. For him, each house that he worked on was a chance to develop prototypes which he could then use in further work. He spent some of 1934 in Cucq supervising the work, and developed a very good relationship with the Lahousse family, with whom he stayed in contact for many years.

Between 29 July and 14 August of 1933, Ernö attended CIAM IV, the famous congress that took place on a Mediterranean cruise ship, the SS *Patris II*, on the round trip between Marseilles and Athens. The congress was originally to have been in Moscow, but communications broke down and CIRPAC, which was dominated by Le Corbusier, decided to change the venue. As secretary for the French division of CIAM, Goldfinger was responsible for making the travel arrangements to Marseille for the French party – another pressure on his time in an extremely busy year.

More than a hundred delegates attended the congress. These included architects, designers and artists such as Pierre Chareau, Jean Badovici, Charlotte Perriand, Le Corbusier, Wells Coates, van Eesteren, Alvar Aalto (who joined the cruise in Athens), Ferdinand Lèger and László Moholy-Nagy. Many of these were already Goldfinger's friends or acquaintances. Others, such as Wells Coates and Moholy-Nagy, he met on board for the first time, but maintained a friendship after the cruise. If, however, there was a risk of the young Goldfinger getting self-important as a result of mixing as an equal in such company, despite not yet having completed his first building, the letter waiting for him in Athens from Ursula would have helped to bring him down to size. It reveals how important in grounding and supporting him their relationship would become. She began:

> I wonder if you collected all your little architects together in the end – and if you had tummy aches of emotion.[36]

But by the next page she is praising the shop front he designed for Helena Rubinstein:

> We passed Rubinstein's today. I was all thrilled – as if I suddenly saw a bit of you. It really looks marvellous and might have been done yesterday.[37]

In Athens, Ernö displayed his plans for a twenty-seven-storey block of flats, but the design made little impact at the time.[38] Some of its features, such as the rooftop nursery, recur in Le Corbusier's Unité d'Habitation in Marseilles.

It is easy to idealise this fortnight's cruise: many of the century's most remarkable architects were on board. But in a letter from Athens, Ernö reveals the 'perfect disorganisation' of the congress, and sums up the event as 'much fuss, not much work'. Le Corbusier's speeches were long and boring,

4.7
Alvar Aalto and László Moholy-Nagy on the deck of SS *Patris II*, Ernö's snapshot from the CIAM cruise, 1933

as were most of the others.[39] For him, and for many of the young architects involved this was a place to make connections, something that was in some ways obstructed rather than facilitated by the day-to-day business of CIAM. Even the self-important Athens Charter was, according to Goldfinger at least, an afterthought, not something concocted during the event.

Ernö was working in Paris and Cucq or travelling for most of Ursula's pregnancy, much of which she spent in England at the family home in Oxhey, and later in a rented cottage in Burford near Oxford. She wrote regularly to him about the pregnancy, talking about the baby-to-be as 'Jennifer John' or sometimes 'Jane John'. 'Darling – come back as soon as you can' she wrote, 'but it is wonderful to have a little deputy Ernö kicking about inside – only I still like the real one best.'[40] Her serious interest in architecture and design is apparent in a letter describing her visit to Lubetkin and Tecton's recently completed Gorilla House at London's Regent's Park zoo:

> It is good, rather Le Corbusier – badly so about two little businesses stuck on at the sides like ears where the public goes in when it is closed – also there is an impossible concrete seat in between [. . .] We saw the house being closed – all the wall and ceiling moves out together pushed by several men.[41]

4.8
Ernö at the Parthenon, 1933

The Gorilla House was one of very few modern buildings in London that excited Ernö – he had a higher regard for it than he did for most of Lubetkin's buildings for human beings. The only other building that excited his architectural imagination here was the Isokon Flats at Lawn Road, designed by his new friend Welles Coates.

Ursula had strong family ties in England and it would have been natural for her to gravitate in pregnancy towards her family home, where she could be sure of support, particularly given Ernö's work commitments in 1933. But the more immediate reason for giving birth in England rather than in France was to avoid his being called up for French National Service. At the time there was no British National Service and by being born in England, he would have been able to avoid call-up papers in France (Peter was in fact later called up to do National Service in Britain). Even during the later stages of Ursula's pregnancy, they were still entertaining the possibility of returning to Paris and living permanently in France, possibly building a family home there.[42] Ernö had even begun the process of taking on French nationality. Had he decided to settle there, he would, as a conspicuous Jew with communist connections, have been lucky to survive the war. A comment in a letter from Ursula indicates that as early as 1933 they were both aware that the political situation was unstable:

> When does the Franco-German war start? You'd better not be a Frenchman too quickly?[43]

This may in itself have been enough to prevent Ernö going through with French naturalisation. But there were also financial obstacles to remaining in France.

On 10 September 1933, less than a month after Goldfinger's return from the Athens conference, and on the day before Ernö's own thirty-first birthday, their first son, John Peter Gordon (known as Peter), was born in hospital in Oxford. Ernö was present at the birth.

The Goldfingers constructed Peter's name in the same rational spirit as Ernö constructed buildings and furniture: 'John' and 'Peter' were chosen because they translated easily into French. If they decided to carry on living in France, then he could become 'Jean-Pierre' – in fact Max Ernst refers to him as 'Jean-Pierre' in a letter to the Goldfingers written in 1936.[44] 'Gordon' was included as an alternative surname that would allow Peter to become John Peter Gordon at a later date if he so chose, without sacrificing his initials. Shortly after Peter had been born, Mr Parsons, the local clergyman came to visit Ursula in Burford. She described the encounter to Ernö in a letter:

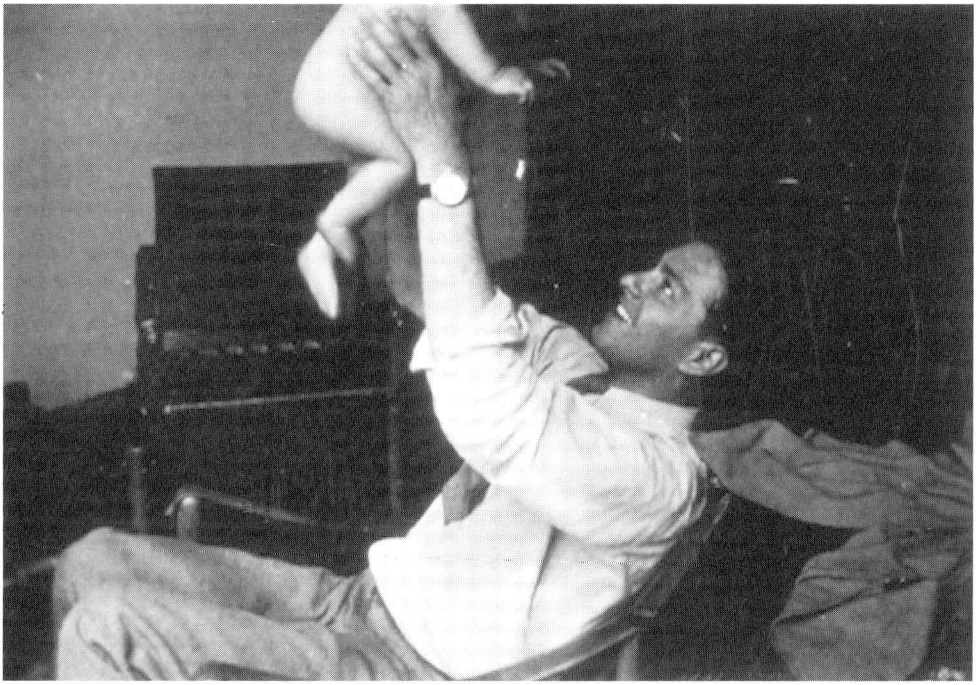

4.9
'It's a boy!' Ernö with his first child, c.1933

> He was very nice. Told me to try to imagine that God's relationship to me was the same as mine to John. I at once pictured God as an enormous pair of tits![45]

Ursula had a substantial inheritance in a trust fund following a legal settlement of her parents' estate in September 1930. Her Uncle Geoffrey and Cousin Philip had been appointed as trustees. In order to gain access to any of the money Ursula, who was still only twenty-four, needed to persuade them that she wasn't going to fritter it away and that any business venture she invested in was a sound one. In 1933 she met with her Uncle Geoffrey to investigate the possibility of releasing money to set up a design business with Ernö, to buy a building that could serve both as an office and home and, ultimately to build a family residence. Ursula's impression was that Uncle Geoffrey had a prejudice against investing any of the money in France – still their first choice at the time. The message she was left with was that it would be easier to persuade the trustees to release the money if it was to be used in England.[46] Her Uncle Geoffrey's worries about the stability of France were well-founded: by the end of 1935, Ernö was writing of the difficulties in Paris for foreigners caused by fluctuating exchange rates in the aftermath of the Wall Street stock market crash.[47] It was probably the combination of the greater likelihood of financial security, and the awareness of the changing political climate in mainland Europe, that eventually led to the Goldfingers setting up home in London, though Ernö had been a lifelong Anglophile. He later claimed – disingenuously perhaps – that he was attracted to Britain because it did not have any modern architecture, and so would be a land of opportunity for an innovative architect, and that it was only subsequently that he learned that the reason there were no modern buildings here was that the British didn't particularly like them.

Once they had made the decision to leave Paris, Ernö tied up the loose ends of his design practice in Paris, arranged for huge crates of furniture and drawings to be shipped to England, and finally set sail himself. He did not sever his connections with Paris – for both he and Ursula it was the 'moveable feast' that Ernest Hemingway described in the sense that it stayed with them forever.[48] They revisited Paris often, and many of their friends and colleagues from those days passed through London or, like them, settled there. Many of the paintings on their walls were by surrealist friends, painted in the Paris years.

When Ernö left Paris in November 1934, the main structural elements of his personality as an architect and as a man – scarcely distinguishable in his case – had been formed and were starting to find their expression. He had all the benefits of a rigorous Beaux-Arts training in planning, drawing, and the use of materials. At the same time he had a tradition to react against, again provided by the Beaux-Arts. He had a favoured medium – reinforced concrete – that provided exciting possibilities, and principles for its use, in particular a commitment to the visible expression of the supporting structure of anything that he built. This came from his master, Perret. He was firmly within the Modern Movement in architecture, and, particularly through his CIAM connections, he knew and understood the major proponents of the emerging International Style; also, like most members of CIAM he had a commitment to improving social conditions through good design. Yet his knowledge of the history of architecture, and his own strength of character, stopped him becoming a slavish follower of 1930s architectural fashion. Unlike many of his contemporaries, he completely rejected the Corbusian use of white rendering to hide the structure of buildings. He had a political stance – he was a Marxist, and remained a Marxist throughout his life. And he had a commitment to solving architectural problems in a rational way: human reason was the best hope for the future.

Notes

1 Reported in conversation with James Dunnett who had asked him about this, London, 23/12/01.
2 This was his reply to John Allen when he asked Ernö how he came to meet so many of the major artists in Paris. Author's conversation with John Allen, 28/9/02.
3 From John Cage, 'Lecture on Commitment' in *A Year from Monday*, London: Calder and Boyars, 1968, p.113.
4 See also the account in Joan Retallack (ed.) *Musicage: Cage Muses on Art and Music*, New England, Hanover: Wesleyan University Press, 1996, pp.83–4. Although Goldfinger made a lasting impression on Cage, the effect was not mutual. When James Dunnett asked Goldfinger about Cage in later life, Goldfinger had no recollection whatsoever of him. Conversation with James Dunnett, 17/7/02.
5 For example, letter from F. Gillion dated 21/12/25, in GolEr 530/2.
6 Mary McBrady, letter to Ernö Goldfinger, 4/1/28 in GolEr 530/2.
7 Dunnett, conversations with Ernö Goldfinger, unpublished manuscript, 30/9/83.
8 Dunnett, conversations with Ernö Goldfinger, unpublished manuscript, 30/7/80.
9 Oskar Nitzchke, interviewed by James Dunnett, unpublished transcript, 9/3/85.
10 This is mentioned in Daniel Snowman, *Hitler's Émigrés: The Cultural Impact on Britain of Refugees from Nazism*, London: Chatto & Windus, 2002, p.25.
11 AEAR Manifesto, 13/3/33 in GolEr 492/1.
12 See correspondence in GolEr 395/3.
13 Letter from Margot Monclus to Ernö, dated 12/7/30 in National Trust 2 Willow Road collection.
14 Charlotte Perriand, preface to James Dunnett and Gavin Stamp, *Ernö Goldfinger: Works 1*, London: Architectural Association, 1983, p.5.
15 Report of a conversation with Frances Goldfinger, private conversation with author, October 2001.
16 Yet another version is that they met in Ozenfant's studio – something that seems to contradict Goldfinger's claim that he introduced her to Ozenfant.
17 He kept the name 'Ernest' on his British passport until 1958 when he reverted to Ernö.
18 Recalled by Oscar Nitzske, interviewed by James Dunnett, 9/3/85.
19 Letter from Ursula in Assisi to Ernö in Paris, 17/5/31, in National Trust 2 Willow Road collection.
20 Letter from Ursula in Florence to Ernö in Paris, 1/6/31, in National Trust 2 Willow Road collection.
21 Letter from Ursula in Florence to Ernö in Paris, 1/6/31, in National Trust 2 Willow Road collection.
22 Oscar Nitzchke, interviewed by James Dunnett, 9/3/85.
23 Margot Monclus, letter to Ernö, 27/12/37, in GolEr/276.
24 Letter from Ursula to Ernö, undated, from Sandhurst, in the National Trust 2 Willow Road collection.
25 Letter from Ernö to Ursula, 30/5/31, in National Trust 2 Willow Road collection
26 Letter from Ernö to Ursula, 15/7/31, in National Trust 2 Willow Road collection.
27 Letter from Ernö to Ursula, 18/7/31, in National Trust 2 Willow Road collection.
28 Letter from Ursula to Ernö, 1931, in National Trust 2 Willow Road collection.
29 Letter from Ursula to Ernö, 1931, in National Trust 2 Willow Road collection.
30 Letter from Ursula to Ernö, 18/9/31, in National Trust 2 Willow Road collection.
31 Letter from Ursula in The Berkeley Hotel, London W1, to Ernö in Paris, 24/11/31, in National Trust 2 Willow Road collection.

32 Letter from Ursula to Ernö, 1933, in National Trust, 2 Willow Road collection.

33 The basic design of the heliometer bears a quite close visual resemblance to the design of the latest tilting flat screen iMac computer.

34 The most detailed illustration of the workings of the heliometer is in *Architectural Design*, January 1963, pp.53–54 (this issue has an extended feature on Goldfinger's work). The heliometer drew the attention of the *Daily Express* reporter at the Olympia Building Exhibition in London in 1936 (*Daily Express*, 17 September 1936), where it is described as the work of 'a brilliant European inventor'.

35 This information comes from James Dunnett, *Conversations with Ernö Goldfinger*, unpublished notes, 19/2/83.

36 Letter from Ursula to Ernö in Athens, 29/7/33, National Trust 2 Willow Road collection.

37 Letter from Ursula to Ernö in Athens, 29/7/33, National Trust 2 Willow Road collection.

38 As described by Goldfinger in *Conversations with Ernö Goldfinger*, James Dunnett, unpublished manuscript, 20/2/82.

39 Letter from Ernö to Ursula, undated, August 1933, National Trust 2 Willow Road collection.

40 Letter from Ursula to Ernö, undated, 1933, National Trust 2 Willow Road collection.

41 Letter from Ursula to Ernö, undated, written from Burford, in National Trust 2 Willow Road collection.

42 This is clear from several undated letters written in 1933 from Ursula to Ernö, in National Trust 2 Willow Road collection.

43 Undated letter from Ursula, presumably 1933 or early 1934, in National Trust 2 Willow Road collection.

44 In GolEr/269/2.

45 Ursula to Ernö, undated letter from Burford, 1933, in National Trust 2 Willow Road collection.

46 Recounted in Ursula's letter to Ernö, 1933, in National Trust 2 Willow Road collection.

47 In a letter to Charles Reilly, 10/12/35, requesting a reference for Ozenfant to help him set up an art school in London, Ernö refers to the exchange rates and political instability as reasons why Ozenfant's former pupils cannot stay in Paris. In GolEr 278/2.

48 'If you are lucky enough to have lived in Paris as a young man, then wherever you go for the rest of your life, it stays with you, for Paris is a moveable feast.' This is from Hemingway's letter to a friend in 1950, inspired by his experience of Paris in the 1920s. It is printed as the motto of Ernest Hemingway *A Moveable Feast*, London: Arrow Books, 1996, first published by Jonathan Cape in 1936.

Chapter 5

Making a home

A young architect ought to be made to build his own house first.

The early 1930s saw a number of the most distinguished modern architects and designers emigrating to England, though few remained here. In several recent studies these architects have been described as in flight from Hitler, particularly since a number of them, like Goldfinger, were Jewish. This explains why, by the time war was declared, some of them had moved on to the relative safety of America. It also explains the artistic and cultural influx from the rest of Europe from the mid-1930s onwards. Yet in the early 1930s, very few people outside of Germany accurately foresaw the course of events. And in many cases the reasons for flight were overdetermined, with economic factors playing as great a role as political ones.

Many of the first wave of émigrés were seeking out new opportunities in what was then the largest city in Europe. Berthold Lubetkin was one of the first to settle in London, followed by Erich Mendelsohn in 1933, and Walter Gropius and Ernö Goldfinger in 1934. Marcel Breuer came in 1935. England for them was a powerful nation with interesting if somewhat staid architectural traditions and a shining industrial past. Pre-war London was the centre of a great empire, and had a larger population than New York.

Ernö joined Ursula and their son Peter in rented accommodation in Markham Square, off the King's Road in Chelsea. As a foreign national, however, he was initially only given a residency permit: the Home Office did not grant him official permission to carry on his profession until August 1935.[1] Even then, as a foreigner, he could not become a member of the Royal Institute of British Architects, or any other English body, and could not describe himself as a 'Registered Architect'.[2] Goldfinger didn't stop being an architect in the meantime – how could he? Architecture was his life. He had no hobbies, no other serious passions – apart from his interest in art. He lived for his work.

He always dressed like an English gentleman, perhaps influenced by Loos' and Gropius's preference for the English style of suit. This to some degree eased his integration into London life. He bought suits from Sandon Cie Ltd in Savile Row, with special pockets put in to accommodate his array of pens and pencils. He had his shoes handmade on a personal last in St James. This traditional style of dress may seem at odds with his commitment to rational modernism, but he argued that the English tradition in suits – tweeds, Oxford cloth and other traditional fabrics – was perfectly adapted to the English climate and one of our finer achievements. He was not alone among the avant-garde in admiring the English tailoring tradition – Coco Chanel, for instance, was greatly influenced by it. His unwillingness to jettison a successful and tested formula for the sake of novelty alone was also characteristic of his general approach to design.

5.1
Solarised Portrait of Ursula Goldfinger, c.1935
© Man Ray Trust/ ADAGP, Paris and DACS, London 2003

Like many of his fellow émigrés, Goldfinger adopted English mannerisms and customs partly out of a desire to be accepted and integrated into his new chosen country, though he always remained exotic and to some degree an outsider. His strong accent and idiosyncratic English revealed his origins as soon as he opened his mouth. And his unusual name immediately announced his Jewishness. When, soon after coming to England, however, someone suggested that he might find it good for business to change his name, his response was 'Marvellous! Let's change it to Cohen then!'[3] As an atheist, he had no time for religion, and thought the notion of Jewishness unscientific, both from a racial and from a biological point of view.[4] But he wasn't prepared to disguise his background and ditch the family name to minimise anti-Semitism. At least, this is the story he told in later life. However, in 1935 he did initiate investigations into the possibility of changing his name. This proved awkward in English law due to his Polish nationality. Although the Home Secretary was prepared to consider Goldfinger's desire to use a different name in connection with his profession as a special case, it seems that in the end Goldfinger decided not to proceed.[5] Writing to him in 1941, his brother George wanted to know if Ernö still planned to change his name. George was on the verge of gaining US citizenship which would allow him to change his surname and he wanted to keep the same surname as Ernö. In a practical spirit that Ernö no doubt appreciated, he hoped that Ernö would select a name beginning with 'A' as this would allow George to be the first author on co-authored scientific papers (his usual collaborators at the time had surnames beginning with 'B' and 'C').[6]

The Blackwell family at first disapproved of him. They had not expected Ursula to marry a foreigner with Marxist tendencies and surrealists for friends, and they shared some of their class's unthinking anti-Semitism. In the initial stages of the relationship, Ernö's continued involvement with

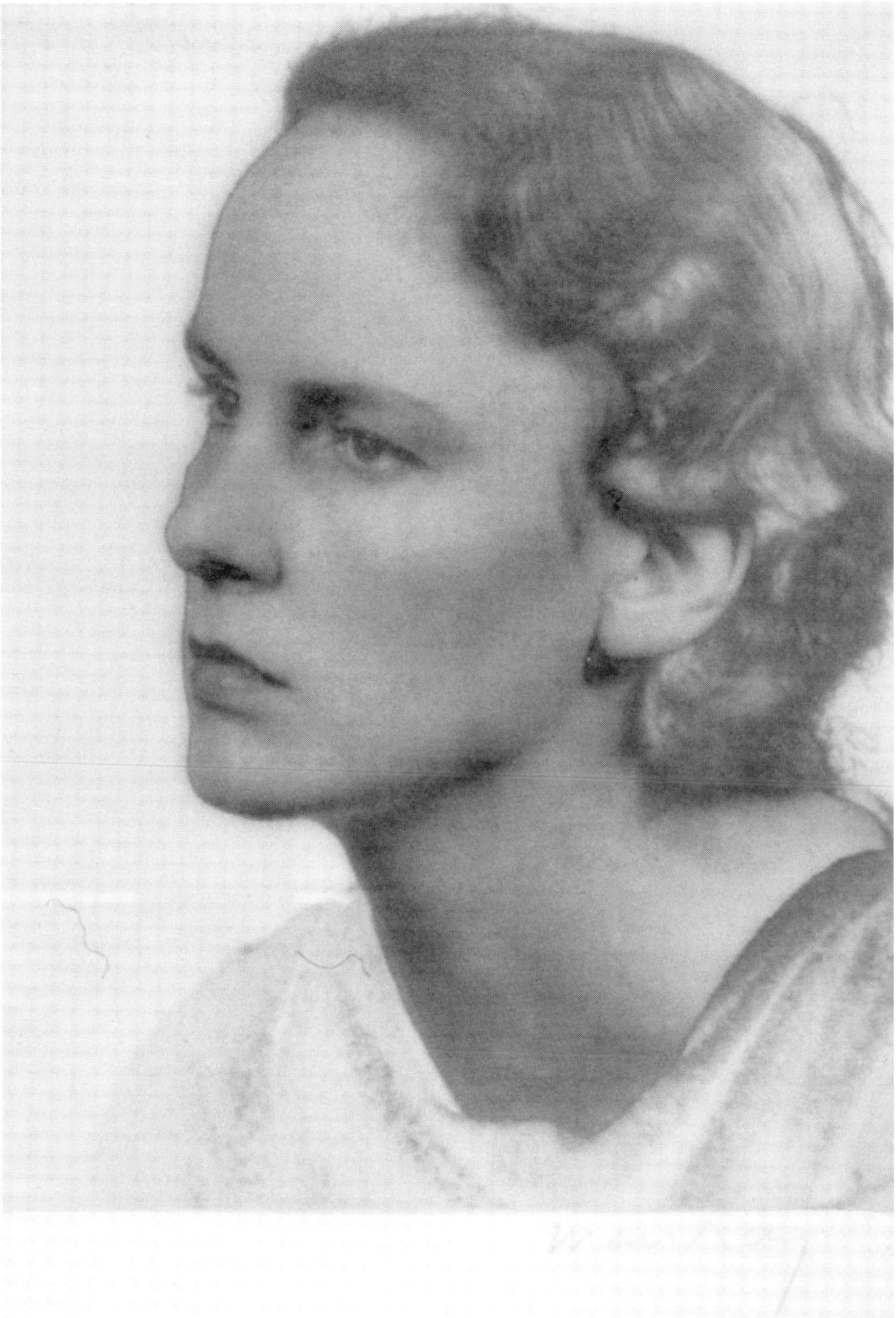

Margot must also have been a source of concern. But he soon managed to charm them.[7]

From Chelsea the Goldfinger family moved into 20 Springfield Road, St John's Wood, where Ernö set up an office in the front room and where they stayed until July 1935. Subsequently he rented an office at 7 Bedford Square. At this time Goldfinger commissioned portraits of Ursula and of Peter from Man Ray, whom he'd met in Paris. The resulting portraits show Ursula radiant and elegant, both when photographed alone and with her son. At this time Ernö and Man Ray were friends, having met in Paris through Lee Miller. They later fell out when Ernö made some remarks at the opening of Man Ray's photographic exhibition in London which Man Ray took to be disparaging.[8] Ernö pronounced that Man Ray was a photographer rather than a painter. This did not go down well. Ernö's comments were based on his ignorance of Man Ray's paintings, which he later saw and thought very good – but the damage was done.[9]

Setting up an architectural practice was not straightforward, particularly in the face of institutionalised xenophobia and widespread anti-Semitism. In May 1935, following up the discussions she had been having since 1933, Ursula wrote a formal letter to the trustees of her settlement, her Uncle Geoffrey Blackwell and cousin Philip Brooke, to release ten thousand pounds from the trust fund that had been set up for her.[10] Her stated reason for this was to help her husband in his profession. This money, when released, gave them the freedom to begin plans for building their own home which was to be both an architectural statement and the hub of their family life.[11] It also gave Ernö a security that many of his contemporaries lacked. Wells Coates, for instance, was on the verge of bankruptcy in the 1930s;[12] Goldfinger, in contrast, would frequently exclaim 'I have no need to make money out of architecture,'[13] though this may have been a self-serving justification for his reluctance to fawn to potential clients or to compromise his plans for their buildings.

In the meantime, while waiting to begin work on their family home, the Goldfingers moved once more, this time to become the first tenants in Berthold Lubetkin's and Tecton's Highpoint I in Highgate,[14] the building which Le Corbusier described as a garden suburb in the sky. Lubetkin himself was not at that time living there, though he later moved into a penthouse apartment. Highpoint I was a built manifesto for the modernist apartment block. Goldfinger, however, was not overly impressed with it. For him, Lubetkin's vision was an example of the 'Kasbah' gleaming white box school of architecture that disguised the building's structure and materials. Despite Lubetkin's pedigree in the Atelier Perret, this was not a building of which Perret could have approved. More than that, Ernö found it quite uncomfortable to live in. There were a number of practical shortcomings: the layout of the flats, for instance, required everyone to go through the main living room to get access to any of the other rooms. As for Lubetkin the man, Goldfinger had a long-running antagonism towards him, though he acknowledged that some of his buildings were very good.

Like many of the new generation of architects, Ernö had admired the famous Penguin Pool and Gorilla Houses at Regent's Park zoo. These buildings can now seem barren environments with an implict disdain for animal welfare that put animal display and geometrical wizardry above comfort. When first built, though, they demonstrated radical new possibilities for reinforced concrete. The nature of the buildings is a reminder of changing attitudes to animals in captivity. For Lubetkin's daughter, Louise Kehoe, writing more than half a century after their first tenants moved in, they were the product of her father's extreme rationalism:

> His animal houses were designed unapologetically as theatres, circuses; they made no attempt to simulate the natural habitat of their intended occupants. Instead, by juxtaposing the cool, mathematical precision of pure geometric shapes – cylinders, spirals, ellipses, cast in thin sections of white reinforced concrete – with the lumbering gait and awkward, unrefined behaviour of the captive tenants, he made clowns and performers of them in spite of themselves. The animals became living monuments to rationalism, imprisoned not so much by bars or cages, but their intellectual inferiority to humankind, whose hand had wrought the seamless, soaring canopies that sheltered them.[15]

Ernö had known Lubetkin very well in Paris, living in the same apartment block. He had even introduced Lubetkin to the Atelier Perret. Yet Ernö often referred to him privately as a scoundrel or a rogue. This may have been simply an expression of resentment that Lubetkin had been given so many opportunities to build in England despite his never having qualified for the DPLG. Perhaps it had something to do with Lubetkin's incredible stinginess too: he would, for example, instruct his chauffeur to pawn and later redeem his expensive astrakhan coat at a nearby pawnbrokers when he went to his club rather than pay for the coat check in the cloakroom at the club.[16] Another explanation is that Ernö had recognised that Lubetkin was a Jew who had gone to incredible lengths to hide this fact from everyone else, including his own children. Lubetkin told a web of lies, including that he had bought the name 'Lubetkin' and forged identity papers to allow him to pretend to be Polish – a prerequisite of entering Warsaw University where he had studied architecture before coming to Paris. Ernö might even have known about

Lubetkin's psychological cruelty to his children, the details of which have been made public by his daughter, Louise Kehoe, in her disturbing memoir *In This Dark House*.

Highpoint I attracted an interesting variety of tenants. The Goldfingers' neighbours included the Mendelsohn family. Erich Mendelsohn, whom Ernö had first met at the Stuttgart Weissenhof in 1927,[17] had, with Serge Chermayeff, recently completed the De La Warr Pavilion at Bexhill-on-Sea. The Mendelsohns' daughter, Esther, used to babysit for the Goldfingers and the families stayed in touch with each other long after both had moved from Highpoint and the Mendelsohns had emigrated to America.

While living in Highpoint, Ernö designed a sideboard with sliding doors for his own use. Like several of Goldfinger's furniture designs, such as a large table on a stand made from a cast-iron tool stand which is in Willow Road, this used an existing industrial metal part as its base. In this case the sideboard stands on legs made from mass produced RSJs (rolled steel joists).[18]

Ernö's main architectural project in 1935 was the design of a shop front, showroom and fittings for the Weiss lingerie shop, a conversion of an existing building in Golders Green. Jim Cadbury-Brown, who later went on to design the new buildings for the Royal College of Art, was then studying at the Architectural Association. He had heard about Goldfinger from a friend of

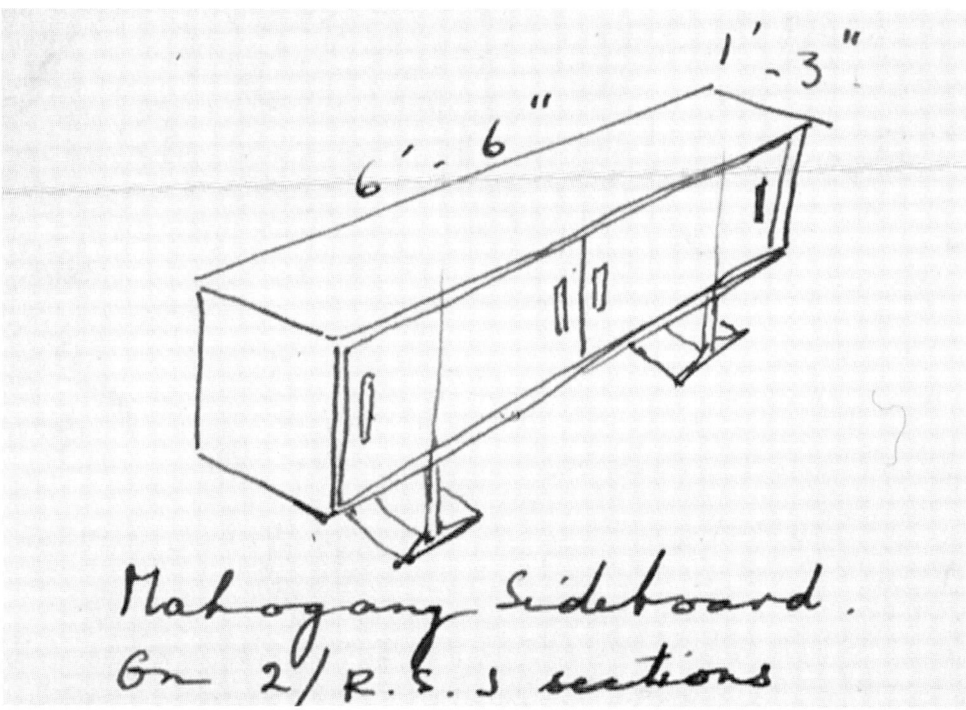

5.2
Reference card drawing for mahogany sideboard, on RSJs

Ursula's and had been excited to find a modern architect working in London as, in the mid-1930s, there were barely half a dozen modern practices of any standing there. Goldfinger invited him to work in his office, but wasn't yet in a position to pay him – Cadbury-Brown was subsidised by his father. The relationship was essentially one of teacher and pupil, and Cadbury-Brown later said that he learnt almost everything about architecture from Goldfinger:

> Grammar of detailing, grammar of composition, the way to use materials, how they come together.[19]

The division of labour was that Goldfinger would tell Cadbury-Brown precisely what he wanted in a design, and then Cadbury-Brown would make drawings instantiating Goldfinger's thoughts. This was to be Goldfinger's preferred working method in his office throughout his life. The dynamic of teacher and pupil was also a recurrent model for his working relations. Goldfinger always felt that there was a right way to do things, and did not hesitate to intervene and correct whenever he saw someone using a tool or method inappropriately, whoever they were. Yet despite being a skilful draughtsman himself, he almost always delegated detailed drawing to his assistants.

The Weiss shop had begun as an ambitious design for a women's hairdressing salon with specially designed taps, basins and mirrors, and two large 'photo-frescos' designed by László Moholy-Nagy, who was at that time based in London. Ernö had met him on the CIAM cruise to Athens.[20] The photo-frescos were to have been two surrealist-inspired collages of a mannequin's head and a hand – one in profile, the other facing the viewer. The designs were made from a combination of photographs, paper, foil and acetate, and were drawn over. It is hard to imagine what the ladies of Golders Green would have made of this kind of innovative composite art as they had their hair permed. To appreciate how radical Moholy-Nagy's art appeared in 1935, consider Frank Pick's thoughts about the artist. Pick had commissioned many of London Transport's innovative designs in the 1930s: but even he was suspicious of Moholy-Nagy's approach. In this he voiced a distinctively British fear of invasion by European avant-garde art. He declared Moholy-Nagy:

> . . . a gentleman with a modernistic tendency who produces pastiches of photographs of a surrealistic type, and I am not at all clear that we should fall for this. It is international, or at least continental . . . Let us leave the Contintent to pursue their own tricks.[21]

When the salon project fell through, Goldfinger tried to rechannel his enthusiasm into the lingerie shop project, but ultimately he had less scope for interior design, given that much of the space had to be taken up with places to hang the shop's wares. He kept the designs for the photo-fresco prints, eventually selling them in 1973.[22] He did however engage in an uncharacteristic flamboyance in the design of the lift, which was highly elaborate, using a variety of different mirrors.

Goldfinger had a particular interest in modern flats and had just received a contract from the publishers B.T. Batsford to write an illustrated book entitled *Modern Flats in England and Abroad*. The covering letter from Harry Batsford outlined its contents:

> The book is to deal, within the limits specified, in a thorough manner, with the modern developments of flats in England, Europe and America within the last few years, from working-class flat housing schemes to large blocks of luxury flats, though concentrating largely on the kind of medium flat of fair accommodation available at moderate rents.[23]

Ernö began the research for this book – not least by living in Highpoint I – but like many of his writing projects, it was never completed, perhaps because he'd become immersed in building his own house at Willow Road. In temperament he was better suited to writing shorter reviews and articles than books. He only published two books during his lifetime, one of which was co-written; the other was mostly a picture book. Nevertheless he began work on many others. In 1939 he had started to write *How Man Uses Water* for Country Life Publishers, then a book on timber to be published by Crosby Lockwood and son. Other proposed books which remained incomplete included *Building a House*, a translation of Perret's aphorisms, *The Growth and Planning of Towns*, and books on neighbourhoods, French furniture and kitchen planning.[24]

Ernö continued his interest in furniture design after coming to England. Inspired by observation of his son Peter, and later his daughter Elizabeth, who was born in September 1936, he developed toys, cupboards, chairs and tables for children. He had strong views about the need to design furniture on a scale that would allow children to interact with it. He wasn't interested in creating a quaint miniature world that would set the child apart, rather he wanted homes and schools to provide children with an appropriate environment, built on a scale that they could inhabit and handle. The point was to facilitate a smooth transition to the adult-scaled world. As he put it, taking the child's viewpoint:

> How would you feel, for instance, living among furniture made for a 12 foot man? Result: all sorts of things the child could, would and should do for himself are forbidden him. Or, if he attempts them, lead to ructions.[25]

One clever innovation was his 'growing table'.[26] The idea behind this was that as the child grew, so the table supports could be unscrewed and replaced with taller ones, allowing the table to be extended as a child's seat on a bicycle might be. His designs were made and sold by his good friends Paul and Marjorie Abbatt.[27] He avoided anything remotely sentimental: most of his toy designs were versions of modern transport. Notable among them were a wooden aeroplane, and a wooden train with the goods carriages linked by dowel and socket couplings. He also designed a toy workbench, and a children's alphabet and number sets that fitted into boards which were thinner than the characters to allow the child to lift them out and replace them easily. At home he designed a doll's house for Elizabeth – no ordinary doll's house, but rather a modernist one, with a spiral staircase and miniatures of his own furniture designs.

The Abbatts had opened their first toyshop in 1932 in Tavistock Square. When they moved premises to Wimpole Street in 1936, Goldfinger was commissioned to re-design their shop. The result, as with Helena Rubinstein's salon, was a thoroughly modern and uncompromising shop front. It incorporated several novel ideas. The window was set back from the road so that children and parents could peer in through the large plate glass window without obstructing the pavement, sheltered from rain. Behind it there was a well-designed and light interior intended to encourage children to interact with the toys and furniture on show – a radical idea at the time. The door was made from plate glass, with no frame. The glass in the door wasn't toughened, but gained its strength from a top to bottom tubular metal handrail. The result was surprisingly resilient. It survived Queen Mary (the Queen Mother) trying to walk straight through it without opening it on a visit – an event that amused Ernö, though he wasn't there to witness it. More impressively, during the war, a bomb exploded in the street outside – the door was the only piece of plate glass to remain intact, suffering only a minor crack across one corner.[28]

In 1937, Ernö had a chance to put some of his furniture designs into production on a large scale with a commission to create a range of modular furniture units for the London-based Easiwork Limited.[29] Easiwork had been founded in 1922 by a Canadian, G.E.W. Crowe,[30] who imported refrigerators and kitchen cabinets from Canada, specialising in labour- and space-saving designs. From the early 1930s, Crowe began to commission new furniture from designers based in Britain, specialising in kitchen furniture, which he sold from a sleek chrome and glass modern showroom, designed by Raymond McGrath at 242 Tottenham Court Road, a few minutes walk from Goldfinger's Bedford Square office. McGrath was, with Serge Chermayeff and Welles Coates, responsible for the interiors of Broadcasting House, a commission which he fulfilled at the same time as the Tottenham Court Road showroom.[31]

5.3
Abbatt toy shop interior, London, 1936

Crowe relished the opportunity to employ top designers and had a mission to educate the general population about the virtues of high-quality design. He was also keen to form working relationships with architects because of the potential for repeat business and design collaboration. His clients included Welles Coates, who had used Easiwork cupboards for kitchens.[32] Crowe approached Goldfinger to design built-in furniture for an 'All-in Bungalow' exhibited at the Ideal Home Exhibition at Olympia and this led to his being invited to act as adviser on the design and manufacture of the Easiwork Furniture Elements (EFE). Crowe had devised the EFE range around standard modules of 3 feet by 2 feet by 18 inches. These included cupboards, wardrobes, chests of drawers and bookshelves, some with tambour fronts and removable shelving, some built to half the standard module height. The underlying principle was that standardisation of modules, or 'sectional units' as the advertisements described them, allowed re-arrangement in new permutations, avoiding the problems of most built-in furniture. It was both space-saving and adaptable. Unlike fitted furniture, these units could be re-arranged and moved from house to house. The cupboard units could even be stacked to divide a room.[33] Such modular furniture is now commonplace in Habitat and Ikea, but in the 1930s this was a novel approach.

Goldfinger's rectilinear designs for EFE, along with McGrath's, were manufactured in Easiwork's Shepherd's Bush factory in waxed oak and sold through the West End showroom. The EFE catalogue stressed that the units were 'architect-designed', presumably an indicator of quality. As with many of Goldfinger's collaborations, however, the business side of the arrangement with Easiwork was not straightforward. Unwilling to lose control of his designs, Ernö insisted that all enquiries about the range should be referred directly to him rather than to Easiwork. This allowed him to control business with his own architectural clients, but may well have undermined the range's commercial potential.[34]

With a growing family, Ernö focused increasingly on designing his own home. He had found a site overlooking part of Hampstead Heath with four small Georgian cottages on it. The cottages were undistinguished and in a state of disrepair – in no way comparable to the fine Georgian buildings round the corner in Downshire Hill. Despite his admiration for high-quality Georgian architecture, Goldfinger had no compunction about clearing the ground of these less impressive relics of that age. What really appealed to him about the site was the view over Hampstead Heath. He later declared that 'the most significant thing about a house is the view from within it'.[35] By October 1936 he had, with Gerald Flower, begun drawings for a block of three terraced houses. The central and larger of the three was for the Goldfingers' use.

The block was to be a combination of manifesto, practice piece and advertisement:

> A young architect ought to be made to build his own house first. It is the only way to learn. And at his own expense. I don't know in all cases, but he ought to have the chance to show what his ideas really are.[36]

In fact, though, his first complete house, built with Flower in 1937, was in Broxted in Essex, commissioned by the artist Humphrey Waterfield and built on a site of five acres of hill pasture. The first designs were for a two-storey building with a double monopitch roof that echoed the design of the Le Touquet studio. The site vendor, however, insisted that Waterfield's combined house and studio should conform to 'the old Essex type' of exterior, with tiles or thatch since it would be visible from his new house – 'a masterpiece of stockbroker's gothic' according to Waterfield.[37] The compromise was to remove the first floor and redesign the house as a flat-roofed bungalow with a covered walkway and semi-enclosed garden.[38] This incorporated Goldfinger's only acknowledged surrealist influence in all his building: a front door that isn't a front door. The main entrance to the house is through a door in a brick wall that you expect to lead directly into the house. Instead you find yourself still out of doors, having to walk up a further path to the front door proper. That he should include an overtly surrealistic gesture at this time is probably no coincidence: in April 1937, Ernö exhibited 'Topgraphique Sentimentale'[39] – a contour model of the Phillipeville site in Algiers where he had hoped to build a hotel, with small white-headed drawing pins stuck into it[40] – in the surrealist section of the 'Artists for Peace' exhibition held at Grosvenor Square. This was shown alongside work by his friends and acquaintances from his Paris years, Max Ernst, S.W. (Bill) Hayter, Eileen Agar, Man Ray, Julian Trevelyan and Joan Miró, and also by Roland Penrose, whom he'd met in London through Lee Miller. Paul Klee, Pablo Picasso and René Magritte also had pieces in this exhibition – so he was in excellent company. Two more friends from Paris, Amédée Ozenfant and Ferdinand Léger had work in the Abstract section, as did László Moholy-Nagy, Ben Nicholson, John Piper and Wassily Kandinsky.

Although sceptical of the idea that a small group could carry out any serious empirical research into architecture, Goldfinger was also an active member of MARS, the Modern Architectural Research group which counted Wells Coates, Maxwell Fry, Serge Chermayeff, Misha Black, John Betjeman and Herbert Read among its sixty members. He organised the 'mother and child' section for the influential 1938 'New Architecture' exhibition at the New Burlington Gallery in London. Although only open for three weeks, this exhibition attracted more than 7,000 visitors.

As the house was completed at Broxted, a surge of anti-modernist feeling broke in Hampstead in reaction to Goldfinger's planned home in Willow Road. There were already several remarkable modern houses in the area, most notably Maxwell Fry's Sun House, completed in 1936 at 9 Frognal Way. Many of the local residents despised this invasion of modern architecture. Their aesthetic objections were in some cases tinged with xenophobia, since modernism was linked in their minds with continental Europe and not with the English architectural tradition. They felt that modernist houses were angular and 'out of keeping' with the elegant Georgian and Victorian buildings that flanked them. In late 1937, the Hampstead Heath and Old Hampstead Protection Society, led by Henry Brooke, their Honorary Secretary, mounted a protest against the proposals that Goldfinger had submitted to the London County Council and Hampstead Borough Council. Brooke railed against what he saw as desecration:[41]

> The erection of a building of that kind, even if faced with brick in the upper storeys as this is proposed to be, would damage irretrievably the 'atmosphere' of the approach from the Heath to Downshire Hill, one of the most beautiful roads in Hampstead.[42]

The protest was directed at the buildings that were to be erected rather than towards preserving the existing cottages. The Protection Society's wish was to protect Hampstead from an invasion of modern architecture rather than to preserve buildings irrespective of their quality. The worry was that an alien aesthetic would destroy the beauty of the neighbourhood. The main objections to the proposed houses were that they would be 'disastrously out of keeping' with the houses in the area, that they would be made of concrete, that the windows were too large, and that the houses were rectangular. Brooke and his fellow protestors seemed to be basing their expectations about Goldfinger's design not so much on his submitted proposals but rather on other modern buildlings in the area. Goldfinger defended himself against the various charges in the *Evening Standard*. He stressed that his own designs were an adaptation of the eighteenth-century style, and as such in keeping with the beautiful houses in Downshire Hill. Goldfinger always found the English tendency to worry about how a building fits in with its neighbours irritating and irrelevant: for him a good building fitted in anywhere. And usually 'fitting in' meant 'looking just like all the buildings in the neighbourhood' – hardly a formula for progressive architecture. But by drawing attention to the pedigree of his designs and their continuity with Georgian terrace architecture, he sought to undermine some of his opponents' prejudices about modern architecture. To the concern that his houses would be made of concrete, he retorted:

> The concrete that people seem to be afraid of is, in my case, invisible to the public save for the partitions between balconies.[43]

Besides, there was already at least one modern concrete house 'to which no possible aesthetic objection can be taken' in the middle of Downshire Hill.[44] He dismissed the worry that his houses would be rectangular with pseudo-anthropological rhetoric:

> Only the Eskimos and the Zulus would build anything but rectangular houses.[45]

Elsewhere he defended the large windows on the grounds that he needed the best possible light for the studio at the front of the house. And, as he pointed out:

> . . . the windows will not be as large as some in the lovely old houses in Bedford Square, which is usually considered the finest square in London.[46]

These responses did not assuage the protestors and a fiery debate ensued.

As might be expected of an area in which some of the most forward-thinking contributors to the arts had settled, many eminent neighbours rallied to his support. The actress Flora Robson, whose Downshire Hill house overlooked the site, spoke out in favour of his design, as did the surrealist Roland Penrose, who had recently moved there with Lee Miller. Julian Huxley, the distinguished zoologist and brother of Aldous Huxley, was moved to write to the *Daily Telegraph*, attacking unthinking conservativism about architecture:

> Let the Hampstead Heath and Old Hampstead Protection Society protest against the ravages of sham Tudor and nondescript villa architecture, as perpetrated only too frequently even on the borders of the Heath, but let them refrain from hindering the development of a true 20th-century British style.[47]

Defenders of modern architecture saw this as a battle that needed to be fought. Members of the Isobar Club in the Isokon Flats, not far from the intended site, invited Goldfinger to display plans and elevations as part of a counter-attack.

Goldfinger and his allies' counter-campaign, both locally and in the national press, was effective and he was given permission to build despite the opposition. Work on the block began. Like most of Ernö's projects it was potentially a prototype – although it remains a one-off terrace, drawings show that he conceived it as a unit which could be expanded along a street, or form part or all of a square.[48]

Ernö took his son Peter, then only five, to inspect the progress, and he still remembers the thrill of the building site and the evocative smell of concrete being cast. Ernö couldn't resist intervening to tell builders how to mix cement.[49] Gradually the reinforced concrete frame of the houses took shape – concrete floor slabs were supported by pillars, allowing for maximum window space at front and rear – an important feature for Ursula's painting and Ernö's drawing, much of which he did from home. The load-bearing columns also gave great freedom about the division of rooms within. This permitted folding room partitions opening out to create large open rooms if desired, or, as happened over the years in number 2, the Goldfingers' house, changes in the floor plan layout. A spiral staircase, made from cast concrete, runs from basement to top floor in each of the three houses, providing an internal core, lit from above by a circular skylight. The concrete drum of the staircase formed one of the supporting columns for the house. It also made highly efficient use of the available space, since its location in the centre of the house minimised the need for corridors. In the Goldfinger's house, the banisters are connected to the staircase with a zig-zagging tensioned hemp rope balustrade, reminiscent of Barbara Hepworth's use of tensioned wires in some of her sculptures. The Goldfingers' was the largest of the three houses, the other two being approximately two thirds its size and with half the main window area.

Because of the slope of the land, there were three storeys at the front, and four at the rear. The basement, or lower ground floor at the rear of the Goldfingers' house consisted of a garden room, a store room and a maids' bathroom. On the ground floor there were two maids' rooms and the kitchen with a service lift or dumb waiter to all floors. In the Georgian tradition, the main living room and dining room were on the first floor. There was also a studio at the front of the house with a large step intended to provide a convenient place for models to hold a pose, and doubling as a storage space for paintings and other large materials in the deep drawers beneath. Almost all of the first floor could be opened by folding back hinged partitions to provide a large space for parties.

Like most modern architects in the 1930s, Goldfinger put great emphasis on creating light-filled rooms. This was not just an aesthetic consideration: it was a moral imperative. Adequate sunlight was a prerequisite for healthy living, as Maxwell Fry noted in 1934:

> In the last few years the medical profession has seriously awakened to the therapeutic effects of daylight, and the call for larger areas of window space.[50]

The living room at the rear of the house has a balcony and a large window that can be folded back to open the room in the summer. The window of the dining room, at the front of the house, incorporates what was to become a recurrent feature in Goldfinger's design: a photobolic screen. Goldfinger coined this term at the suggestion of the classicist Reg Winnington-Ingram who occupied number 1 Willow Road. A photobolic screen is a shelf which offsets the top part of the window – in Willow Road it is made of concrete. Provided that this shelf was kept clean it bounced light onto the ceiling and thus further back into the room than would a conventional window. It seems, however, that its invention was pure serendipity. Serge Chermayeff, the architect and designer, visited Willow Road soon after it had been built and noticed the quality of light in the dining room. He pointed out that light must be reflected and redistributed from the top of the horizontal transom and from the back of the room.[51] Goldfinger had not appreciated this effect at the time he designed it – its inclusion in the design was probably a way of dividing a very large window into a more human scale – but once discovered, he made repeated use of it in subsequent buildings.

5.4
Topping out ceremony, Willow Road, Hampstead, 1938

There is very little that is arbitrary about the Willow Road design. Goldfinger thought through everything; he could provide a justification for each element of the building. The bathroom, for example was small because a bathroom is 'simply a place to wash' and so should not waste space.[52] The same principle was used for the WC: 'A lavatory. Minimum width and area. Space is for living.'[53] Throughout his domestic architecture he applied this same rationale. Even in the larger houses and apartments, bathrooms and WCs use the minimum amount of space that make them functional. Generous space is reserved for the living areas.

The house was a focus for the Goldfingers' new life in England bringing together family, architecture and artistic vision. They brought with them their collection of paintings by their friends Max Ernst, Amédée Ozenfant and Robert Delaunay, and photographs by Kertész and Man Ray. Soon the drawers under the living room were full of paintings, photographs, sketches and posters. Bookcases were filled with magazines and art books, many given by friends. Goldfinger's own furniture prototypes were used throughout the house and the modern aesthetic extended even to using laboratory conical flasks as carafes. Charlotte Perriand wrote that the Goldfingers 'built their nest in accordance with their fine principles'. For her it encapsulated the essence of an age:

> It is not without emotion that I stay there, surrounded by friendship, objects, books, paintings, rediscovering the spirit of that unique period, for it was then that the modern age was built.[54]

5.5
The houses at Willow Road, from the Heath, photographed by Colin Penn, 1941

Yet events in Germany and beyond meant that this unique period, with its optimism and energy, was about to end. Like so many Europeans, the Goldfingers were forced to set aside their ambitions and personal projects as the war moved closer.

Notes

1 The letter granting permission to reside and the later one giving permission to work in Britain are in GolEr/271.

2 Letter from W.H. Court and son solicitors, 16/1/35 in GolEr 279/2, a letter which presents Goldfinger with the results of their enquiries as to his status makes this clear.

3 Recounted by Nick Goldfinger, private conversation.

4 He stated this explicitly in a letter to S.W. Hayter, dated 14 June 1955 in GolEr 271/4.

5 Letters from W.H. Court and Son (solicitors) 2/1/35 and 8/1/35 in GolEr 279/2.

6 Letter from George to Ernö, 19/1/41 in National Trust 2 Willow Road collection.

7 Peter Goldfinger on F7576 side B.

8 Probably Man Ray's solo exhibition at the Institute of Contemporary Arts in 1959 – the offices of the ICA were then below Goldfinger's office.

9 James Dunnett, *Conversations with Ernö Goldfinger*, unpublished notes, 30/10/83.

10 Copy of letter from Ursula to Geoffrey Blackwell and Philip Brooke, 1/5/35 in GolEr 279/2.

11 To get a sense of the value of ten thousand pounds, the four-storey Isokon Lawn Road block of flats, opened in 1934, was built for approximately £14,800, see Laura Cohn, *The Door to a Secret Room*, Aldershot: Scolar, 1999, p.127.

12 This is documented by his daughter, Laura Cohn, 1999, pp.115–126.

13 Remembered by John Roberts, NSA Architects' Lives, F11528.

14 They changed flats in Highpoint I shortly after moving there. They took out a lease on flat 40 on the fourth floor on 10/10/35 and then subsequently for Flat 3 on the first floor from 2/12/35 until June 1938.

15 Louise Kehoe, *In This dark House: A Memoir*, London: Penguin, 1995, p.39.
16 See Louise Kehoe, 1995, p.12.
17 Recorded in Joyce Lowrie's chronology in *Architectural Design*, January 1963, p.9.
18 This cupboard is now in the dining room at 2 Willow Road.
19 Cadbury-Brown, F5679, side B.
20 Letter from Moholy-Nagy, 4/10/35, in GolEr 276. This is also mentioned by Cadbury-Brown on F5679, side B. Ernö kept the preliminary photomontage for his private collection when the project fell through.
21 Quoted in Daniel Snowman, *The Hitler Emigrés*, London: Chatto and Windus, 2002, p.58
22 Photographs of Moholy-Nagy's *maquettes* are in the National Trust 2 Willow Road collection.
23 Letter from Harry Batsford, 26/6/35, in GolEr/266.
24 Drafts of parts of some of these are to be found in GolEr 348. The book on French furniture is mentioned in a letter to Jean Royere, 18/9/52, in GolEr 278/3.
25 Quoted in article in *The Star*, 8/1/1938, in GolEr 389/1.
26 Advertised in the Abbatt Catalogue for December 1938, in GolEr 394/12.
27 The Abbatts were profiled in an article for The *Observer*, 'Idealists in the Toyshop', 2/12/62. Peter Abbatt was Peter Goldfinger's godfather (mentioned by Peter Goldfinger on NSA 7577).
28 Interview with John Roberts, NSA Architects' Lives, F11529, side A.
29 These are co-credited to his architectural partner Gerald Flower, though he later suggested that it was important at this time for his name to be accompanied with an obviously English one – presumably because of widespread xenophobia and anti-Semitism – and that Flower's input was negligible. This was Ursula's recollection when interviewed by G.E.W. Crowe's grandson Simon Willey in 1989.
30 Misnamed as 'CEW Grove' on p.48 of Robert Elwall's otherwise excellent book on Goldfinger *Ernö Goldfinger*, RIBA Drawings Monographs no. 3, London: Academy Editions, 1996.
31 The Tottenham Court Road Easiwork showroom was completed in September 1931; the BBC project was commissioned in 1929 and completed in 1932.
32 Simon Willey, unpublished undergraduate thesis, 'Housework Made Easiwork: Easiwork Limited: The Ideal Modern Kitchen 1919–1939', Department of History of Art, Edinburgh University, 1989.
33 Described in *News Review*, 7 April in GolEr/394/10 and also featured in *Picture Your Bungalow By the Sea* (March 1937) a pamphlet produced for Boulton and Paul Ltd, Norwich, which offered furniture units designed by Goldfinger with Gerald Flower. This pamphlet is in the National Trust 2 Willow Road collection.
34 This information comes from Rebecca Milner's important article on Goldfinger's furniture, 'Ernö Goldfinger: The Architect as Furniture Designer', in Edwin Heathcote (ed.) *Furniture and Architecture*, London: John Wiley and Sons, 2002, pp.9–10.
35 Recalled by James Dunnett, Centenary Conference, Architectural Association London, 28/9/02.
36 From Clisby Kent, 'Goldfinger: Britain's Most Consistent Modernist', *House and Garden*, February 1965, p.34.
37 Quoted in Elwall, p.45.
38 The house did eventually get a second storey in 1955, designed by Gerald Flower – to Goldfinger's chagrin. Flower wrote to Ernö about his client's intentions to extend the bungalow upwards. For Ernö, the prospect of the extension was 'a very sad story' that would completely spoil the building. He urged Flower to try to persuade Waterfield to add a further ground floor bedroom. Letter from Ernö Goldfinger to Gerald Flower, 16/3/55, in GolEr 269/6.
39 'Topographique Senitmentale' was catalogue no. 243 in the Artists' International Association Third Exhibition, 14 April–5 May 1937. This catalogue is in the National Trust 2 Willow Road collection.

40 Described in James Dunnett. 'Conversations with Ernö Goldfinger', unpublished notes, 15/8/83.

41 As Robert Elwall (1996, p.52) points out: 'Ironically 2 Willow Road was formally handed over to the National Trust by the Heritage Secretary, Peter Brooke, son of the scheme's most voluble opponent.'

42 Letter to *Hampstead and Highgate Express*, 18/12/37.

43 *Evening Standard*, 22/12/37.

44 A reference to 13A Downshire Hill, built by Michael and Charlotte Bunney.

45 *Evening Standard* 22/12/37.

46 *Hampstead and Highgate Express*, 25/12/37.

47 *Daily Telegraph* 11/1/38.

48 See, for instance, the drawing reproduced in F.R.S. Yorke *The Modern House in England*, 2nd edn, Surrey, The Architectural Press, 1944, p.94, which Yorke describes as 'emphasising the architect's attempt to design a façade capable of serving as a unit in street design, whilst expressing the individual house'.

49 Peter Goldfinger, NSA F7580 (C467/44/05) tape 5, side B.

50 Maxwell Fry, quoted in Glendinning and Muthesius, p.35.

51 This information comes from James Dunnett, 'Conversations with Ernö Goldfinger', unpublished notes, 7/3/83.

52 Ernö Goldfinger quoted in Stephen Gardiner 'Goldeneye' *The Times Magazine*, 16/11/1996, pp.44–48, p.45.

53 Ernö Goldfinger quoted in Stephen Gardiner 'Goldeneye' *The Times Magazine*, 16/11/1996, pp.44–48, p.45.

54 Charlotte Perriand writing for the catalogue for the AA exhibition, May 1983 in GolEr 399/1.

Chapter 6

War work

In 1939 when Hitler entered Poland, I occupied the house. I am still here![1]

Ernö had already applied for British nationality in 1939 as soon as he had achieved the necessary five consecutive years of residency. This resulted in a notice being placed in *The Times* as early as 23 August 1939 (between an advertisement for Nescafé instant coffee and a begging letter from a woman with cancer whose husband was unemployed and ineligible for dole money). The notice declared that Goldfinger was applying to the Home Secretary for naturalisation and that:

> Any person who knows any reason why naturalization should not be granted should send a written and signed statement of the facts to the Under Secretary of State, Home Office.

His application was going smoothly, and it looked as if he would be naturalised in September of that year. But, with the outbreak of war, this was the very moment when all applications for naturalisation in process were suspended. This bad timing put Goldfinger in a difficult situation.

From mid-May 1940, the British government interned huge numbers of foreigners, many of whom were already refugees from Nazi barbarity. Although he had been resident in England for six years, had married an Englishwoman, held a Polish passport and hated Nazis with venom – he had, for example ripped a swastika flag from a German embassy car long before the outbreak of war – Goldfinger nevertheless was at risk of police interrogation and possibly even deportation. Hampstead, with its high proportion of refugees, was a dangerous place. On 13 July 1940, for example, a group of CID officers walked into Hampstead Library and arrested all the Germans and Austrians who were there. They were given very little opportunity to gather belongings and to speak to relatives before being sent away. People were also stopped in the main streets of Hampstead and, if found to be 'enemy aliens', were taken off to the police station.[2] This sometimes happened even if they were deemed 'friendly enemy aliens'. From there, the next destination could be the Isle of Man, or internment in the distant colonies. Goldfinger's connections probably protected him to some extent, as did his Polish nationality. Nevertheless, acutely aware of the dangers associated with being labelled an alien, he devoted his energies to becoming naturalised. He called upon his political and family connections, but to no avail. He remained an alien throughout the war, though he escaped internment. A Hungarian acquaintance John Vago, nephew of the architect Pierre Vago, was much less fortunate: he wrote in utter amazement to Ernö from a camp where he had been detained under the Aliens Order:

> To be quite correct the Home Office order my deportation, and owing to the safe defence of the realm, my detention. It is absolutely fantastic.[3]

In October 1940, while he was still interned, Vago's flat in Maddox Street suffered bomb damage, and his solicitor wrote to Ernö asking him to recover some of Vago's papers. The inventory of possessions included an Easiwork cupboard. Ernö, however, was unable to gain access.[4]

Despite his best efforts, Ernö's application was not accepted until eight years later in 1947.[5] Ursula kept the Polish status she had acquired by marrying Ernö for several years after that, so that for a time, by a bizarre quirk of bureaucracy, the couple had effectively swapped nationalities. One contact Ernö called on to help him achieve this naturalisation was the journalist and MP Tom Driberg, whom he'd met in 1936 when they were both opposing the Franco rebellion.[6] He wrote to Driberg in 1945, asking him to put in a word with the future Home Secretary. Driberg shared Goldfinger's pro-Soviet stance – in 1999, the former Soviet Agent Vasili Mitrokhin revealed that this left-wing politician and former member of the Communist Party had worked during the cold war as a spy, codenamed 'Lepage', following a homosexual entrapment on a visit to Moscow in 1956. Whether he continued to work as a double agent is unclear, nor is there any evidence that he followed up Goldfinger's request to put in a word for him in high places.

As an official alien, travel could be difficult for Goldfinger. When, for instance, he was invited to give a talk on the social background of planning to the Workers' Educational Association in late 1941, he had to write to the Chief Constable of Bristol in advance to seek permission to make the journey.[7]

While being denied British nationality, Goldfinger made a point of collaborating in his work with English nationals, making sure that his name appeared coupled with an English name wherever possible. When Ursula's name appeared alongside his on drawings, for example, she was always 'Ursula Blackwell' rather than 'Ursula Goldfinger'. This was at least in part from fear that his obviously foreign name would undermine the educational purpose of his wartime work.[8]

Marriage to Ernö presented problems for Ursula's contribution to the war effort. She was keen to help by working in soup kitchens, but was more or less prevented because from a bureaucratic point of view she was Polish, despite being English by birth, upbringing and inclination. As a Polish national she had to convince officials of her loyalty to Britain through filling in a questionnaire with thirty-eight different questions. The process of getting clearance even for such menial work was exasperating for Ursula who, despite having passed her wartime canteen training, had to wait almost six weeks to have her application considered for work as a dishwasher in the Euston YMCA canteen when she applied in 1942. Exasperated, she wrote an acerbic letter to the General Secretary of YMCAs:

> As we are given to understand that during this war time is valuable I am sure you will agree that it is far better that no more of mine or yours or the Authorities is wasted and that I should immediately undertake some other job and leave dish-washing to others who are unquestionably reliable for such confidential work.[9]

Despite his lack of British citizenship, Ernö found numerous ways to contribute to the war effort. He put together educational exhibitions, designed evacuation camps and air-raid shelters, lectured and contributed to plans for the post-war renovation of bomb-damaged London. He also acted as an air raid warden and was able to join the Home Guard from 1941. He summarised his contribution up until early 1942 in a letter to his brother George in America. It is clear that Ernö, like so many Londoners adopted a spirited attitude to life in the wartime capital:

> Life in London is practically normal. There has been no 'Blitz' since last May, and I can assure you that even the worst blitz is much less bad when you are in it than it appears to be from far away. We have practically never missed a London Air-Raid except in December 1940 the big raid on the City, at that time we were in Scotland, and the last big raid in May when we were in the country for the weekend. I am an air-raid warden but besides going to the post one night a week have nothing to do. The only disagreeable thing about the raids is when you or your friends get hit or otherwise messed up, but you can't help that. I think Schiklgruber highly miscalculated the character of the British in this respect. The morning after a raid is generally pretty messy, but a day or two

later (in some exceptional cases a little longer) the whole thing is nicely cleared up and does not look worse than a building site at various stages of the building operations. Sometimes you see odd things like a lavatory basin, a WC or an unbroken mirror suspended in mid-air four or five floors up. The Civil Defence Services are extremely efficient without any of the German Drills.

My own position is less satisfactory as you can imagine how keen I am to do my part to get at old Schikl: In the beginning of the war I offered my services to the War Office, but there were all sorts of difficulties. Architecture has ceased to exist in my sense, everything is done by official bodies, and it is not easy for me to fit in there. The jobs which are going are mainly junior ones and they hesitate to take one in such a capacity. I have now a splendid offer to conduct the Reconstruction Research for an East End Borough, but it takes a long time for them to decide. In the meantime I do a lot of journalistic work in the technical press, they seem to like my stuff and pay well, what more can you want?

[. . .]

I understand that a friend of ours, Serge Chermayeff, has got a job at Brooklyn Polytechnic. He is rather pompous and thinks a lot of himself (not quite justified) but is all right and his wife is charming. Look him up if you want. Erich Mendelsohn is also in America, he lectures a lot, you may come across him, if so give him and his wife our love. He can even be quite useful as he has a lot of connections in industry.[10]

Some of the Goldfingers' friends were not so fortunate in their wartime experiences. In late September 1939, Ernö and Ursula received a letter from 'Prim' (Leonora) Carrington, care of Roland Penrose.[11] Leonora Carrington was a young surrealist painter and author. Leonora's brother, Noel Carrington of Penguin Books, was a friend of Ursula's – Ursula suggested the idea of using a puffin as the trade symbol for the children's imprint Puffin Books. Max Ernst, a German citizen, and with whom Leonora had been living, had been put into a concentration camp by the French when war had been declared between France and Germany. There was some irony in this since he was also on the list of 'degenerate' artists compiled by the Nazis. He was set to work cutting brambles and wood, had to sleep on straw, and was prevented from painting. Leonora could only see him for ten minutes twice a week and was clearly under great strain. The money that Ernö had been sending Ernst as payment for a picture he had bought was being confiscated. Unfortunately, Leonora's letter came after Ernö had dispatched his final payment.

Ursula had introduced Leonora to Max Ernst in 1937 when Ernst had been staying in England during the opening of a surrealist exhibition. At that time both Ursula and Leonora were studying painting with Ozenfant, who had transferred his academy to London. Ursula had invited Carrington and Ernst to dinner, knowing that Ernst would far prefer to spend an evening with a young art student than some old intellectual. She had perhaps underestimated the degree to which this was so: Ernst and Carrington became lovers almost immediately. Ernst left his wife, Marie-Berthe Aurenche, for the young beautiful artist. Carrington followed him back to Paris, much to the consternation of her supposed guardian Serge Chermayeff, who called her a 'cheap slut' to her face.[12] Julian Trevelyan summed up the episode in a very short, understated paragraph in his autobiography *Indigo Days*:

> Max Ernst came over but did not stay long. He carried off Leonora Carrington from Ozenfant's academy, and there was some ill-feeling.[13]

Ernst and Carrington had moved from Paris to St Martin d'Ardèche and had lived in a rural idyll, painting, writing and entertaining themselves in surrealist fashion by serving an unwelcome guest an omlette containing locks of Leonora's hair. Then Ernst had been arrested.

Ernö wrote back to Leonora, promising to do everything he could to help secure Ernst's release, contacting friends in France and meeting with Roland Penrose to see if there was any way to help. The story has both a happy and a sad ending. Happy for Ernst in that he was released a year later in the winter of 1940 and Peggy Guggenheim, who became his lover, secured a passage to New York for him in 1941. In the meantime, Leonora had fled Ardèche, selling their house for a bottle of brandy, and escaping to Madrid where she was found at the British Embassy, threatening to murder Hitler and calling for the metaphysical liberation of mankind.[14] Her mental breakdown was compounded by a later painful meeting with Ernst and Guggenheim in a Lisbon market.[15]

In occupied Belgium, meanwhile, Ernö's brother Paul was active in the Resistance. Putting his chemical knowledge to good use, he was making bombs in jam jars, using a paper divider between two chemicals which, when mixed, triggered an explosion: the thickness of the paper determined the time the bomber had to escape. The Gestapo searched his house one day when the bombs were in clear view on a shelf, but they didn't understand what they were looking at, and left him to carry on his work.

In contrast to this, the Goldfingers had a straightforward wartime experience, though enduring the Blitz in London was more difficult than Ernö's cheery letter would suggest. Fear of invasion was real, and as a Jew with communist connections, he wouldn't have expected to survive for very long in such an event. There was, however, an extremely painful consequence for the family: the evacuation of their children, Peter and Elizabeth (usually known as Liz) aged only six and three.

At the beginning of the war, in the winter of 1939–40, Ursula and the children left London for a rented bungalow, known as 'Holly Frindle' in Whipsnade, in order to avoid the bombing. It belonged to Ida Mann, an eminent ophthamologist whom Goldfinger had met through Peter Chalmers-Mitchell, a friend and fellow supporter of left-wing causes. 'Bungalow' makes this sound like a modest suburban dwelling, but in fact it was a stylish modernist building and, like their Highpoint flat, designed by Lubetkin, and built between 1933 and 1936. It was one of three bungalows grouped on a hillside in the Chilterns. Lubetkin had designed two of these, the third having been built by Chalmers-Mitchell himself. The Lubetkin bungalow was a place of light, white walls and right angles. In other circumstances it would have been an idyllic retreat. Goldfinger built an Anderson air raid shelter for his family with a corrugated iron roof piled up with earth. Liz and Peter made the mistake of telling Chalmers-Mitchell that they liked the mixture of milk and soda water that he gave them the first time they visited them – after that they had to endure this 'treat' at every visit. Nevertheless, when he was introduced as 'Sir Peter', they heard it as 'Saint Peter' and were duly impressed.

Meanwhile, Ernö continued to work in London, escaping to Whipsnade at the weekends when he could. This was not entirely satisfactory, as Ursula made clear in a letter:

> On the whole it is a pretty poor solution you being away all the time war or no war.[16]

In 1940, however, the Goldfingers quite reasonably feared for their children's safety. There was the threat of heavy bombing, but more worrying still was the likely invasion with all that that might entail for Jewish children. The name Goldfinger advertised their Jewish origins, and Ursula and Ernö were under no illusion about what the likely consequences of this would be for Peter and Liz. An opportunity to evacuate them to Canada arose through the school Peter attended, Byron House in Hampstead, and the Goldfingers felt they had to take it, agonising as this decision was.

Parents of children at Byron House had not been taken in by the 'Peace in Our Time' claims of Neville Chamberlain, and had begun early to think about evacuating their children from Hampstead should war break out. Initially they had found accommodation in Cambridge, where the school officially moved to three days before war was declared, some of the children staying in Lady Darwin's house on Silver Street. At this point Liz and Peter remained in London. Many parents, however, realised that Cambridge would not be much safer than London when, as seemed inevitable, the Germans invaded. Senator Wilson, the only female senator in Canada at the time, sent out invitations to six schools in England to evacuate to Canada. By this time Byron House had a list of more than a hundred children whose parents wanted them to escape overseas. Berths to Canada were offered on the *Duchess of Atholl*, and these went to the first twenty-eight children on the list, aged between three and eleven. Three female teachers could accompany them. Peter and Elizabeth Goldfinger were on the list. The Goldfingers had twenty-four hours to decide whether to send their children away or not. There had only been one air raid in London at this time, but this was enough to persuade them to make the agonising decision to put them on the ship to Canada.[17] There was no question of parents being allowed to accompany them. More children were expected to follow later, but time was short.

Preparations were swift. Ernö photographed Peter and Liz on the balcony at Willow Road on their last day together, a sunny evening.[18] They are smiling, cherubic, happily unaware of the possible tribulations ahead and the impact of such a separation. They were used to their father spending time away from them, but could hardly have understood the implications of a transatlantic voyage in wartime, and the impending threat to those who stayed in Britain. For Peter, certainly, this was an adventure. Their parents had clearly managed to maintain a front, behind which their emotions must have been churning.

Almost before they realised what was happening, the children, along with their school friends and teachers, boarded a train at Euston Station to take them to Liverpool. Peter was given solemn instructions to take care of Liz. And that was the last the children saw of their parents for four years. It is hard to imagine how painful the goodbyes must have been for the parents. A few made the journey all the way to Liverpool. Most, but not all, managed to maintain some control for the sake of the children; but there was a point where they were not allowed to follow. To see these very young children led away, possibly forever, was agony for any parent. They must have questioned whether this was the right decision, whether they shouldn't have risked keeping the family together. Then the children were gone. A poignant memory for most of the children was that they had to give up their gas masks as they left. Even though they had been drilled to carry them wherever they went, they could not take these life-savers abroad: they were the property of the British government and had to be returned before they embarked.

The ship, a former troop carrier, set sail on 26 June 1940, with about six hundred children on board and the result was – not surprisingly – chaotic. At times the teachers tied the younger Byron House children together

6.1
Peter and Elizabeth on the balcony at 2 Willow Road, the evening before evacuation, 1940

in a line with a skipping rope for fear of losing them in the mêlée. On the first day all the children were seasick – some spectacularly so. The ship was alone without a convoy, and there was a real risk from German U-boats. Willie Hooper, one of the teachers, wrote the first letter back to parents from on board the ship, using a typewriter perched on suitcases. She tactfully omitted to mention that one day of the voyage was spent circling to avoid going into waters where a German submarine had recently been spotted. A later evacuation ship, the *Benares*, was sunk, and this stopped plans for further transatlantic evacuation of children.

After ten days at sea, they docked in Quebec, and travelled on to Montreal and eventually Ottawa. There was no fixed plan of what was to happen to the children when they arrived, and there were problems getting money from London to Canada. As a consequence, the evacuated school had to be run on local charity. No money was released from the trust set up to run the school for two years.

Peter enjoyed the adventure of travelling to a new country; but Elizabeth, who was one of the youngest in the group, was more deeply affected by the separation from her parents at such an early age. Contact between the Goldfingers and their children was difficult – letters took at least six weeks to arrive. Twice a link was set up so that the parents' voices could be broadcast to their children in a collaboration between the BBC and the

'Hello Children' programme in the North American Service. Peter recognised his father's distinctive voice, but Elizabeth's memory did not stretch far enough back.[19]

For the most part, interaction was limited to sporadic letters and exchanges of photographs. Ernö, whose letters were generally functional – brief and to the point – sent typewritten messages, discussing such questions as whether it was possible to build houses with flat roofs in Canada given the weight of snowfall (the answer was yes, it is possible, if the roofs are made strong enough). Ursula's letters were always handwritten. The children wrote home every Sunday. When, four years later, the Byron House children returned to England to be reunited with their families, the children had changed so much that one mother from the group went up to the wrong child on the station platform.

Shortly after Peter and Elizabeth set sail for Canada, Ernö's cousin, Gladys Goldfinger, who lived in the United States and had US citizenship, sent affidavits for the whole family that might in principle have allowed them to emigrate there together, although it is very unlikely that Ernö would have been given an exit permit to travel even if they could have found transport.[20] The children were able to visit Gladys in New York on a couple of occasions during their evacuation. They also spent two Christmases with her in Pennsylvania, appropriately in Bethlehem.

Separated from his children, Goldfinger immersed himself in war work. Soon after the outbreak of war, he had transferred his practice to his studio at home in Willow Road, sub-letting his 7 Bedford Square offices to the newly formed Industrial Camouflage Unit. The name suggests a highly-organised military operation, but in fact the unit consisted of four key members of the English Surrealist Group: S.W. Hayter (known as Bill), Roland Penrose, Julian Trevelyan and the engraver John Buckland Wright. Goldfinger was their official technical advisor. The sculptor Helen Phillips, who had recently married Hayter, and Denis Clarke Hall were also associated with the unit, though their names did not appear on the letterhead. The surrealists had all been connected with Atelier 17 in Paris, Hayter's printmaking workshop which had been frequented by the likes of Max Ernst, Oskar Kokoschka, Joan Miró, Salvador Dalí, and Picasso. They had also exhibited at the International Surrealist Exhibition of 1936 at the New Burlington gallery – London's first major surrealist exhibition. Goldfinger knew most of them from his time in Paris. Ernö was, at least initially, pleased to provide the unit with a place to work and to act as their adviser. Here was a practical way in which he could contribute to the war effort and help his friends at the same time.

The unit's main aim was to produce appropriate camouflage designs for factories, and for this Goldfinger's heliometer (or 'sun machine' as they called it, preferring the poetic to the scientific description) was a particularly useful device since it gave them a reliable indication of how shadows would fall on buildings at different times of the day and in different seasons. Hayter, who had been in Madrid during the Spanish Civil War, already had some experience of camouflage, and had theories about how it could be improved; the rest of the group were very much beginners. Nevertheless, they began eagerly constructing models and painting them in various abstract patterns. Julian Trevelyan described camouflage in those early years of the war as 'a perfunctory ritual', which had little to do with protecting buildings from becoming targets for bombing:

> Much of it was done in an uncoordinated freelance way; the little corner garage in a housing estate was quickly painted in wiggly lines, and so was the laundry and even the roof of the cinema. People seemed to feel that the green stripes were a charm that somehow bought them immunity from the unknown hazards of war; like the paper strips on the windows, it made them feel that they had done their little bit, had invested in their small piece of twentieth-century magic. In those early days it was easy to sell any kind of camouflage.[21]

As Trevelyan came to realise, no one in the unit knew much about what buildings looked like from the air, and many of their designs were based on false assumptions about how patterns of paint would be read from above. Nor did they give any consideration to fundamental questions such as whether they were disguising buildings from night-flying bombers at high altitude, aerial photographers, or low-flying daytime raiders. Despite this they managed to persuade Player's Imperial Tobacco cigarette factory in Bristol to commission a camouflage scheme from them. Members of the unit visited the factory, clambered over it taking measurements and sitings, and returned to London where they produced a model complete with an abstract camouflage design. In the meantime the factory owners' fear of bombing had receded: they paid the unit well for their design work, but never used it. The unit carried on with its experiments and model-making, concentrating on camouflaging guns and other military equipment, but they did not receive any further commissions.

As far as Goldfinger was concerned, the other members of the Industrial Camouflage Unit were not good tenants. They were late paying rent and other bills. And they didn't share his respect for tools and materials – the secular equivalent of the sin against the Holy Ghost for him. A rift between Goldfinger and the group grew, fuelled by his discovery that a typewriter and trestle table had gone missing, and lamps had been damaged. Worst of all they were using one of his best drawing boards as a table to make models on. He distanced himself from the unit, sending them a bill for his services as technical advisor and demanding the return of his equipment, including the sun machine.[22] One of the items requested was Peter Goldfinger's toy aeroplane, a toy that Goldfinger had designed in 1936 for the Abbatt toy company, and which hung suspended from the ceiling in the studio. With Peter evacuated in Canada, this toy must have had a particular emotional charge for Ernö. The surrealists had taken it down and practised their camouflage painting on it. The request for its return triggered an irreverent response from Buckland-Wright:

> We shall be returning your aeroplane in the course of the next day or so. Naturally the camouflage will have to be taken off it as such designs are the property of the Unit. However, it will be painted silver and has now acquired wheels, tail runner and a propellor all of which it lacked before. Several members of the Unit have suggested a particular use for it which might be to your advantage but you would naturally have to detach the wings before employing it in this manner.[23]

Soon after, the group dispersed. Most of its members carried on their work in camouflage design. Roland Penrose, for example, went on to lecture on camouflage at the Home Guard School at Osterley Park[24] and even wrote *The Home Guard Manual of Camouflage* (1941) and Julian Trevelyan studied camouflage at Farnham; he was later invalided out of the forces after suffering a nervous breakdown. Both came to realise the limitations and false assumptions of many of their early experiments. In retrospect, in private, Goldfinger described the unit as 'the biggest con I was ever involved in'[25] – presumably a reference to the substantial payment from the Player factory for what was probably an interesting large three-dimensional painting, but which was of dubious value as camouflage.

Ernö's wartime connections extended beyond the visual arts. His friends included poets, writers, and politicians. When the poet Stephen Spender married for the second time, Ernö attended the party held in the South Kensington studio that Spender shared with Peter Quennell and Arthur Koestler. Cecil Beaton's photograph of the event shows him alongside the philosopher A.J. Ayer, Cyril Connolly (editor of *Horizon*), Sonia Bronwell (who would marry George Orwell), the poet Louis MacNeice and Guy Burgess, who would later be revealed as a spy.[26]

The conditions of war and the limitations they put on Goldfinger's intentions to build, and on his ability to fight the fascists, left him with time to focus on organising exhibitions. His combination of artistic and practical skills, together with his incredible network of friends and acquaintances in the visual arts, soon led to work. He had hoped to secure a job with the BBC Overseas Service, but when he was turned down for this he looked for other ways in which to channel his energy and earn a living. One of his main outlets was organising and designing a string of educational touring exhibitions for the Army Bureau of Current Affairs (ABCA) – part of the education section – and the Admiralty and Air Force Education section.

His exhibitions for the ABCA included 'Cinema' (1943), 'Food' (1943), 'Health Centres' (1943), 'The County of London Plan' (1944) and 'Planning Your Kitchen' (1944). Some of these were co-credited to Ursula. Gordon Cullen did many of the drawings.[27] Goldfinger planned these exhibitions with great skill, combining photographs, captions, drawings, diagrams and informative maps. They were designed to a standard format on 20 inch by 15 inch cartridge so that they could easily be transported. Multiple copies were made of the panels so that an exhibition could be shown simultaneously to several different army units, if necessary fitting into a box on the back of a motorcycle.[28] These exercises in visual communication were a poor substitute for architecture, but they did allow Goldfinger to contribute to the war effort.

In the case of 'The Two Mrs Britains',[29] an exhibition created for the London Women's Parliament, an organisation which had published pamphlets such as ''You CAN get a war-time nursery in your district', Ursula took the lead role. The idea of the exhibition – which was held in Boots the chemist on Piccadilly – was to show two ways of coping with changes brought about by war. One Mrs Britain (Mary Britain) moaned and resented doing factory work, whereas the other (Betty Britain) was a dynamic organiser and all-round contributor to the war effort. The visual argument was carried by Edith Tudor-Hart's photographs. The Goldfingers had found suitable models for these photographs from among the 'clippies', the female conductors on London buses.[30] The propaganda message was hammered home: 'Women! – Fight now for victory as you have seen Betty Britain doing!' Yet there was a more radical message too: 'Equal opportunities and Equal Pay for Victory and Reconstruction'.[31] One reviewer pointed out that some of the drawings and graphics that Ernö had designed gave the exhibition 'a politically pink hue'.[32]

The Goldfingers' most distinctive contribution to the war effort, however, stemmed from their enthusiastic support for the Soviet Union. In June 1942 they opened up their own home as an exhibition space for a remarkable show of modern painting known as 'Aid to Russia'.[33] The Goldfingers had been committed members of the intellectual opposition to fascism from the time of Franco's rebellion in Spain. They had been active in the Holborn and Hampstead Spanish Aid committees, which had drawn upon the support of artists to help their cause. Fundraising activities had included exhibitions of paintings by the likes of Ben Nicholson, Roland Penrose, Paul Nash, Eric Gill and Mark Gertler, and even raffles of drawings and paintings. The National Joint Committee for Spanish Relief had even brought Picasso's *Guernica* to London, exhibiting it in the New Burlington Galleries in October 1938.

These earlier fundraising exhibitions provided the models for 'Aid to Russia'.[34] The immediate stimulus for fundraising was the Anglo–Soviet Treaty which Churchill and Molotov had signed in May of the same year. There was already substantial public sympathy in Britain for the Russian people who were suffering the full force of the Nazi war machine. Tales of unprecedented barbarity were emerging and there was genuine compassion for ordinary Russians. In this atmosphere, pro-Soviet fundraising activities were popular. Memories of the Nazi–Soviet pact were erased, and there were calls to open a new front to dilute the force of the Nazi attack on the Eastern Front. The Soviet Army's resistance in the winter of 1941 offered hope that Hitler might yet be defeated. Everything connected with Russia became popular: a play by Turgenev was a sell-out, the Red Flag flew over Selfridges, and the Soviet Ambassador Ivan Maisky was elected to the Athenaeum.[35] Unlike many Londoners, however, the Goldfingers had long been aware of Russia's power. The confirmation of the Anglo–Soviet Treaty now provided them with the stimulus to contribute to the war effort in a way that made use of their remarkable network of artistic connections.

Nearly seventy works were put on display in 'Aid to Russia', most for sale, and visitors were charged an entry fee of one shilling. The quality of the art was exceptionally high. The organising committee included Peter Watson. Watson was a member of the editorial board of *Horizon*, and had a wide range of artistic contacts which supplemented the Goldfingers'. He and Ursula were the driving force behind the exhibition: they wrote to most of the major artists based in Britain and invited them to submit two pieces. Very few refused, perhaps in part because they were allowed to keep half of any money received from sales (though some, like Julian Trevelyan, waived this, and donated the entire amount to the cause), the rest going to the Aid to Russia fund and minor organisational expenses. They borrowed additional paintings, including a Picasso and a Henri Rousseau, from friends or friends of friends. The exhibition was sponsored by the Association of Architects, Surveyors and Technical Assistants (AASTA) of which Colin Penn, a member of the Communist Party, was the president.

On display were drawings, prints, paintings and sculptures by most of the significant European artists alive in 1942: Hans Arp, Jacob Epstein, Max Ernst, Barbara Hepworth, Augustus John, Rita Kernn-Larsen, Paul Klee, Ferdinand Léger, Joan Miró, Henry Moore, Paul Nash, Ben Nicholson, Amédée Ozenfant, Roland Penrose, John Piper, Henri Rousseau, Kurt

Schwitters, Graham Sutherland, Julian Trevelyan and others were all included. Naum Gabo would also have sent some work, but the invitation letter reached him too late.[36] Many of these were already personal friends of the Goldfingers. Pride of place in the main living room was given to a Picasso portrait borrowed from Hugh Willoughby. This has subsequently been thought to depict Nusch Eluard (the wife of the poet who had been a good friend of Ernö's in Paris), but at the time was simply known as *La Niçoise*, a reference to the straw hat worn by the sitter. The painting had to be insured for the exceptionally high sum of £1,500 (most of the works for sale in the exhibition were under 20 guineas). The Goldfingers' own collection already included three works by Max Ernst, a collage by Hans Arp and a drawing by Ozenfant, and these were all on display; Roland Penrose lent works by Klee, Miró, Picasso, Moore and Rousseau's *The Actor*.

'Aid to Russia' had a special appeal as this was the first time a representative range of modern art had been exhibited in a modernist house in Britain. The contemporary conventions of display involved lavish frames and cluttered hanging, typically on patterned walls. The clean fresh lines of the newly built Willow Road house, in contrast, were the ideal complement for the art and provided a foretaste of the style of presentation now common in major galleries. For the exhibition the moveable wall partitions on the first floor were all opened up. From a different angle, the exhibition of modernist art in wartime was a defiant counter to the Nazi Degenerate Art exhibitions that had tried to undermine the careers of such artists as Ernst, Klee, Picasso, Miró and Schwitters. All these artists had work in the Goldfingers' exhibition.[37]

The organising committee took their work seriously, with a poster campaign at local underground stations and in shops.[38] The exhibition was opened on a warm summer's day by Mme Maisky, the wife of the Russian Ambassador, with the Goldfingers' friend Sir Peter Chalmers-Mitchell, Treasurer of the Joint Committee of Soviet Aid, in the chair. Mme Maisky focused the proceedings, declaring:

> As you will all realise the burden of war is very heavy upon my countrymen and women.[39]

Here was an opportunity to contribute to the Russian resistance to the Nazis. Half of Hampstead jostled to see the show and to support the cause, with many eminent visitors and a number of the artists visible in the crowd. The Goldfingers opened their house to the public every afternoon and evening from 3 p.m. to 9 p.m. on weekdays, and 11 a.m. to 6 p.m. on Sundays from 5 to 21 June. These generous opening hours resulted in more than eight hundred visitors in the first week; ten paintings were sold in that time. The

6.2
La Niçoise featured in a photograph of Ernö Goldfinger showing the painting to Madame Maisky at the opening of 'Aid to Russia' exhibition, 1941
© Succession Picasso/DACS 2003

exhibition was widely reviewed in both local and national newspapers and magazines, and the critics were unanimous in their praise for the show and its venue.[40] Evening talks on Soviet music, Soviet architecture and Soviet cinema and theatre drew more people in. By the end of the nineteen-day exhibition, 1,778 visitors had passed through, an average of almost a hundred a day. In all, eighteen works of art were sold raising a profit of nearly £250, a substantial sum. Buyers included Edward Hulton of *Picture Post* (who bought a Léger engraving for four guineas), Goldfinger's friend the toy manufacturer Paul Abbatt, Ursula's step-brother Michael Strachan (who bought a Henry Moore drawing of Londoners sheltering in the underground)[41] and F.R.S. Yorke, the architect and author of the influential book *The Modern House in England* (1944), who also bought a work by Moore. The Goldfingers themselves bought several pieces, including a carved elmwood head by Henry Moore for £25 which is still in the house (they even kept the price tag). Yet many works by artists of the calibre of Ben Nicholson, Barbara Hepworth and Kurt Schwitters failed to find buyers; it fell to Ursula to write sensitive letters informing the artists that they should make arrangements to collect their work.[42]

Most of the émigré artists and art-lovers of London had come to lend their support to the cause – or at least to see some outstanding art. For some of them this was not just a way to raise money, but a public and symbolic expression of anti-Fascism by artists. Penn wrote in the catalogue, justifying the support of the building association:

> . . . if culture is to develop, flourish and become part of the life of the people, it is necessary first that Fascism be destroyed.[43]

Ernö himself managed to maintain an inspiring optimism, and even in June of 1941, when there was very little to be hopeful about, he was looking to the time when architects and planners would be able to transform and rebuild the cities and, through the rational application of technology, improve the quality of life of ordinary people:

> The cities can become centres of civilization where men and women can live happy lives. The technical means exist, to satisfy human needs. The will to plan must be aroused. There is no obstacle, but ignorance and wickedness. Planning means freedom.[44]

For Ernö, the artist's role in wartime was not that of an ivory tower individualist: artists of every variety should pull together to fight Fascism. This message came out most strongly in an extended review of the poignant 'For Liberty' exhibition that Goldfinger wrote for Communist newspaper *The Daily Worker* in March of the following year (*The Daily Worker* had been closed down in early 1941, but had then been reinstated when the Soviet Union became an ally). His review of this exhibition which was held in the basement of a bomb-damaged building off Oxford Street, and which included works by Augustus John and Oskar Kokoschka, was Ernö's pretext for a manifesto for artistic solidarity. It suggests very strongly that the 'Aid to Russia' exhibition was about much more than simply fundraising. This was an opportunity for artists to pull together in the fight for civilisation. For him artists were like seismographs, registering and recording the underlying turmoil of their times:

> In our society, with its infinite cleavages and chaotic confusion, there is an endless number of tendencies in art. This is precisely because art reflects these historic facts. For twenty years the greatest artists of the interwar period painted, in isolation, decay, rottenness, erotic escapism. They painted ruins and destruction well in advance of the real happenings. They felt it coming, it was in their bones.
>
> Today the scene has changed. We are in a life and death struggle. Everything becomes clear. The fascist cannibals are on the prowl.

> A thousand years of European civilization is at stake. The Nazi hangmen, after raping and murdering, turn their bloodstreaming claws on the most treasured possessions of the downtrodden nations and land they run over. They plunder Peterhof, they destroy Yasndya Polyana; paintings join the books on the bonfire of destruction.
>
> Fascism must be destroyed or civilization will perish . . . This becomes clearer every day to the artist . . . Fascism can be destroyed by combined action . . . This becomes clearer every day to the most individualist and sectarian artist in his ivory tower. Ivory towers will crumble if the bastillions of freedom fall on the Donetz or on the Straits of Dover . . .
>
> [. . .]
>
> Those who are not there [i.e. in the exhibition] should remember that the 'avant garde' of humanity and art is not fighting in the drawing rooms of Mayfair nor in the picture galleries of the West End nor in the shelter of country seclusion, but in the hills of Savoy, the olive groves of Tunisia, the snowcovered planes of Vyasna and also in the factories and blitzed cities of Britain. And that the job of artists is to understand this as Picasso did when he painted the agony of Guernica.[45]

The general ignorance of the power of the Russian army and people and their willingness to fight Hitler is evident in Ernö's comments in a letter to his brother George, written in early 1942:

> Since the entry of Russia into the war the attitude here is, at least on the surface, quite amusing. Old Joe is a kind of national hero like Joan of Arc or Walt Disney or even Greta Garbo. Last August of course when some of us referred to the possibility of the Red Army not being defeated straight away or even possibly licking the Nazis, one was rewarded with a compassionate smile, and treated as a hopeless visionary. Now it is quite different. It is far from being over but judging from what people say who have just come back there is an even chance, not to say more, that total war really means something and the chaps know what they want to do, and even know what they can do.[46]

Goldfinger threw himself into the pro-Soviet cause in 1942, rightly seeing our new allies as the most likely force to halt the Nazis. In late June 1942, while the 'Aid to Russia' exhibition was still running, the 'Eastern Front Exhibition' opened in Devonshire House, Piccadilly. Ernö had designed the exhibition, which was put on by the Society of Cultural Relations with the USSR and which was intended to cultivate Anglo–Soviet friendship by displaying to the British public the Russian contribution to the war effort, in terms of raw materials, military and medical equipment – from anti-tank guns to x-ray machines.[47] The exhibition was designed to travel round the country and reach a very wide audience and in the process promote Anglo–Soviet friendship. Key sections were labelled 'What we are Fighting For' and 'What we are Fighting Against'. In the autumn of 1942, Goldfinger followed up this exhibition by designing 'Twenty-five Years of Soviet Progress', shown at the Wallace Collection in Manchester Square in London. Again the aim was to foster understanding and appreciation of the Soviet contribution to the war:

> The twenty-fifth anniversary of the Soviet Union sees many of the misunderstandings between us swept away. May our alliance of friendship grow ever stronger as we fight together for victory.[48]

Goldfinger's drawings, maps and charts complemented the sometimes gruesome images, such as those of charred, raped, tortured and hanged Soviet victims of the Nazis. For Goldfinger the message was clear, and his wall displays communicated it effectively.[49] The Soviet army was well-trained and well-led, with a twenty-five year history and a heritage to defend. Brave Soviet soldiers and civilians were giving their lives to save the world from barbarism:

> Today the Soviet People win the admiration of the world for their heroic resistance to the Fascist aggressor. In the name of the British People we greet them as the defenders of civilization.[50]

Goldfinger's skill with visual symbols was apparent in exhibits such as a map demonstrating the location of the USSR's chief fur-producing centres. Silhouettes of elk, sable, polar fox, seal, beaver, and so on provided effective visual indicators of the relevant species.

The publishers Penguin seriously considered producing a book based on the exhibition, with Goldfinger as its sole author. This was to be called *Twenty-five Years of Soviets*. They went so far as to produce a dummy book, with a hammer and sickle on the front cover, but finally shied away from the project.[51] The editor who wrote to Goldfinger could not commit herself one hundred per cent to the book – no doubt she shared many of her contemporaries' concern that Soviet allies could once again become enemies and that the fervour for all things Russian might be short-lived. Or perhaps her caution simply reflected wartime paper shortages.

The exhibition was opened by the Soviet Ambassador, M. Maisky, and by the architect Sir Edwin Lutyens in his role as president of the Royal

6.3
Opening of 'Twenty-five Years of Soviet Progress' exhibition: Ernö, Lutyens, Maisky

Academy. This led to an unlikely friendship. Ernö showed the distinguished guests around the exhibition. On entering a room devoted to Soviet buildings, Ernö turned to Lutyens and told him 'I think you'll like this' and then added 'I'm an architect you know'. At this Lutyens extended his hand in a mock serious gesture: 'So am I. Shake!'[52] They then toured the exhibition deep in discussion for an hour and a quarter. Despite their differing architectural sensibilities and standing, the two would meet regularly for lunch. Goldfinger knew and admired Lutyens' early work, such as Deanery House. He had originally come across it in Muthesius's *Das Englische Haus*, the book that had inspired him to study architecture. The two architects got on surprisingly well, Goldfinger, as he had done with Walter Gropius, once again finding it easy to mix more or less as an equal with an architect who at the time was far more eminent. Goldfinger warmed to the man as well as to the architect: 'He was a charming person, and funny. He didn't take himself seriously.'[53]

The Goldfingers continued their energetic support for the Soviet army and people throughout the war – in Red Army Week, for example, in early 1943, they again opened their home as a venue for fundraising activities as part of Hampstead's tribute to the Red Army.[54]

Before the end of the war the family was finally reunited. Most of the children from the evacuated group returned from Canada in late June of

6.4
Ernö dressed for Air Warden duties, outside Willow Road

1944, shortly after the D-day landings. They made the journey in a ship that was in a convoy bringing supplies from Montreal. Almost unbelievably, though, the father of one child whose mother had died during the war, never sent for his daughter to return to England.[55]

Ursula and Ernö met their children at Euston station. Peter had been old enough when he left to remember his parents well, but Liz was disconcerted by Ernö's accent: for a while she was convinced that he was a foreign spy. She had become so used to Peter being responsible for her, that when Ursula asked her to do something shortly after their return she replied that she had better ask Peter if that was alright.[56]

London was still far from safe. Doodlebugs, the unmanned V1 aircraft-bombs launched from France and Holland, which might arrive at any time of day or night, were still falling from the sky, some of them on Hampstead. Then came the V2 rockets. Ursula, meanwhile, was pregnant again. The Goldfingers' third child, Michael, was born in July 1945. The family was once more a unit, and the war was about to end. Ernö would at last be able to get back to the real business of architecture.

Notes

1 Goldfinger in Hungarian television documentary, transcript in National Trust 2 Willow Road collection.
2 This is described in F. Lafitte, *The Internment of Aliens*, London: Penguin, 1940, p.76. Philip Ziegler also mentions Hampstead as a favourite target for alien-hunting and points out that the raids on the library 'may have eased pressure on the library's newspapers, but does not seem to have contributed notably to national security', *London at War 1939–1945*, London: Pimlico, 2002, p.96.
3 Letter from John Vago to Goldfinger, 16/7/40, in GolEr 281/8.
4 Letter from Pritchard and Co. solicitors, 9/10/40, in GolEr 281/8.
5 He was sent the appropriate certificate of naturalisation on 8 May 1947, and swore allegiance to King George VI the next day. The papers are in National Trust 2 Willow Road collection.
6 The Goldfingers had been active in raising funds for republicans in the Spanish Civil War, and this had brought them in contact with most of the prominent members of the London left wing intelligensia, including Stephen Spender and Cyril Connolly.
7 See letter to Chief Constable of Bristol, 21/11/41, in GolEr 273/5.
8 Author's telephone conversation with James Dunnett, 2002, who recalls Goldfinger making this point.
9 Letter from Ursula Goldfinger to General Secretary of YMCAs, 5/2/42, in National Trust 2 Willow Road collection.
10 Goldfinger's letter to his brother George in New York, 24/1/42, in National Trust 2 Willow Road collection.
11 Letter from Leonora Carrington, 27/9/1939, in GolEr 269/2.
12 See 'An Interview with Leonora Carrington', by Paul de Angelis from *El Paseante* 17, trans. Martinz, ed. Van Hussell, on http:/www/kalin/.lm.com/carrint.html at 26/10/01.
13 Julian Trevelyan, *Indigo days*, London: Macgibbon and Kee, 1957, p.70.
14 Described in Whitney Chadwick, *Women artists and the Surrealist Movement*, London: Thames and Hudson, 1985, p.84.
15 Chadwick, 1985, p.85.
16 Ursula, letter to Ernö, 5 December 1939, in National Trust 2 Willow Road collection.
17 See Goldfinger's letter to his brother George, 9/7/40 in National Trust 2 Willow Road collection.
18 These photographs are in the National Trust 2 Willow Road collection.
19 Reported in 'Family Transatlantic Link: local children away for nearly four years, hear their parents' voices' *Hampstead and Highgate Express*, 21/1/44, in GolEr 389/1.
20 These affidavits are in the National Trust 2 Willow Road collection.
21 Trevelyan, 1957, pp.112–113.
22 GolEr 272/2. Letter from Goldfinger, 11/4/1940.
23 GolEr 272/2. Letter from Buckland-Wright, 6/5/1940.
24 See Antony Penrose, *Roland Penrose The Friendly Surrealist*, Munich: Prestel, 2001, p.101.
25 James Dunnett, 'Conversations with Ernö Goldfinger', unpublished notes, 15/8/83.
26 This photograph is described by Ben Rogers, *A.J. Ayer: A Life*, London, Architectural Press, 1999, p.170.
27 Dunnett, unpublished notes, 30/7/80.
28 For an example of a drawing from one of these exhibitions and further information about the ABCA, see R. Elwall, *Ernö Goldfinger*, RIBA Drawings Monographs no. 3, London: Academy Editions, 1996, p.61.
29 Elwall reproduces a coloured drawing of the layout of this exhibition with its characteristic Goldfinger use of pointing fingers, p.59.

30 As Helen Langley has pointed out, there may be an updating of 'the man on the Clapham omnibus' implied here – or it might just have been a convenient source of possible models.
31 Both are captions from the exhibition. See GolEr 400/3. Ernö and Ursula subsidised the exhibition, contributing £42.80 to pay off the Women's Parliament's debts.
32 *News Review*, 7/9/1943. In GolEr 394/18.
33 The National Trust has recently staged a re-creation of this exhibition in Willow Road ('Art for Russia' 9 Novermber to 14 December 2002). My understanding of the content and significance of this exhibition has been greatly enhanced by discussions with Helen Langley and Barbara Pezzini, both of whom have conducted interesting research on the topic. The National Trust's exhibition pamphlet, *Art for Russia*, 2002 includes short essays contextualising the exhibition.
34 The Goldfingers' was not the only 'Aid to Russia' art exhibition: another larger, more diluted exhibition with similar aims was staged in the Wallace Collection, London, between 1 July and 4 August 1942.
35 See Ziegler, 2002, pp.223–4.
36 Letter from Naum Gabo to Mrs Penn, 2/6/1942 in National Trust 2 Willow Road collection.
37 I owe this point to Barbara Pezzini who has extensively researched the 'Aid to Russia' exhibition and the background to the Goldfingers' collection of works of art.
38 Letter from Mrs Penn to London Underground, 22/5/1942, in National Trust 2 Willow Road collection.
39 Quoted in review in *Hampstead and Highgate Express*, June 1941, in GolEr 389/1.
40 GolEr 389/1, a scrapbook of cuttings, includes reviews in the *Tatler*, *Country Life*, the *Manchester Guardian*, *The Glasgow Herald*, *Studio*, *New Statesman and Nation*, *News Chronicle*, The *Daily Telegraph* and The *Observer*.
41 This topic was also photographed by Bill Brandt, a friend of the Goldfingers, who also attended this exhibition.
42 Copies of these letters are in the National Trust 2 Willow Road collection.
43 From Colin Penn, '"Art Too is A Weapon": Pravda', introduction to 'Exhibition of Modern Painting and Sculpture at 2 Willow Road Hampstead on behalf of the "Aid to Russia" Fund of the National Council of Labour' catalogue, June 1942, in National Trust 2 Willow Road collection.
44 From Goldfinger's review of 'Living in Cities', a travelling exhibition, in *Horizon*, June 1941, in GolEr 389/2.
45 Typescript version of Goldfinger's review of 'For Liberty' for the *Daily Worker* 31 March 1943, in GolEr 338/6 – this is a longer and more impassioned version of the review that was printed.
46 Goldfinger's letter to his brother George in New York, 24/1/42, in National Trust 2 Willow Road collection.
47 Reviewed in *The Times*, 23/6/1942, cutting in GolEr 394.
48 From exhibition captions, photograph in National Trust 2 Willow Road collection.
49 A review in the *Architectural Review*, December 1942 singled out Goldfinger's graphical and statistical charts for special praise. Cutting in GolEr 394.
50 Caption from a wall display for the '25 Years of the Soviet Union' exhibition, November 1942, from a photograph of the installation, in National Trust 2 Willow Road collection.
51 Letter from Eunice E. Frost of Penguin Books, 3/2/43, in GolEr 399/5.
52 Reported in *Architect's Journal*, 19 November 1942, cutting in GolEr 394. It is not clear whether this refers to the Eastern Front Exhibition or the 25 Years of Soviet Union – which the dates fit better.
53 Quoted in Gavin Stamp, 'Conversation with Ernö Goldfinger', *Thirties Society Journal*, no.2, 1982, pp.19–24.
54 Reported in *Hampstead News*, 4/3/43, in GolEr 389/1.
55 Conversation with Peter and Nick Goldfinger, Soho, 28/11/02.
56 Conversation with Peter and Nick Goldfinger, Soho, 28/11/02.

Chapter 7

The sensation of space

Architecture masters space, limits it, encloses it.

In the first few years of the Second World War, with no buildings to build, no regular job, the difficulties of being an alien, his children evacuated to another continent and a real risk of Nazi invasion, it might have been reasonable for Goldfinger to feel frustrated, bitter and pessimistic. In fact though, he threw himself into a range of writing and research with tremendous energy and optimism for the future.

Photographs by Bill Brandt of Ernö and Ursula in their Willow Road study in around 1940 shows Ernö seated at a typewriter – not the obvious symbol for a practising architect.[1] But for several years his incredible energy was channelled principally into writing. He published articles and reviews on architectural and town planning issues in a number of papers and magazines. He also found time to clarify and articulate his vision of the nature of architecture and of urban planning. He published three important articles in *The Architectural Review* on this subject: 'The Sensation of Space' (November 1941), 'Urbanism and Spatial Order' (December 1941) and 'Elements of Enclosed Space' (January 1942). Together these articles constitute his most fully developed theoretical statement.[2] They appeared alongside a series on bomb damage to buildings of architectural value. In contrast, Goldfinger's articles make no mention of the war or its implications for architecture. They focus on perennial themes relating to the human experience of enclosed space.

There is nothing in his subsequent writing to indicate that Goldfinger changed his views about the nature of architecture and art from this moment on. Indeed, many of the talks he gave on the subject in later years were summaries of the ideas more fully expressed in these articles. As with his building solutions, when he found a technique or device that worked, such as the photobolic screen, he saw no reason to look for alternatives, but reused it wherever appropriate with only minor modifications.

7.1
Ernö and Ursula photographed by Bill Brandt, Willow Road, c.1940

His main contribution to theory is his incisive analysis of the sensation of space. His basic thesis was that architecture is a way of enclosing space and that the way in which space is enclosed has a psychological effect on anyone within that space, at least at a subconscious level. This echoes Perret's aphorisms:

> Architecture is the art of organising space. It is through construction that it expresses itself.[3]

and:

> Architecture masters space, limits it, encloses it, circles it. It has this prerogative to create magical places totally the work of the intellect.[4]

7.2
Ernö the writer, photographed by Bill Brandt, c.1940

In his article 'The Sensation of Space', Goldfinger used the word 'subconscious' to describe the effect of enclosed space on the person within it, but this is best understood as meaning pre-conscious – that is, not currently conscious, but capable of being brought to consciousness.[5] This is clear from his analogy with listening to music:

> It is not necessary to listen (consciously) to be affected by music, it is equally not necessary to be consciously scrutinising spatial relationships to be affected by them.[6]

By focusing on the sensation of space rather than on the outward shells of buildings, Goldfinger put the emphasis on lived experience of architecture rather than aesthetically pleasing formal masses. As we move through a building we are aware at some level of the way in which space has been enclosed, and this produces an emotional effect in us. True to the rational spirit of his approach, Goldfinger gives a hard-headed analysis of the sources of this emotional response. He is scathing about the invocation of mystery to account for the spatial sensations triggered by buildings. Spatial sensation is a natural phenomenon. We are always in some sense within enclosed space – even our experience of the horizon and the sky contribute to a feeling that we are not entirely free of enclosure. We always have some spatial sensation whether we are consciously aware of it or not. Yet there is no single organ by which we perceive this sensation. The sensation of space is not simply a visual sensation: it is in part the product of what Goldfinger calls 'memorised analogies'.[7] At some level, our experience of the enclosure of the womb may be relevant too – Goldfinger in fact produced an illustration of a foetus in a womb to accompany 'The Sensation of Space', but it was considered too risqué to publish in *The Architectural Review*.[8] Our sensations of space, then, come from a range of sources, and are experienced through several senses, and memory too:

> The spatial order is built up by an amalgamation of a multitude of phenomena, the perception of which, subconsciously integrated, helps in building up the sensation of space. Memories and experience, not only of visual sensation but also of sound and touch and smell, enter into it. The sound and vibration in a hall; the physical touch of the walls of a narrow passage; the atmosphere and temperature of a stuffy room; the smell of a damp cellar; all are, in various degrees, components of spatial sensation. Every element, plastic or pictorial, partially obstructing the view, and people in the crowd rubbing against you, are part of it.[9]

The two main determinants of the spatial sensation are (1) the 'enclosing agent' – that is, the wall, fence or window that surrounds the person; and (2) the enclosed space itself, its shape, height, and so on. Qualitative and quantitative aspects of these two determinants also affect the sensation of space: the dimensions and materials affect the percipient, again usually at the pre-conscious level.

One aspect of his account explains why clients were such poor readers of plans and models, something Goldfinger often remarked on. When you reproduce a painting you reproduce it in two dimensions. Consequently the reproduction gives rise to sensations which are in many ways similar to those created by the original image – they are at least sensations of a similar kind in reaction to a similar stimulus. In contrast, a three-dimensional object can only be hinted at in a two-dimensional representation of it, such as a photograph or perspectival drawing. Indeed, Goldfinger pointed out that the illustrations accompanying the article 'The Sensation of Space' were only intended as depictions of situations in which particular spatial sensations would be experienced: they were not themselves meant to evoke any sensation of space. The logical implication for an architect trying to communicate the sensation that a building creates might seem to be the use of scale models. But Goldfinger points out the serious shortcomings of models as a way of producing spatial sensations: they cannot give the sensation of being *within* enclosed space that is fundamental to our experience of buildings:

> A scale model only adds confusion to the other difficulties by introducing a three-dimensional element of an utterly different order and scale which then gets confused with spatial order.[10]

The measure of man that so occupied Goldfinger in his planning could not be replicated adequately on a smaller scale: the whole point of scaling buildings to people would be lost once the scale was reduced.

Having outlined the basic features of enclosed space and its psychological effects on the person within it, Goldfinger, ever systematic, analysed enclosed space in relation to architecture in his article 'Urbanism and Spatial Order'. He had a very clear vision of the goal of architecture:

> The object of architecture is to fulfil a specific social function, i.e. to provide an ordered enclosure for human activities.[11]

That is architecture's main aim, but beyond providing physical shelter, it is 'an instrument of psychological effect': it produces the spatial emotion. In the process it may also be art.

Goldfinger explained architecture as the result of three integrated factors:

1 functional needs (why it was made)
2 constructional means (the available technological resources)
3 emotional effect (how it is experienced).

For Goldfinger, aesthetic issues arise as a normal part of human activity and, like our experience of space, do not require any mystical explanation. The appreciation of beauty is a human phenomenon. Underlying Goldfinger's whole approach is a historical determinism. Aesthetics must be understood within the 'general pattern of social conditions and their historic evolution'. Goldfinger was a lifelong Marxist, and his commitment to socio-economic explanations is consistent with this; though, diplomatically, he avoided explict references to Hegel or Marx in this suite of three articles.[12] In the same spirit, he reminds us that[13] human beings are 'time and space bound'; they are 'chained to the fate of the human adventure'.

This adventure unfolds for architecture as a result of the constant struggle of the conflicting factors outlined above: function, means and the human experience of enclosed space. These conflicting factors impinge on one another and change over time. Consequently, there is no unique and static correct way to build that, once discovered, would bring about the end of architecture:

> New technics of construction make new functional demands possible and new functions engender new technical answers; interlocked and ever-changing they produce enclosed space which at its best, is architecture.[14]

From the outside, a building has purely *plastic* effect on the spectator: it is a work of abstract sculpture:

> The play of light and shade, the massing of volumes and shapes, can be observed and appreciated.[15]

So, for example, looking at Trellick Tower from the Westway coming into London, the building can be appreciated for its sculptural qualities, just as we might appreciate a sculpture by Max Ernst, except that, unlike Ernst's work, this is not a representational object.[16] Closer to a building, Goldfinger points out that the eye cannot take in the whole, and so the effect is different: it becomes not plastic but *pictorial*. The building is experienced as an organised surface rather than as a three-dimensional mass.

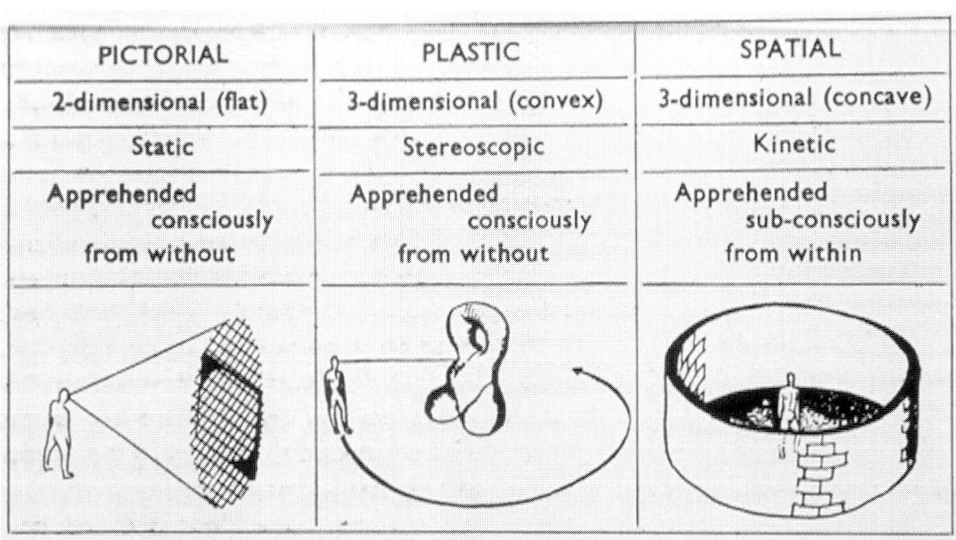

7.3 Goldfinger's summary of 'The Sensation of Space'

But it is only when the spectator enters the building that he or she will feel the sensation of space in relation to that building. Before that moment the experience of the building is not an experience specific to architecture. The plastic and pictorial sensations, important as they are to the overall effect of architecture, by no means exhaust our experience of architecture. For Goldfinger, the sensation of space is all-important. The building experienced from within evokes in the spectator a spatial emotion, possibly in a pre-conscious form.

The building can of course itself evoke spatial emotions even when the spectator is outside the building, since the building's exterior may be part of a street or conglomeration of buildings that enclose the spectator. The ways in which buildings are placed relative to each other enclose the spectator, providing spatial organisation analogous to the spatial organisation within a building. This is particularly so in a city: 'you are *in* the street even if you are *out* of doors'.[17]

Furthermore, new forms of transport have affected the sensation of space in the city: we can approach by air, travel through it at high speeds by train or car. These new forms of travel create entirely different sensations of space from those experienced by the pedestrian. What seems solid and monumental at walking pace can feel light and open when passed by at 50 miles an hour. Within buildings too, technical developments have affected the direction in which people move through buildings: for example with escalators and lifts, devices which, as he explained in 'The Elements of Enclosed Space', 'alter completely the speed and effort involved in displacement and the direction of penetration.'[18] Consequently, urban planning needs to reflect the ways in which space in cities is now likely to be experienced: the medieval street was built for pedestrians and horse riders. Goldfinger suggested that urban planners needed to be sensitive to these factors, just as architects need to be sensitive to the effects their buildings have on those who enter them. When cars and buses started to use streets designed for horses in the early twentieth century, few problems were anticipated; in the modern world, in contrast, Goldfinger argued for 'the complete segregation of traffic according to speed'.[19]

As we have seen, for Goldfinger, architecture creates a spatial emotion by enclosing space: but that is not its *purpose*: the purpose of architecture is 'to fulfil a social function with the best means of an up-to-date technology'.[20] When architecture fulfils or attempts to fulfil this purpose, the sensation of space is inevitably evoked almost as a by-product. But it is in the way that the architect approaches the shaping of space and the evocation of spatial emotions that he or she rises above mere technical proficiency. Goldfinger ends the 'Urbanism and the Spatial Order' article by hinting at the relationship between the sensation of space and architecture as art:

> It is the artist who shapes this space, to develop it from the crude, mere by-product of enclosure into spatial order, not by adding frills or ornaments, but by making the very enclosed space self-evident and clear i.e. by making it Architecture.[21]

In a letter to the architect John Brandon-Jones, Goldfinger expanded these intriguing comments about art and architecture. For Goldfinger, the essence of art is that it must be a creation which produces a specific artistic emotion in the experiencer of the work, one which the artist intended to evoke through the work:

> This 'artistic emotion' may be delight, humour or any other emotion which, if the artist were successful, is the one he wished to produce.[22]

In an aside he explained that he tried to analyse 'what constitutes the essence of architectural emotion, i.e. the sort of art side of architecture'. The letter to Brandon-Jones goes some way to clarifying how he saw the relationship:

> I therefore consider it to be playing with the unprecise [sic] meaning of the word 'art' if the practice of medicine or engineering is described as art. While the primordial function of architecture is to put one in a state of mind (architectural emotion) the two other 'human activities' have quite different objects, which are not sensual. The fact that the exercise of a profession fills you with delight (and by Jove don't I think architecture does . . .) is not a criterion of it being a work of art.[23]

In the last of his three theoretical articles, 'The Elements of Enclosed Space', Goldfinger again hinted at the relationship between architecture and art, this time suggesting that, in order to produce a specific emotional effect through the sensation of space in a building, the emotional effect must itself be anticipated by the architect. Furthermore:

> It seems to be a constant coincident that only if persons creating a work of art experience an artistic emotion while doing so, are those undergoing its effects enabled to experience an emotion of a similar nature.[24]

Goldfinger, then, saw his role as an architect as one of fulfilling the social role and finding elegant and rational solutions to the problems set by means and ends; but also as an artist evoking emotions by enclosing space. For him the artist–architect is a kind of champion:

> It is the artist who comprehends the social requirements of his time and is able to integrate the technical potentialities in order to shape the spaces of the future.[25]

Although he fails to explain precisely why the evocation of specific spatial emotions is such an important achievement, it is clear that for him this is at the centre of his life's work.[26] His friend Erich Mendelsohn wrote to him from New York, to say that he was following Goldfinger's series of articles with great interest (and correcting the caption on one of the illustrations):

> Remarkable statements for the brain. Guard of functionalism, pure and true. Congratulations . . .[27]

Goldfinger's reply indicates his reservations about the term 'functionalism' and how his adherence to the view that architecture is an art set him apart from the mainstream of modernist architectural theory:

> With regard to 'functionalism pure and true' I think you are completely mistaken about me, if you associate this term with the efforts of some of your friends. I have been fairly unpopular for the last ten years amongst these very advanced gentlemen as I still believe that architecture is an art, although not of the order termed 'dynamic' propagated by some other friends of mine.[28]

Despite the importance of the evocation of emotions to his understanding of his own activity as an architect, he believed that the *techniques* by which he enclosed space and, by implication, how he created the specific emotions that are at the core of architecture were an entirely personal affair and not anyone else's business.[29]

This approach to his own architecture has had a consequence that he would not have wanted. His attitude to those who worked and lived in buildings he designed was that they would feel the effects at a 'subconscious' (i.e. pre-conscious) level. How these effects were produced was not something he ever communicated to them. When he did disclose, for example, the range of rectangles on which his designs were based, it was almost as if he were a magician revealing how a trick had been performed – a matter of letting the listener in upon an arcane 'secret'.[30] Indeed, when, in later years he gave talks on his theory of the sensation of space, the title evolved to become 'The Magic of Enclosing Space' – in part to emphasise the excitement of the process, but also, perhaps hinting at this secret knowledge shared by good architects, like members of the Magic Circle. Yet when repairs and renovation to buildings have subsequently become necessary, the clients have often been ignorant of just how important, say, the proportions of a window frame or the lack of ornament are to the overall experienced effect of the building. It is no surprise then that many of Goldfinger's buildings have been significantly altered, with local builders and carpenters opting for the most convenient solution, rather than necessarily the most appropriate in terms of the building as enclosed space and ultimately as work of art.

Notes

1 Brandt took a series of photographs of the Goldfingers at home shortly after they had moved into the house at Willow Road. These now exist only as contact prints in the National Trust 2 Willow Road collection and have not previously been known about by the photographic historians who have documented Brandt's work. Dedicated copies of Brandt's first two books, *The English at Home* and *A Night in London*, are also in the collection.

2 Translations of these articles appeared in the French journal *Architecture* in 1953. Goldfinger continued to lecture on the topic throughout his life. He also produced an abbreviated version of his ideas which was used in the catalogue for *This is Tomorrow* and in a privately printed pamphlet.

3 Perret in *Contribution to a Theory of Architecture,* reprinted and translated as an appendix to Britton, *Auguste Perret*, London: Phaiden, 2001, p.231. Goldfinger made his own translation of Perret's aphorisms which he intended to publish. His draft of this translation is in his desk in the National Trust 2 Willow Road collection.

4 Perret in Britton, 2001, p.232.

5 In the Freudian sense, 'subconscious' refers to aspects of our psyche which are not directly available to consciousness, but are typically discovered through the indirect means of dream analysis or parapraxes ('Freudian slips').

6 'The Sensation of Space', reprinted in J. Dunnett and S. Stamp, *Ernö goldfinger: Works 1*, London: Architectural Association, 1983, p.48–9.

7 Dunnett and Stamp, p.50.

8 Recounted to James Dunnett by Ernö Goldfinger. Dunnet recalled this at the Goldfinger Centenary Conference, The Architectural Association, London, 28/9/02.

9 Dunnett and Stamp, 1983, p.50.

10 Dunnett and Stamp, 1983, p.47.

11 'Urbanism and Spatial Order', reprinted in Dunnett and Stamp, 1983, p.51.

12 I have resisted the temptation to describe the series of articles as a 'three-piece suite' except in this footnote.

13 Dunnett and Stamp, 1983, p.51.

14 Dunnett and Stamp, 1983, p.51.

15 Dunnett and Stamp, 1983, p.51.

16 James Dunnett has made an explicit link between the sculpture of Goldfinger's friend Max Ernst and the appearance of Trellick Tower from a distance.

17 'Urbanism and Spatial Order', reprinted in Dunnett and Stamp, 1983, p.52.

18 'The Elements of Enclosed Space', reprinted in Dunnett and Stamp, 1983, p.57.

19 Dunnett and Stamp, 1983, p.57.

20 'Urbanism and Spatial Order', reprinted in Dunnett and Stamp, 1983, p.54.

21 Dunnett and Stamp, 1983, p.54.

22 Letter dated 17/12/42 to John Brandon-Jones, who was then based at the Naval Base in Orkney. Goldfinger's copy of the letter and the letter to which it is a reply are held in GolER 266/4.

23 From letter to John Brandon-Jones, 17/12/42 in GolEr 266/4.

24 'Urbanism and Spatial Order', reprinted in Dunnet and Stamp, 1983, p.58.
25 'The Elements of Enclosed Space', reprinted in Dunnett and Stamp, p.58.
26 As a philosopher of aesthetics I can't resist pointing out the main philosophical criticism of the type of theory Goldfinger is putting forward here: it is a circular argument. The two key terms, 'spatial emotion' and 'Architecture' (with a capital A) are each defined in terms of the other: spatial emotion is the type of emotion that Architecture (i.e. Art) arouses; Architecture as opposed to mere building is the enclosure of space capable of arousing the spatial emotion. However, by fleshing out what the spatial emotion was, giving independent criteria for recognising it; or similarly by giving independent criteria for recognising Architecture as art without bringing in spatial emotion, he could have got round the criticism of circularity (he might well have done this had he expanded these articles into a fully-fledged theory).
27 Letter from Erich Mendelsohn (then signing himself as 'Eric'), 8/1/42, in GolEr 276. Another admirer of Goldfinger's theory of architecture was Herbert Read, to whom Goldfinger sent copies of the articles when Read was writing a piece about him in 1962 – see letter from Herbert Read, 5/11/62 in GolEr 279/1.
28 Letter from Goldfinger to Erich Mendelsohn, 22/2/42, in GolEr 276.
29 Interview with James Dunnett, in GolEr 397/3.
30 See, for example, corrections to interview, April 1983, in GolEr 397/3.

Chapter 8

Rebuilding

The Blitz has cleared some sites and we must clear many more – but for what?

Once the Second World War ended, rebuilding began on a massive scale. Much of London had been demolished or was in ruins. Architects were in demand. And with the election of a Labour government, there was a particular commitment to finding better solutions to social housing. Between the end of the war and 1969, more than four million public dwellings were built, and social housing represented some fifty-nine per cent of all new housing in that period. In November 1945, Ernö wrote to his brother George:

> I have a tremendous amount of work to do and hope to have even more in the near future. Building has been at a standstill for the last four years, and there is heaps to be done. There is a Government which seems to mean business.[1]

The post-war optimism was infectious. Goldfinger, who had been frustrated by the lack of building work available for him during the war, was full of energy and passion for the task of rebuilding Britain. Indeed, in the last years of the war he had thought deeply about the most effective ways of using the scarce resources to create a better environment for Londoners and had, with the structural engineer Ove Arup, worked on a number of projects for post-war housing, details of which were published in pamphlets, but were never built.[2] When the war ended he had an opportunity to explain his ideas to a wider public as co-author of a Penguin book, *The County of London Plan Explained*.[3]

The County of London was created in 1889. It is an area of 117 square miles that takes in the city and surrounding areas from Hammersmith in the west to Woolwich in the east. In 1938 it had a population of just over four million. From the early days of the war it became clear that substantial reconstruction and re-planning of London would be necessary as part of the

8.1
Ernö's first book
© Penguin/Allen Lane, 1945

post-war recovery. The devastating effect of the Blitz left acres of wasteland. Bombsites provided a challenge and an opportunity for planners to reconstruct a new and better-organised city.

In April 1941, Lord Reith, who was then Minister of Works and Planning, asked the London County Council (LCC) to devise a plan for reconstruction. J.H. Forshaw and Patrick Abercrombie worked on the plan, together with a number of specialists, producing a substantial volume in 1943, known as *The County of London Plan*. They later expanded this into *The Greater London Plan* (1944). Goldfinger had applied, unsuccessfully, to work on *The County of London Plan*. Towards the end of the war, however, he had the opportunity to interpret the plan for the wider public, a project that played to his strengths as a visual communicator and as a passionate advocate of rational planning. With the librarian of the Royal Institute of British Architects, E.J. Carter (known as 'Bobby'), who was a co-member of the MARS group, he wrote and illustrated an enthusiastic explanation of the key themes of the *County of London Plan*. This little book caught the imagination of the public and briefly became a bestseller – on 5 August 1945 the *Sunday Express* listed it as one of the books most in demand in the previous week. Charles

Reilly described it in *The Tribune*[4] as 'a grand piece of condensation, easier to read and almost better than the original'.

The success was well-deserved. The text was clear, passionate and to the point. It caught and helped to fuel the post-war desire for improved living conditions and for a new social order. Goldfinger and Carter argued that Londoners could build a better future for their children if only the principles of rational planning were applied. This is encapsulated in the caption to two drawings, one of a bombsite, the other of the same site redeveloped with modern buildings:

> The opportunity? The Blitz has cleared some sites and we must clear many more – but for what? Has the Blitz cleared our vision too and made it possible to see what London might be? And, if we can see this, have we the imagination and power to realise our hopes, or shall we just return to the old unplanned city blocks, to the same old wild activity of private speculation, to recreate the same old jumble of courtyards and streets and competing facades? An inheritance for the future as grim as anything we know to-day. The land speculator's boards are up . . .
>
> OR can we plan our London; give it order and efficiency and beauty and spaciousness? Can the County of London Plan become the real plan of London?[5]

Part of the book's success was due to its visual design. It included coloured maps as well as Goldfinger's own illustrations and diagrams. It also used photographs of Londoners at work and play, many taken by Bill Brandt. Goldfinger had known Brandt since the 1930s, and they may have met earlier in Paris when Brandt was working in Man Ray's studio as an assistant in the late 1920s. Goldfinger greatly admired his work – he owned a photograph of a seagull over the Thames that Brandt had given him in 1937 and which he described as 'marvellous'.[6] Through his books *The English at Home* (1936) and *A Night in London* (1938)[7] and through photo-stories for *Weekly Illustrated* and *Picture Post* magazines, Brandt had built up a substantial portfolio of images of London life and buildings. Many of these are reused in The *County of London Plan Explained* to make points about East End slum conditions, crowded streets, and the life of Londoners at work and leisure. Another photographer whose work appears in the book, Edith Tudor-Hart – sister of the photographer Wolfgang Suschitzky – was also in the Goldfingers' social circle.

The County of London Plan focused on four chief defects of London: traffic congestion, poor housing, inadequate open spaces and the juxtaposition of houses and industry. A fifth problem was the suburban sprawl, the tendency to build more and more housing in the country towns surrounding London. For each defect, the original plan had a solution. Perhaps of most interest is the argument that Carter and Goldfinger (and presumably the driving force here was Goldfinger) put forward about high-rise building in relation to the plan (which only envisaged a maximum of eight to ten storeys):

> It is necessary to emphasise that almost without exception all city flat building in Britain has been second rate mainly because the conditions in which local authorities have had to work, [. . .] have never allowed free and open mixed development of flats and houses over large enough areas to make really good schemes possible. There has however been much good small house development. People are thus limited in their experience and are not free to form a fair picture. Naturally they compare sub-standard flat building with moderately good small houses and as naturally vote for the latter.[8]

Goldfinger, who had already designed high-rise flats for the CIAM congress, could justifiably hope to play his part in building for Britain's future if he could only persuade the wider public of the potential benefits of well-designed blocks of flats.

His first chance to build on a large scale after the war came in late 1945 with a commission to convert a bomb-damaged Victorian warehouse into the new offices and printing press of the *Daily Worker* newspaper at 75 Farringdon Road, London. The *Daily Worker* was controlled by the Communist Party and owned by a cooperative: 'The only paper owned by its readers.' It had been banned during the early years of the war, but pressure from the Labour movement, and the fact of the Soviet Union becoming an ally, resulted in the ban being lifted in 1942. William Rust, its editor, had plans to turn what was then a four-page newspaper into a more substantial mass circulation daily that might ultimately challenge the monopoly of the press barons. The paper had collected a substantial amount of money from donations to fund the expansion. Donations had continued to flow in during the war. The move from Gray's Inn Road to Farringdon Road was to be a symbolic part of the transformation of the newspaper, but it was important for practical reasons too: it would allow the installation of a new and faster rotary press.

Goldfinger, as we have seen, considered himself a Marxist throughout his life, though like most young revolutionaries, he became more conservative with age. He took the communist *Daily Worker* as his newspaper and had even written art reviews for it during the war. He also donated to the newspaper's Fighting Fund.[9] He had impeccable pro-Soviet credentials through his highly visible contributions to three fund- and awareness-raising wartime exhibitions, and through Colin Penn, who had helped to co-ordinate the 'Aid to Russia' exhibition, he had a range of contacts within the Communist Party. He also counted Harry Pollitt, the general secretary of the Communist Party of Great Britain, among his friends. But he never joined the Party. He stated this explicitly in a letter to Godfrey Samuel, when Samuel was putting him up as a possible member of the Reform Club in 1954:

> To put your mind at rest I must tell you that I never was a member of the Communist Party, nor am I a member now. I contracted freely to be a subject of Her Majesty and, although I do not always agree with the politics of Her Majesty's Government, I think I am a loyal subject, in spite of rumours which go around about me.[10]

Over the years various people asked him why he never joined the Party, and his standard answer was that he didn't want to be bossed around by a bunch of trade unionists.[11] Nevertheless, as we have seen, he had been an active member of a revolutionary Marxist organisation in France until 1934, a fact that if it had been more widely known could easily have caused him problems while trying to establish himself in London and gain citizenship.

He was pro-communist because the communists were the main group standing up to Fascism. This was particularly so in Britain, were he was conscious of the Fascist sympathies and connections among the upper classes, something which appalled him. He proudly recalled ripping a swastika flag from the front of a German Embassy car in the 1930s. Before the 1956 Soviet suppression of the Hungarian uprising, he was pro-Russian, too. After 1956, his attitude to Russia was more ambivalent. But, like so many of his peers among the intelligensia, he remained sympathetic to the core Marxist ideology. Ernö's political stance was no secret – it even influenced his children: Peter Goldfinger remembers as an eleven-year-old scratching a hammer and sickle into the plaster of his bedroom at Willow Road.[12]

Ernö, in collaboration with Colin Penn – who *was* a member of the Communist Party, and who had been chief assistant for the De La Warr pavilion in Bexhill-on-Sea[13] – began to rebuild around the old warehouse, replacing timber floors with reinforced concrete. The work was in part funded by donations from *Daily Worker* readers.[14] Due to weakness caused by bomb damage, the building started to move, and a more substantial conversion was needed. What began as a relatively simple commission became a major building task. As work dragged on and the costs rose, the *Daily Worker* appealed to its readers, encouraging them with a cartoon captioned 'Alfie says put your money in Farringdon Road' and by giving the assurance that:

> By filling in the form on page six you will be making a safe investment and ensuring that the new paper appears on time.[15]

The architectural task was far from straightforward. The River Fleet ran underground close to the level of the floor in the sub-basement and there was a risk of flooding. The building itself integrated the Victorian warehouse's ground floor. Goldfinger's relations with a succession of clerks of works and with the builders themselves were also strained: as soon as Goldfinger opened his mouth it was obvious that he was foreign, and many of the builders objected to being told what to do by a foreigner.[16] Despite furious arguments, Goldfinger managed to cajole the workers into completing the task in 1948 – the first edition of the redesigned *Daily Worker* rolled off the press on 1 November of that year.

By the time the building was finished it was scarcely recognisable as a conversion, and looked more like a Perret-inspired original design. Goldfinger removed most of the Victorian mouldings from the lower façade so that it would not clash with the modern structure. Niklaus Pevsner could not resist a barbed aside when he described the finished building as:

> very different from the style a Communist newspaper would care to display in Russia.[17]

8.2
Daily Worker Building, Farringdon Road, London 1946

From the journalists' point of view there were two major faults. First, the toilets were very low. When they complained to Goldfinger about this he gave them a lecture about the benefits of squatting low when defecating as in the French style of hole-in-the-ground WC. The low WCs he'd had installed had the luxury of allowing you to sit in a near squatting position, combining comfort with the much more complete bowel evacuation in the French style. As in so many aspects of life, Goldfinger believed that there was a correct way of doing things and that rational planning would lead to a better quality of life – low WCs were a feature in most of his buildings. The journalists were not convinced.

The second fault they described was that the main newsroom was completely open plan – a radical concept at the time, and one that allowed its users to discover most of the problems of this style of office layout – particularly the problems of noise – long before it became fashionable.[18]

Goldfinger's left-wing contacts resulted in another commission. With Colin Penn he renovated and restructured the headquarters of the Communist Party in Covent Garden. Here Goldfinger used glass bricks in an echo of Charreau's Maison de Verre, while Colin Penn redesigned the interior. Although obviously glad to win commissions from Marxist comrades, from a professional angle Goldfinger was wary of becoming openly associated with the extreme left wing in politics. In applications for various jobs in the late 1940s, he described the *Daily Worker* and Communist Party headquarters projects in purely architectural terms on his curriculum vitae, carefully omitting mention of his clients' names. In an article in *Building*, showing photographs of the completed Communist Party headquarters, it is described as 'Offices in Covent Garden, London', and although the author mentions that glass bricks were used 'to provide lighting with reasonable protection', there is no explanation of why the building might be particularly prone to broken windows.[19]

Most of Goldfinger's smaller domestic buildings were commissioned by contacts, friends or family. In 1947, he built a semi-detached pair of houses in Henley-in-Arden for a Colonel W.B. Fletcher.[20] Post-war building restrictions limited the size of houses, but Goldfinger got around this by building two houses with a joining wall that could later be removed to form one house. He also built two adjoining three-bedroomed houses for his brother Paul and for his father and mother at 74 Avenue des Chênes, in Brussels, and designed another house for his brother George, to be built in Buffalo, New York. Another family contact, John Boyce, commissioned four staff houses for the Wellesley House School at Broadstairs in Kent. In every case he lavished the same attention to detail that he devoted to his larger commissions.

In 1950 Ernö completed two primary schools, at Brandlehow Road in Wandsworth and at Westville Road in Hammersmith. For these he devised a clever prefabricated system that allowed the framework of the buildings to be constructed cheaply and swiftly, using brick infill. Ernö employed his son Peter in the office working on drawings. He later built a comprehensive school in Haggerston in the East End of London (1963). Office building work came his way too, for Carr and Co. in Shirley in Birmingham – a scheme he completed in 1954. But these were relatively small projects given the scale of post-war reconstruction.

Having established himself as one of a handful of architects working in a consistently modern style in Britain, Goldfinger might reasonably have expected to play a significant role in the 1951 Festival of Britain. He drew up plans for a fun fair and restaurant on the edge of Hampstead Heath, but these were rejected. The commission for the major project on London's South Bank, the Dome of Discovery, went to a young former assistant of his, Ralph Tubbs. Another former assistant, Cadbury-Brown, was also given large-scale work. Goldfinger himself, in contrast, was asked to design the kiosks used to sell programmes, and also the telephone booths. The latter

8.3
British Furniture Today, 1951
Tiranti publishers

designs were rejected by the Post Office on the grounds that they weren't properly sound-proofed – perhaps another example of Goldfinger being somewhat ahead of his contemporaries, since open telephone booths are now commonplace. The Festival of Britain should, Goldfinger felt, have been a celebration of the great achievements of British design. Britain had produced the best ever aircraft, the Spitfire, and the best car, the Rolls Royce. But, to his dismay, the festival organisers chose to focus on skills such as basket-making.[21]

By the late 1950s, Goldfinger's office in Piccadilly had become a magnet for a succession of young architects who were drawn to work for him, despite his reputation for tantrums. Jacob Blacker, a young architect recently arrived from Cape Town, decided he wanted to work for Goldfinger. He phoned for an appointment. At the arranged time he nervously climbed the wooden stairs of the slightly run-down offices in the building facing on to Piccadilly and Albermarle Street opposite the Ritz. The offices were mysteriously silent. No one was at reception on the second floor. No one was in the first room he entered on the next floor. He looked into the studio, and saw Ernö and Ove Arup totally engrossed, sketching at drawing boards. He knocked on the door, but they ignored him completely. Unsure what to do next, he waited outside the door. Then the telephone in the office began to ring. No one answered it. So Blacker picked it up and said 'Ernö Goldfinger's office, can I help you?' A voice asked 'Can I speak to Mr Goldfinger?' Blacker replied 'I'm terribly sorry, but he is in a conference. If you give me your name and number I'll get him to ring you back.' At which point the voice said 'This is Leslie Julius [Blacker's current employer]. You're fired!' Blacker put the phone down. It rang instantly and an unmistakable heavily-accented voice boomed: 'Here, Goldfinger. You're hired! You can start tomorrow.' Then Julius phoned back saying 'You're hired again, just in case Goldfinger doesn't take you.' The whole episode had been an elaborate test of initiative which Blacker had obviously passed.[22]

Ernö's presence in the office was forceful. He was a dominant male animal at the top of the pecking order. Something drove him repeatedly to reassert this pre-eminence at every available opportunity, typically at the expense of those lower down the hierarchy. His imposing physical presence combined with his intellectual rigour and explosive personality terrified some of his employees. The sound of his heavy footstep on the staircase brought genuine fear to some of them. There was the risk of being fired if he was dissatisfied with their work; though also the possibility of being re-employed the next day if he needed them. One Australian assistant began work at 9 a.m. and had quit voluntarily by 2 p.m. the same day after hearing Goldfinger shouting at another assistant. He couldn't face stepping into the firing line.[23]

Goldfinger was most brutal when he felt that someone was not doing exactly what they should be. He had an uncanny knack of being able to see errors or fudges from the other side of the room and would stride across the office, snatch a drawing in progress from under the pen of an assistant and tear it to shreds if anything was in the slightest bit careless or imprecise. This office was no place for the sensitive and emotionally vulnerable. Ernö would attack and attack again without compassion. This was part of his philosophy that if you wanted to be an architect you had to live and breathe architecture. There was no compromise. It was a matter of integrity that you got it right. No errors were permitted. Anyone who couldn't cope with this should get out. Those who survived this sort of scrutiny internalised Ernö as a kind of superego or architectural conscience for the rest of their careers.

In the office he explained the right way to punch holes in drawings mounted for exhibition, six sheets of card at a time, so that the holes matched up perfectly. Ernö was the only one in the office strong enough to put this into practice – perhaps an indirect way of reaffirming who was in charge. He would even take people to task for not tearing up their drawings correctly. He never doubted for an instant that there was a right way to do everything, whether it was using a T-square or wrapping a drawing. And it was not just architects and assistants that he would berate for doing things wrong: he was just as likely to take the accountant to task for not doing the books in the right way or a builder for failing to mix cement in the correct proportions. Yet this was not simply an arbitrary exercise of power. Most of those corrected admitted – often to their chagrin – that he was right. He had a mission to teach rigour and rationality about the use of tools and materials wherever he went. People's feelings were no consideration. He would allow himself to be challenged on anything, but if the person challenging him proved confused or mistaken, he would humiliate them. Sloppiness or irrationality in anything that related to architecture was a moral fault. One former assistant, John Winter, summed up the atmosphere and ethos of the Piccadilly office:

> Goldfinger was a difficult man, explosively impatient of any shortcoming, and the mood in the office was often uneasy but the standard was never allowed to falter and respect for the art of architecture and the quality of construction was absolute.[24]

His utter conviction that he was right on all matters gained Ernö a reputation for arrogance and rudeness. Yet on rare occasions those he respected could pull him up for this. When visiting Amédée Ozenfant, for instance, Goldfinger began a tirade against someone who had disagreed with him, dismissing this person as 'an absolute fool'. Ozenfant responded, 'You must accept that people who disagree with you aren't necessarily fools.' Ernö

– uncharacteristically – was quite squashed by this remark.[25] On the whole, though, he was not renowned for humility. This did not turn all those he berated into enemies, though one site agent was heard to mutter 'One day he will fall off a roof!'[26] Because they understood that Ernö was completely consistent in his outbursts, and that he would say what he thought to anyone, no matter what their rank or reputation, many of his victims regarded him as an eccentric genius or, at worst, an interesting if explosive character. He could be charming and affectionate too, and seemed to want people to stand up to him. Fools, however, received no quarter.

The force of Ernö's personality exerted such a pervasive influence over those who worked for him that all the talk in their lunch hours at the local pub was of what Ernö had said and done that day. Stories about his outbursts circulated around the profession, many of them sounding far-fetched. Jacob Blacker, whose experience with fiery Eastern European relatives had prepared him well for coping with Goldfinger, rode the storms, but as he later commented: 'All the crazy stories are understatements! It was much worse!'[27]

Perhaps the most extreme event occurred when two representatives of an American department store visited the office. They had arranged a meeting to investigate the possibility of Goldfinger's practice designing new stores for them. Ernö listened as they laid down more and more conditions about what the stores should look like, how they had to have a big red banner outside, how they should be organised, and so on. At a certain point, Goldfinger buzzed through to Jacob Blacker on the office intercom and barked: 'Jack! Open the door.' Blacker obliged, and Goldfinger emerged holding the startled Americans by the scruffs of their necks, pushed them hard down the steep staircase and frog-marched them out onto the street. 'Nobody tells me what to do!' he fumed. He didn't care that he was losing clients. It was a matter of architectural self-respect that he was in charge of the design. Clients either trusted the architect or they didn't. As he once put it, 'If they trust you they are wonderful, and if they don't trust you they are bastards, and what can you do?'[28] As far as he was concerned he had treated the potential clients exactly as they deserved to be treated. They, of course, took their lucrative contract elsewhere.[29]

On another occasion, Goldfinger had kept his assistant Douglas Stephen working late in the office and left him to lock up when he had finished. The phone rang. Stephen picked it up and answered in a heavy Hungarian accent 'Here Goldfinger!' only to get the emphatic response from the caller '*Here* Goldfinger! You're fired!'.[30] This is probably the most frequently recounted anecdote about Goldfinger – and it captures something of the style of the man. Goldfinger did actually fire Stephen – it wasn't a joke for him.

8.4
'Here Goldfinger!'

Anthony Short joined Ernö's office in February 1955. Ernö asked him how much he had been earning before he did his national service. To which Short replied 'Ten pounds'. Ernö's response was 'I'll pay you eight and you will have to wait a month as I'll have to sack someone to give you a place.'[31] Short himself only lasted until November of the same year – he was the thirteenth employee to leave that year and the twenty-sixth in two years – an amazingly high turnover in a very small office. When Jim Scott first visited the office in 1960, he was surprised to find a secretary celebrating her 'centenary' – she'd managed to stay a year without being sacked.[32] This relentless cycle of hiring and firing left no one in any doubt about who was in charge or of the consequences of falling short of his high standards – or of just disagreeing with him or catching him on a bad day. He even once attempted to sack a visitor who didn't even work for him. A friend had come up to the office to wait for one of Goldfinger's assistants and was leaning against the wall grinning. Goldfinger took one look at him, didn't like what he saw (because, after all, architecture is a serious business), and shouted 'You're fired!'

The flow of young assistants who wanted to work with Goldfinger – despite his ferocity – is testimony to the creative excitement associated with his practice and the high esteem in which he was held. His enthusiasm and energy for architecture could be immensely stimulating for young architects just learning the practicalities of their profession. Many would put up with the stormy atmosphere of the office as a small price to pay for such an education in what architecture was really about. John Roberts was not alone in feeling that he learnt more in a year in Ernö's office than he learnt in seven years at schools of architecture.[33] And much of the bluster was an act. After ranting and huffing about an assistant's drawings, Ernö would say with a twinkle in his eye 'Well, that's my morning shout over!'[34]

The Goldfinger office was run with a brutal efficiency. Employees were expected to work hard for very little money. If they wanted a rise, they'd have to argue the case with Goldfinger, and often only the threat to leave would get the desired result – a risky game of double bluff. It was not surprising that he gained a reputation for stinginess. Yet at the same time he could be incredibly generous. When Jacob Blacker got married, for example, Goldfinger organised a lavish reception party in his own house at Willow Road, providing champagne and smoked salmon at his own expense (though, consistent with his atheism, Goldfinger refused to go to the synagogue for the wedding itself). When an assistant, John Roberts, was having trouble getting to work because of a rail strike, Goldfinger instantly offered to put him up in his own house. Goldfinger loved to throw parties at Willow Road. They could easily fold back the room partitions on the first floor, making a large open space. Their friends, as in Paris, included many of the most eminent artists and photographers, and also now a number of left-wing politicians and journalists. The party list for 1948–9, for example, included the artists Oscar Kokoschka, Henry Moore and Roland Penrose, the photographers Lee Miller, Suschitzky and Edith Tudor-Hart, the engineer Ove Arup, the flamboyant politician Tom Driberg, and the editor of the *Daily Worker*, Bill Rust.[35]

Throughout his life, this tall, handsome, strong, intelligent forceful and very masculine man was extremely attractive to (and attracted to) women. The secretaries and female assistants in his office would fall for him and stories circulated about alleged sexual liaisons with them and with his assistants. Many of these were probably no more than rumours, based on wishful thinking and his flirtatious charm. He was, though, certainly very aware of attractive women. At lunch one day in Dean Street with Ursula, he pulled her up for staring at the people at the next table, accusing her of giving them the 'Blackwell stare'. Her pointed response was 'It's better than the Goldfinger ogle!'[36] Perhaps stories of Ernö's alleged infidelities were also fuelled by sexual disinhibition towards colleagues and employees of a kind that would today be considered harassment. The architect Jane Drew thought that it was quite hard for a woman to give a fair assessment of Ernö because:

> . . . he was always pawing you. And if you didn't like having your bum pinched and slapped, it was rather off-putting.[37]

The accuracy of this description has been questioned by others who worked closely with Ernö:[38] he was certainly able to maintain deep and respectful friendships with a number of women, including Ylla, Lee Miller, Suzanne Blum and Charlotte Perriand. He also worked successfully with many female clients, and with his associate Mira Molis, and later with his assistant Juliet Leong. Nevertheless, John Roberts described him as 'the world's worst male chauvinist pig'. At times he set out to embarrass or shock women, almost as a game. He used a stencil of a standard French design to label his drawings, the same type of stencil that Le Corbusier used.[39] For amusement, one afternoon, in front of his assistants, he picked up the telephone and shouted at his long-suffering secretary: 'Rosemary! Bring me the *French letters*!' Her embarrassed reaction was to reply 'Don't shout at me!' and to slam down the phone. He turned to his assistants, taken aback, and in a small voice said 'But I didn't shout at her'.[40]

One – possibly apocryphal – anecdote has it that a male assistant had managed to seduce an attractive young woman who was working for Ernö, consummating the relationship in Goldfinger's office while the boss was away. Afterwards the assistant asked how it had been for her. Her reply: 'Very nice, but not a patch on Ernö . . .'[41] Whether she had actually slept with Ernö or not – and perhaps the woman was just teasing her proud seducer – doesn't really matter. What it makes clear is his almost mythical power and charisma. To those who worked in the office at the time it was believable. Rumour had it that his favourite seduction technique was to declare that it wasn't just his finger that was golden.

This reputation as a forceful, explosive, abrasive and lascivious man has at times been in danger of eclipsing Goldfinger's reputation as an architect, at least in the world of architecture, where stories about his antics and outbursts abound. Some are true, some embellished, and some probably based on what he was capable of doing, whether or not he actually did it.

A tyrant in the office, at home – though he could be domineering – he had his match in Ursula. She knew how to handle his moods and cosset him when necessary. She had effectively given up her artistic career to provide him with the emotional support and companionship that allowed him to work. Her great sense of humour presumably helped the marriage survive. One afternoon, Ernö and Ursula were giving Jacob Blacker a lift in their car. Ernö had instructed Ursula to get the garage doors varnished:

'Did you do the garage gates?' he asked.

'Yes.'

'Which colour did you use?'

'Teak.'

'It should be *oak*! I've told you for the last twenty-five years, it's oak, and *it must be kept light oak*. Twenty-five years ago I told you. Twenty-five years!'

There was a pause. Then, Ursula, with impeccable timing, corrected him: 'Twenty-seven years!'[42]

From the mid-1950s, after Ernö's father's death, his mother Regine had come to live in the house. She brought with her an assortment of highly-ornate Austro-Hungarian furniture, including a bureau that the children used to call 'the tabernacle'. This tiny frail woman was not in the least intmidated by her son, and would shout at him when he was being obstinate. When Ernö's brothers came to stay, neighbours were sometimes worried by the volume at which they would harangue each other, though the dispute was more likely to be over an intellectual point rather than stemming from animosity or aggression.

Ernö maintained his lively interest in visual arts throughout his life, through his expanding collection of art, but also through friendships and occasional collaborations with artists. With Victor Pasmore and the sculptor Helen Phillips, he contributed to the 'This is Tomorrow' exhibition of 1956 at the Whitechapel Art Gallery: their combined installation was intended to demonstrate how architects and artists could work collaboratively. Helen Phillips came to stay with the Goldfingers, making her sculpture in the house and covering the place in sawdust in the process.[43] For the catalogue he rewrote parts of his papers on the sensation of space in aphoristic form:

> A particle is snatched from space, rhythmically modulated by membranes dividing it from surrounding chaos: that is Architecture.
>
> There is other enclosed space, not modulated, not rhythmic, but that is not Architecture.
>
> The 'sensation of space'[44] is to Architecture what looking at a picture is to painting. The 'sensation of space' can be a subconscious phenomenon, to undergo its effect it is not necessary to be aware of space.
>
> [. . .] You cannot see Architecture, you can only be in it, as in music.[45]

He extended these ideas to explain how painting and sculpture might work in conjunction with architecture without undermining the sensation of space. Art as decoration might destroy architecture:

> Only if architecture, painting and sculpture are concerned with the same function, is proper collaboration possible. By functioning as a microcosm of the ensemble, painting and sculpture extend and crystalise the architectural idea.[46]

Throughout his life, Goldfinger was interested in finding ways to build affordable high-quality housing. The 1936 Housing Act, with amendments made in 1947, brought in measures which allowed seven or more people to pool their resources and form a housing society – a non-profit association. The housing society could then raise a ninety per cent mortgage on a property. In other words, if a group of seven or more people got together and could find ten per cent of the money needed to build homes, they could jointly borrow the remaining ninety per cent. This scheme was particularly suitable for people with a reliable income but relatively little money available for an initial investment. It also gave members of the housing society significant control over the planning and running of their dwellings.

Goldfinger worked with one such housing association, the Regent's Park Housing Society, which ten families had formed especially to develop a site on Regents Park Road, a few minutes walk from Primrose Hill. The site was due to bomb damage that created a gap in a street of early nineteenth-century stuccoed houses. Either side of the site were three-storied houses with semi-basements. Goldfinger's challenge was to create a block of flats that met his clients needs, did not disturb the rhythms of the street's existing architecture, and yet complied with his own strict aesthetic. The resulting block is an elegant solution reminiscent in many ways of Willow Road. Many of Goldfinger's projects, however, never got beyond the planning stage.

Despite the upsurge in work from the post-war building boom, the 1950s were in some ways frustrating years for Ernö. He received a string of commissions that were thwarted by local town planners' reluctance to allow modern buildings to be built. What was most frustrating was that the planners' objections were usually based on misunderstandings and aesthetic prejudices rather than rational fears about the proposed buildings.

His friends the toyshop owners Paul and Marjorie Abbatt approached him in 1953 to design a farm manager's cottage to be built on Idlecombe Farm in the picturesque Turville Valley in Buckinghamshire. Goldfinger presented the Abbatts with an imaginative design for a bungalow with a butterfly roof, a design that enchanted his clients but, predictably, disconcerted the planning officers of Buckinghamshire County Council. As with the Willow Road objectors, the worry was that a modern design would not 'fit in' with the surrounding scenery. That the nearest neighbour would be seven hundred feet from the house did not prevent the council from blocking planning permission on aesthetic grounds. The Abbatt's appealed against the decision, and the appeal was upheld by the Minister of Local Government on the grounds that:

> the erection of a building in a modern style should rarely be opposed and only on the clearest evidence that the building would be completely unharmonious with its neighbours and entirely out of keeping with its surroundings.[47]

The minister did not find fault with Goldfinger's plans on these grounds.

Another commission for a house, for typographer John Wallis, this time in Old Amersham in Buckinghamshire, produced a similar response from local planners. The site for the house was within a walled garden that had been part of a Queen Anne house known as 'The Firs' on the High Street. Ernö's plans were for a flat-roofed bungalow that would be almost invisible from the other side of the wall and would be screened by trees. The house was meticulously planned around a 2′9″ grid using an approximation of the Golden Section, the square and the 2:3 rectangle. Predictably, the element of the design that angered the local planners, the Amersham Rural District Council, was the flat roof that – in true local planners' style – they considered 'not in character with local buildings'.[48] This seemed to be a purely aesthetic consideration, and so Goldfinger and his client appealed against the refusal to give planning permission. Sir Patrick Abercrombie and J.M. Richards gave evidence in favour of Goldfinger's design, and letters of support by Hugh Casson and John Summerson were read out. The minister, nevertheless, overruled the appeal, and by implication Goldfinger's highly eminent and informed supporters, declaring that the house would be a 'quite incongruous addition to the town'.[49] One worry was that it would be visible from a footpath that went behind the High Street. The minister gave permission to build only on condition that in place of the flat roof, a traditional pitched roof with overhanging eaves should be used. Ironically, this built version of the design made the house visible above the garden wall. The original design would have been far more discreet.

This irony was compounded by subsequent building around Amersham High Street. First a 95-foot gasometer was constructed by the North Thames Gas Board, visible from most of the street. This was exempt from the need for planning permission. Then, a more serious humiliation for Goldfinger, and a clear indication of the planners' anti-modern aesthetic prejudices, a large mock-Tudor house with half-timbering, herringbone brickwork and leaded windows was built for a member of the local council right up against the footpath. Goldfinger had appreciated the way building in Britain was tending as early as 1937 when he had declared:

> I could make lots more money if I designed neo-Tudor or Georgian abominations. But I won't.[50]

To see such a building going up, however, while his own design had to be adjusted to comply with planners' prejudices, galled him. In justifying the Rural District Council's apparently inconsistent planning policies, the chairman Major Boyce clarified the council's disdain for modernist buildings. It wasn't just the flat roof of Goldfinger's design that they opposed: 'These Cubist buildings are bad in this climate. They soon get stained, and look unkempt,' he said.[51] The implication was that such buildings were being imported from a sunnier continent and were uninformed by native building tradition and weather conditions. Perhaps too Boyce and his colleagues had mistakenly assumed that Goldfinger's design was of the white-box modern variety that he in fact despised.

As Goldfinger pointed out at a discussion of planning controls, the real problem with planning in Britain was that local town planners were being allowed to pose as art historians before the work of art had been created. He expressed his exasperation and disbelief at the impudence of the committees that exerted such aesthetic control.[52] In this case the damage was compounded by the government minister's acceptance of the local planner's arguments in the teeth of informed support for Goldfinger's design from the pre-eminent architects and planners of the day. There seemed little hope of building in England evolving if planners preferred stockbroker's mock-Tudor to consistent modern design. Ernö was beginning to appreciate why there were so few successful modern buildings in England.

It was not just small houses that challenged local planners' aesthetic prejudices. In 1958, Goldfinger had the opportunity to design a four-storey apartment block a few minutes' walk from his home. The site on the Vale of Health in Hampstead was a promising one. It would involve demolishing the Athenaeum, a Victorian Gothic-style concert and dance hall that had in later years been used as temporary storage by the Old Vic Theatre. Ernö produced drawings for three dwellings above a car port. To his consternation, Henry Brooke – one of the main protestors against the building of the Willow Road flats, but now risen to the government post of Minister of Housing – used the same arguments against the new building as he had against Ernö's own house twenty years earlier. He mustered the support of fifty-three local residents who felt the building was 'out of keeping' with the locale and the ensuing two-day enquiry was reported by the *Hampstead and Highgate Express*[53] under the title 'Ultra-Modern versus Painters' Paradise'. Goldfinger's designs were euphemistically described by the Hampstead Council's engineering assistant for planning as 'the rigorous end of modern building'. Appreciation of the aesthetic potential of concrete and rectilinear design had not permeated all of Hampstead, despite the area's reputation as a colony of avant-garde émigrés.

As with the Willow Road protest, Hampstead's inhabitants were polarised between the nostalgic and the progressive. Sir John Summerson, who lived in Eton Villas, Hampstead, once again gave a passionate defence of Ernö's proposal,[54] but in terms that would have goaded the nostalgic tendency. He dismissed the greater part of architecture in the Vale of Health as 'rubbish – and rubbish chaotically arranged', declaring that 'A sense of decay pervades it with obsolete buildings which are very bad examples of their kind.' He praised Ernö's proposal as 'good design, logically worked out and well-proportioned', at the same time dismissing the Athenaeum – which some protestors wanted to preserve – as 'a blot on the landscape'. Goldfinger's own reaction to the 'charm' of the existing building was equally undiplomatic. Alluding to the Athenaeum's façade, he asked, 'Perhaps you suggest that my building should be disguised as a gothic church?'

Once again Goldfinger triumphed over the Hampstead conservatives, winning his case against the Hampstead Council and Vale of Health residents. But on this occasion it was a pyrrhic victory. By the time the case was won, and planning permission granted, the opportunity to build had been lost. One of the main clients had withdrawn, and another had become interested in using the site for a furniture depot.[55] Despite being championed by some of the most distinguished commentators on architecture, Goldfinger was being obstructed in his attempt to bring rational principles to bear on English architecture. He could not persuade his critics to see his apartment blocks as a phase in an evolving tradition. For them this was a foreign invasion (both metaphorically and literally) and had no place in prized English enclaves. The Hampstead Council's engineering assistant's comment about Goldfinger's proposed building was revealing in this respect. He declared that personally he thought it would look alright 'in a thickly-wooded setting – possibly in Scandinavia'.[56] The message was clear: not in my garden suburb. The only new buildings that could be sure of gaining approval were pastiches of the styles of earlier ages. The dogma that for a building to be aesthetically pleasing it must look more or less like the buildings around it – what might be dubbed the Prince Charles fallacy – is one that has been substantially refuted in the building patterns in every major city in the world. That most of the buildings now so revered by conservative planners did not 'fit in' in this sense with the buildings that pre-dated them does not seem to occur to such people.

Goldfinger saw this clearly. In a letter to the *Architects' Journal* in relation to a proposed building in Gordon Square, he analysed the ways in which modern architecture might successfully contribute to the existing Georgian squares in London. He stressed the changing character of buildings and new methods of construction and the consequent futility of trying to capture the spirit of nineteenth- or twentieth-century Bloomsbury by attempting some kind of pastiche of a past style:

> The character of Eighteenth Century domestic architecture resides in the rhythm of its façades: ground floor, piano nobile and two or three upper floors. That is to say, the balancing of their horizontal rhythm of function with a vertical system of windows. This does no longer exist in modern institutional, commercial or domestic buildings.[57]

The consequence of trying to make buildings 'fit in' in this context was in many cases ridiculous, resulting in such features as fake balconies and masking of the actual layout of the buildings behind. Nor would eighteenth-century squares bear 'cliffs of curtain walling':

> What is needed is to marry our new structures with our new functional requirements to the fact of urban decency.[58]

As he demonstrated in his Regent's Park Road housing, the way forward was to produce buildings that reflected their use, were built in awareness of the rhythms of the surrounding buildings, yet were not merely imitative of them. For those in thrall to the Prince Charles fallacy, buildings need not reflect their actual use, all that matters is that they look more or less like those around them, where necessary using modern techniques and materials to achieve the effects that were originally produced by the techniques that they have superseded. Goldfinger's approach did not imply 'anything goes' (as his comments about curtain walling make clear) – presumably to achieve 'urban decency' required architectural sensitivity and a deep understanding of the logic of the surrounding buildings. It was Goldfinger's misfortune in the 1950s to have come up against a succession of proto-Prince Charles figures with their ill-thought-out conservative mantras of 'local character' and 'fitting in'.

One of Goldfinger's most successful post-war projects, informed by his sensitivity to Georgian architecture, was the office block he designed at 45/6 Albermarle Street in Piccadilly. Again this was a direct result of the Luftwaffe's transformation of central London. Two Georgian houses had been destroyed by bombing. Goldfinger's brief was to design business premises in their place that were modern yet sympathetic to the eighteenth-century street. The two plots were owned by different landlords: Mason-Pearson the hair-brush manufacturer, and Imry Limited, a development company. Goldfinger treated the project as essentially one building, divided in a way that would allow the two parts to become one at a later date if required (much as the house at Henley-in-Arden). The incentive for combining the buildings in this way came from planning regulations: two buildings would require two fire escapes, but with a single joined building, an escape could be provided via the roof. This allowed him to optimise the profitability of the building, something that delighted his clients since it gave both of them a very high ratio of lettable area to total floor area. As Ernö stated with typical rigour in the *New Statesman* in a letter supporting developers' concerns with the economics of buildings:

> The economics of buildings for whomever they are carried out is the ratio of enclosed space to useable space.[59]

The Albermarle Street block has six floors and a basement, and its façade, clad in Portland stone, is given variety and character by the use of central bay windows on the third and fifth floors, and photobolic screens of anodised aluminium above all the larger windows. These features set Goldfinger's building apart from the Mies van der Rohe-influenced box-building that was so typical of office architecture at the time. Even in this relatively small block he provided the geometrically satisfying variety and harmony that is so evident in his larger-scale plans. The building is topped by a cornice balustrade that was intended to provide an emphatic line against the sky; a feature used in all his larger offices and tower blocks.

As with all Ernö's major projects, the building was not achieved without a struggle. A glimpse of his techniques for dealing with construction workers is provided by John Winter's recollection of an early visit to the site. Ernö examined the first of the concrete columns that had been poured. As far as Winter could tell, this was perfect. Yet Goldfinger ranted at the workers, and demanded that it be smashed and that they should start again, making sure it exactly met the specifications. When Winter later asked his boss what had been wrong with the column, Ernö admitted that it had been faultless, but pronounced his pragmatic principle for keeping builders in check: 'Always take down the first column produced on site'.[60]

The completed offices, used by the Robert Sharp and partners advertising agency and by Taylor-Woods Limited, a hosiery and lingerie manufacturer, were much admired. In an article in the *New Yorker*, Lewis Mumford was effusive in his praise, singling the building out as an example

8.5
Albermarle Street, drawing, completed 1959

of excellent modern design in its use of modern techniques in creating openness and light, while at the same time conforming to the rhythms of its eighteenth-century surroundings:

> Here is a building that has not merely learned the lessons of modern form but has learned them thoroughly enough to feel free to learn, too – from the eighteenth century and the Regency – how to create a lively façade for a street that must be modernised. Here the past has been neither externally imitated nor crassly rejected but

> inwardly absorbed and re-created, and contemporary form, instead of being confined to a handful of easily recognised clichés, is a fresh, supple, and many-toned orchestration of varied instruments.[61]

The architectural correspondent of the London *Times* was equally complimentary, praising Goldfinger's design on the grounds that it was:

> . . . an exact modern equivalent of eighteenth-century street architecture, equally reticent in spite of being developed for commercial instead of residential purposes.[62]

Like Mumford, this writer recognised Goldfinger's achievement in finding an appropriately modern reinterpretation of the spirit of the Georgian street architecture that surrounded it:

> It is not the first time that the architecture which departs from the traditional styles has shown itself to be most aware of the traditional values.[63]

The degree to which Goldfinger was consciously informed by eighteenth-century architectural values is clear from his response to the criticism that he had disguised the true nature of the two buildings behind the joined bay windows:[64]

> The bay windows have primarily an aesthetic function in my façade. It is my belief that the function of a façade, from the aesthetic point of view, is not to 'express' something which is behind it, but to form the enclosing vertical membrane of the street. In the case of London street architecture, I am, of course, in very good company. Since the eighteenth century separate buildings have been designed in London in such a manner as to form, in combination with each other, the architecture of the street. The mere accident that there are also party walls – whatever that may mean aesthetically – is never acknowledged (see Bedford Square, Regents Park, Portland Place etc.).[65]

The crass tendency to label Goldfinger a brutalist – a label he always repudiated on the grounds that, unlike the Smithsons, he took great pains to hide wiring and heating ducts – has made his declaration that he wanted to be remembered as a classical architect harder to understand. Yet in medium-scale projects like the houses at Willow Road and the office buildings at Albermarle Street, Goldfinger's affinities with and sensitivity to the spirit of Georgian architecture is obvious.

Further office buildings for Carr and Co. in Birmingham and the furniture manufacturers Hille in Watford allowed him to explore variations on the elements that he had used in Albermarle Street, but it was with Alexander Fleming House that he won his most important commission of the 1950s.

The Elephant and Castle area on the South Bank of the Thames, towards Battersea, had been severely damaged by the Blitz. It was not until the late 1950s that reconstruction began in earnest. An open competition was held to design quarter of a million square feet of office space on the site, with tenders from architects and developers. Goldfinger had taken Jacob Blacker on as an assistant specifically to work on the competition drawings. Ernö would produce a small sketch, perhaps on the back of an envelope scribbled during a boring meeting. Using a planning grid based on multiples of the 2′9″ dimension, Blacker could develop this sketch into a fully worked out drawing that complied with the complex planning regulations and realised Ernö's intentions. There was no need for Ernö to indicate the width of a door or the height of a ceiling because this could be read off from the predetermined features of the grid. As the competition deadline loomed, Blacker moved in to Willow Road so that he could finish the drawings over Christmas 1958.[66]

8.6
Alexander Fleming House, drawing

Goldfinger won, not just on the basis of producing an economical solution, but also on the superiority of his plans from an architectural point of view. He built three blocks connected by glass bridges, in a complex which became the Ministry of Health. He had wanted a Henry Moore sculpture to be included in the enclosed piazza, and Moore went so far as to visit the Goldfinger office[67] and produce a maquette for this. As late as 1968, Goldfinger was writing to Henry Moore, still hoping that it might be possible to place a sculpture within the complex: 'I have a big reflecting pool in the Piazza of this building and would like to have your 'Three-Way Bronze' in the very middle of it.[68] But the financing for the commission fell through. Alexander Fleming House was never popular with its tenants, who complained of poor temperature control and leaks. Among architects, however, this was a very popular building, much praised for its geometrical subtleties.

With his associate Mira Molis, Ernö completed Phase 2 of the Elephant and Castle project in 1963. He had hoped to win the contract for the adjacent shopping centre, but his proposals failed to gain the commission. He did however, expand the complex in 1965 when he added a free-standing cinema.

8.7
Alexander Fleming House

8.8
Alexander Fleming House, the abstract coloured glass in the entrance hall

The cinema consisted of an auditorium with a single bank of seats with space for 1,044, replacing the 4,000 seater Trocadero, which Goldfinger declared was only ever full for bingo. The problem set by the site and the project was to achieve an unobstructed view for every member of the audience given the relation between the beam thrown by twin projectors and the size of the giant screen. Goldfinger used a wooden mock-up of the interior of the cinema to assure the sight lines worked – lengths of blue string and elastic bands allowing him to test these aspects of the design. The cinema also needed to be soundproofed against the noise of nearby trains. Beyond that, Goldfinger, an enthusiastic filmgoer himself – 'Westerns, nouvelle vague, and damn silly films incredibly well-made in Hollywood'[69] – felt that the only other essential factors were the comfort of the seats and the film showing.

8.9
Model of Odeon Cinema for Elephant and Castle development

His solution to the architectural problem was a concrete cinema that wasn't disguised as something else. When it hasn't been hidden inside the shell of a larger complex of buildings, cinema architecture has for the most part aped or exaggerated theatre architecture. This is particularly true of the interior of cinemas. Yet cinemas don't have live performers, so there is little rational justification for the elaborate proscenium arch and the multiple curtains that have so frequently been used in them. The focus of a cinema should surely be the screen, not irrelevant allusions to theatre design and lavish parodies of rococo. Ernö refused to dress the building up as something else – at last, as Reyner Banham wrote, 'a cinema that is not castrated theatre'.[70]

Even from outside, the shape of the auditorium was apparent as was its supporting structure. The roof was supported by a visible reinforced concrete beam running across the building. Two lesser beams, supported by the main beam, followed the shape of the diverging rays of the projector's light. Thus the whole building, inside and out, expressed and also depicted its function. It was a constant reminder of the projector and the light it casts. The open space underneath the auditorium could, if necessary, provide queuing cinemagoers with shelter before entering through the single entry point. Inside, the projection booth appeared suspended above the auditorium. The large screen was a screen and not a quasi-stage, and it was deliberately made the dominating element in the interior so that the filmgoers were always aware of it, even during the interval. When the lights were dimmed it appeared to float in front of the viewers without visible support. Rather than curtains closing across at the interval in that strange theatrical ritual that still persists, a kinetic light display was projected, much like a present-day screen-saver. True to the spirit of Loos, there were no ornamental intrusions to distract from the point of the cinema.

Architectural historians have an unfortunate mythologising tendency: they rarely mention the flaws in their heroes' designs. Perhaps this is a reaction to the popular press's habit of demonising architects. Yet any major building is likely to be imperfect in some respects. Here the new screen design proved attractive to children for the wrong reasons. They had easy access to the stage and soon discovered that they could run round and hide behind the back of the screen. Worse, when Goldfinger located indirect lighting under the handrails leading down the auditorium, he hadn't anticipated that children would discover how easy it was to unscrew the unprotected lightbulbs. During one day fifty bulbs disappeared, leaving fifty live sockets at hand height in a darkened room.[71] The carpet that Goldfinger had designed for the auditorium had worn out in less than two years and was swiftly replaced with aesthetically inappropriate but hardwearing coloured plastic tiles. Yet these were relatively minor problems once recognised, and for the most part the cinema functioned effectively, though, not, as explained in Chapter 10, for as long as he would have hoped.

Alexander Fleming House incorporated an eighteen-storey office building. But what Ernö really wanted to build was high-rise housing. He still nurtured the Corbusian dream of building streets in the sky and of redesigning the city as a mixture of high-rise living and open parkland as an antidote to suburban sprawl and inefficient land use. As the post-war austerity of the 1950s gradually gave way to the optimism of the 1960s, Ernö's ambitions to build social housing skywards and on a monumental scale would at last be realised in the form of the Balfron and Trellick towers.

Notes

1 Letter to George, 26/11/45, National Trust 2 Willow Road collection.

2 See Goldfinger's essay for Ove Arup's *Festschrift*, 1965, version in GolEr 266/4.

3 Published by Penguin in 1945. This book was actually called *The County of London Plan*, but is usually referred to as *The County of London Plan Explained*, to distinguish it from Forshaw and Abercombie's book, and to reflect the byline ('explained by E.J. Carter and Ernö Goldfinger').

4 21 July 1945.

5 Carter and Goldfinger (1945), p.13.

6 See letter to Bill Brandt, in GolEr 266/4, thanking him for the picture, 1/12/37, and the subsequent letter thanking him again and asking for a copy for a friend, 13/12/37.

7 Brandt personally dedicated copies of both books to the Goldfingers. These are still in the National Trust 2 Willow Road collection.

8 Carter and Goldfinger, 1945, pp.27, 31.

9 For instance, on 29 January 1948 he received an acknowledgement for a cheque for £5 which he'd sent to the *Daily Worker* Fighting Fund. This is in GolEr 277/1.

10 Letter to Godfrey H. Samuel, 13/10/54, in GolEr 279/4. There he wrote in response to a request for a candid response on the subject: his application for membership of the club failed.

11 This, for instance, was the response he gave to James Dunnett when he asked this question.

12 Recalled on NSA F7578 (C467/44/03).

13 Goldfinger and Penn went into partnership in April 1946.

14 See, for example 'Planning New DW Building', *Daily Worker*, 15 December 1945, where the paper appealed to its readership and the working class movement to provide £150,000 – its minimum objective.

15 Sam Russell, 'Three Months to Go – Progress Report on Our Building', *Daily Worker*, 3 August 1948.

16 This information is based on an interview conducted by Kevin Morgan (16/9/94) with Sam Russell, a journalist on the *Daily Worker* at the time.

17 Pevsner, *The Buildings of England: London except for Cities of London and Westminster*, London: Penguin, 1952, p.224. Quoted by Kevin Morgan, 'The Communist Party, and the *Daily Worker* 1950–1956', in G. Andrews, N. Fishman and K. Morgan (eds) *Opening the Books*, London: Pluto Press, 1995, p.151.

18 This also comes from Kevin Morgan's interview with Sam Russell, 16/9/94.

19 'Offices in Covent Garden, London', *Building*, March 1949, in GolEr 389/1.

20 Colonel Fletcher worked as a chemical engineer for ICI and had been involved in commissioning Goldfinger to make an exhibition stand in 1938. Later he commissioned Goldfinger to build a warehouse and offices in Birmingham for his wholesale hardware business. The building has since been demolished.

21 Goldfinger expressed these views to his grandson, Nick Goldfinger.

22 Described by Blacker on NSA F8947 (C467/52/05) and F8112 (C467/52/01–02)

23 Recalled by Jacob Blacker on NSA F8948.

24 John Winter, Obituary of Ernö Goldfinger in *RIBA Journal*, February 1988, p.90.

25 This incident is described by Peter Goldfinger on NSA F7578 (C467/44/03).

26 Quoted by Anthony Short, 'Confessions of an Ernö Employee', *Architects' Journal*, 18/4/96.

27 NSA F8947.

28 From interview with Peter Davey, Dan Cruickshank and James Dunnett, transcript in GolEr 397/3.

29 Recounted by Jacob Blacker on NSA F8949.

30 This anecdote is told by Peter de Francia on NSA F9451, but also by most of those who knew Goldfinger. It was, for instance, recounted to me by the heating engineer Ken Dale, of Dale and Goldfinger.

31 Anthony Short, 'Confessions of an Ernö Employee', *Architects' Journal*, 18/4/96.

32 Recounted at DOCOMOMO conference, the Architectural Association, London, 28/9/02. This was the Goldfinger centenary conference, 'The Measure of Man'.

33 John Roberts, NSA Architects' Lives, F11528.

34 Recounted by Jim Scott, at the DOCOMOMO Goldfinger centenary conference, the Architectural Association, London, 28/9/02.

35 Many of the Goldfingers' party lists are in the National Trust 2 Willow Road collection.

36 Recounted by Peter Goldfinger on NSA F7580.

37 Quoted in Lewis Chester, 'High and Mighty', the *Guardian Weekend*, 16 July 1994, p.28.

38 James Dunnett, who worked in Goldfinger's office, made this point to me in a private letter, 25/4/03.

39 The cover of the first edition of Fleming's novel *Goldfinger* also used a stencil typography for the title. I have not been able to discover whether this was just a coincidence.

40 Recounted by John Roberts on NSA F11527 side B.

41 The anecdote, passed on by Sam Webb, is recounted in Lewis Chester, 'High and Mighty', the *Guardian Weekend*, 16 July 1994, p.29.

42 Recalled by Jacob Blacker on NSA F8949.

43 The sculpture that she produced is still in the National Trust 2 Willow Road collection where it can be found under the spiral staircase.

44 From the catalogue for *This is Tomorrow*, p.97.

45 From the catalogue for *This is Tomorrow*, p.97.

46 From the catalogue for *This is Tomorrow*, p.97.

47 *Architecture and Building News*, 18/3/54, in GolEr 389/1.

48 'Flexible Family Plan', *Architectural Design*, October 1957, pp.79–80.

49 See 'High Street Keeps in Keeping', *Architects' Journal*, 21 November 1957, pp.771–776, in GolEr 389/2. This article provides an interesting account of the planning fiasco at Amersham.

50 Quoted in *Daily Sketch*, 31/12/37, in GolEr 389/1.

51 Quoted on p.775 of 'High Street Keeps in Keeping', *Architects' Journal*, 21 November 1957, in GolEr 389/2.

52 Meeting held at the ICA, London, reported in 'Do Planning Controls Need Revision?', *Architects' Journal*, 1 August 1957, pp.168–170, in GolEr 389/2.

53 *Hampstead and Highgate Express*, 14/11/1958, in GolEr 393/14.

54 Reported in *Hampstead and Highgate Express*, 14/11/1958, in GolEr 393/14.

55 This was reported in *Hampstead and Highgate Express*, 6/3/1959. See also *Daily Telegraph*, 17/11/1958, 'Hampstead Does It Again', both in GolEr 393/14.

56 Reported in *Hampstead and Highgate Express*, 14/11/1958, in GolEr 393/14.

57 Ernö Goldfinger, 'A Problem of Character', letter to *Architects' Journal*, 17/7/58, in GolEr 389.

58 Ernö Goldfinger, 'A Problem of Character', letter to *Architects' Journal*, 17/7/58, in GolEr 389.

59 Ernö Goldfinger, 'Frames for Big Business', letter to *New Statesman*, 10/5/58, in GolEr 389.

60 John Winter at Ernö Goldfinger Centenary Conference, The Architectural Association, 27/9/02.

61 Lewis Mumford, 'The Sky Line', *New Yorker*, 28/9/57, pp.114–123, this quotation on p.118, in GolEr 393/7.

62 'Design of the Small Office Building: A Modest Yet Distinguished Solution', *The Times*, 18/6/57, p.3, in GolEr 389/2.

63 'Design of the Small Office Building: A Modest Yet Distinguished Solution', *The Times*, 18/6/57, p.3, in GolEr 389/2.

64 This criticism was made by J.M. Richards in 'Criticism', *Architects' Journal*, 18/7/57, pp.105–107, in GoLEr 389/2.

65 Ernö Goldfinger, 'The Architect Replies', *Architects' Journal*, 25/7/57, pp.133–4, in GolEr 389/2.

66 Jacob Blacker describes this on NSA Architects' Lives F8948 and a recording of a lecture on Ernö Goldfinger given on 11/11/99 on F8112.

67 Moore visited the Goldfinger office on 3 December 1959, letter to Ernö Goldfinger, 26 November 1959, in GolEr 276/2.

68 Letter from Goldfinger to Henry Moore, 5/8/68, in GolEr 276/3.

69 Quoted in 'A Cinema for the Age of Goldfinger', *Sunday Times*, 24 January 1965.

70 Quoted in R. Elwall, *Ernö Goldfinger*, RIBA Drawings Monographs no. 3, London: Academy Editions, p.90.

71 Mentioned in 'Building Revisited: Odeon Cinema', *Architects' Journal Information Library*, 17 September 1969, pp.709–722, p.722.

Chapter 9

Rising high

. . . the whole object of building high is to free the ground for children and grown ups to enjoy Mother Earth and not to cover every inch with bricks and mortar.

In 1959, Mies van der Rohe came to receive the RIBA Gold Medal. He stayed in London and spent several days in the Goldfinger office. Ernö took him to Cambridge to see in particular the glorious Kings' College Chapel. For greater dramatic effect, Goldfinger had gone ahead and closed the doors to the chapel so that he could throw them open for Mies. As he opened the doors a shaft of light came suddenly through the clouds, lighting up the chapel. 'You see! God is on our side!' declared Goldfinger.[1] And that is how it must have seemed. Like Mies, Ernö had ambitions to build tall buildings, though their architectural sympathies were very different. Ernö held Mies personally responsible for the widespread use of glass curtain walls in modern building, an effect Goldfinger likened to the stocking-masks used by burglars. As they were going through Bowater House near Hyde Park in a taxi, Ernö waved his finger, and declared excitedly 'This is all your fault, Mies!' Mies replied, deadpan, 'I was not the architect for that building'.[2]

Ernö had ambitions to build upwards from a very early stage in his architectural career. In 1933, he had presented his plans for a fifteen-storey 'unite d'habitation', complete with a communal restaurant, a nursery and an infants school, to the CIAM Congress in Athens. In 1955, he and Cadbury-Brown had drawn up plans for a twenty-seven-storey office block in Moorgate in the City of London. Then, backed by Hammerson Properties, in 1962 he proposed a 350-foot high-rise office block for a site on Southampton Place in the heart of Georgian Bloomsbury. None of these projects were ever built. But it was as a designer of high-rise living spaces that he would eventually make his mark on London's skyline.

9.1
Rising high: scaffolding on service tower of Trellick

The basic principle of the tower block as social housing was to provide light and well-planned living space, while leaving room for parks, playgrounds, road access and other amenities at ground level:

> . . . the whole object of building high is to free the ground for children and grown-ups to enjoy Mother Earth and not to cover every inch with bricks and mortar.[3]

This was his ideal for city living, and for offices too. High-rise buildings were not to be seen in isolation from the surrounding land – they should be a way of improving the quality of life of those who lived and worked in them. The declared enemy was suburban sprawl which gradually took over every inch of useable space. Interviewed for the *Sunday Times* in 1960, he declared:

> I would like to see London a park city: not, and I emphasise not, a garden city.

Although he did not spell this out, his preference for parks over gardens was consistent with a concept of social ownership and communal use as opposed to private exclusive fencing of land.

For Ernö, London had great potential to develop vertically:

> In ten years London could be a beautiful skyscraper city, and the view from the river be as it was in Wren's London, except that instead of churches you would have skyscrapers towering over the lower buildings.[4]

Four years later he was declaring that, given a free hand, he would replace most of Hampstead with forty-storey skyscrapers round the edge of the park, and extend the heath south to join with Primrose Hill and Regent's Park.[5] This was his vision for London. In the early 1960s, opportunities to contribute to this vision began to emerge. Goldfinger at last got the chance to put his theories about high-rise social housing to the test.

Ernö's first chance to build high-rise domestic accommodation came with Balfron Tower, and the associated estate at Rowlett Street in Poplar, in the East End of London. On a site next to the busy northern approach road to the Blackwall Tunnel, then known as the Brownfield Estate, he built a twenty-seven-storey block. The name 'Balfron' was borrowed from a town just South of Glasgow, which, according to a GLC press release, perpetuated the Scottish associations with the Poplar area.[6] Completed in 1967 and occupied in 1968, this was the first phase of a three-phase mixture of high, medium and low-rise development of the site by the Greater London Council. This was to provide desperately-needed social housing as part of the extensive clearing of unsanitary East End terraced housing. Goldfinger was responsible for all three phases, which included two-storey housing specifically designed for Old Age Pensioners.

The feature of the block, which gives it its distinctive silhouette, is its separate services tower joined to the main tower by bridge-like walkways. These walkways rest on neoprene which both insulates for sound and allows several inches of movement between the towers. The service tower houses two lifts, the boilers and other services, and is intended to minimise disturbance to inhabitants from the noise from lift motors, and so on. The massive scale of this bush-hammered concrete tower, with its four chimneys, and pattern of what from a distance look like arrow-slits, give this the impression of being a modernist fortress, an effect heightened by the drawbridge-like entrance to the building. The boiler tower overhang could be a modern allusion to the castle parapets designed for pouring boiling oil onto anyone laying siege below. The design even incorporates modernist gargoyle-equivalents. The overall effect, particularly when approaching the building at night – when it is lit from above – is dramatic and uncompromising. Its aesthetic appeal from outside is that of the sublime rather than the beautiful. There is nothing quaint or homely about the exterior. James Dunnett's description of Goldfinger's tower blocks pinpoints this aspect of the buildings:

9.2
Balfron Tower

> It is as though Goldfinger, from among the Functionalist totems, had chosen as a source of inspiration the artefacts of war. The sheer concrete walls of the circulation towers are pierced only by slits; cascading down the façade like rain, they impart a delicate sense of terror. At the summit of the tower the boiler house is cantilevered far out; with its ribbon glazing and surmounted by flues it evokes the bridge of a warship. At night the estate is illuminated by the merciless beam of powerful arclights mounted on the summit of the slab.[7]

Not all external features of the tower allude to martial architecture: a more humane feature is the 'annotation' of the various levels. Goldfinger believed that there was a limit to how many floors of a building someone could take in with their eye. To facilitate perception of the building, he recessed some floors, providing surface variety that allows anyone approaching Balfron to take in, for example, where the twelfth floor begins. Without this differentiation of the surface, the block would be a sheer cliff of concrete and windows.

At midday on 7 June 1967, a symbolic final skip of concrete was slowly hoisted to the roof of Balfron, the crane hook returning to the ground with a barrel of beer. This was the signal for the workmen to retire to the canteen for celebratory beer and sandwiches, and for the invited guests to enter the marquee for a cold buffet lunch. Ernö's vision of social housing had at last been transformed from idea into hard fact. With the opening of the building in late February of 1968, Ernö could now prove to his critics that tall social housing was the way forward.

Ernö grasped the opportunity to make a public commitment to the virtues of high-rise living. The building might look foreboding from the outside but, as he hoped to demonstrate, that was completely compatible with well-planned living spaces, with stunning views across London, daylight, heating and all the prerequisites for twentieth-century city living. In what even his critics conceded was at the very least an inspired publicity stunt, he and Ursula lived for two months in flat 130 on the twenty-sixth floor from February 1968, paying the full unsubsidised rent of £11.10s (compared with the subsidised rent of £4.15s.6d that council tenants would pay for the same flat). This resulted in coverage by the national press, television and radio, almost all of it favourable. Ernö even received fanmail, so unusual was it for an architect to inhabit the building he had designed, particularly when the building was intended as social housing and built on a tight budget. Ernö, Ursula and various members of the GLC posed for photographers on their balcony overlooking the Thames; television and radio interviewers made appointments to visit. But the Goldfingers' stay was more than just publicity and a series of photo-opportunities. It was completely consistent with his view of the art of architecture that Ernö should want to experience the enclosed space he had created from the inside. He had also often declared that he built homes he would himself be happy to live in. He recognised the extent to which his designs would shape people's lives and that this brought with it responsibilities:

> Families will spend most of their lives in the flats I design. I must do everything possible to iron out problems.[8]

He was also keen to answer critics of high-rise living, many of whom had never tried it and so in one sense didn't know what they were talking about. He would be able to give a far more informed opinion of the benefits and problems when he had experienced them himself. Balfron was planned as the first of many high-rises that he would design, and he wanted to benefit from this opportunity to learn about what worked and what needed further thought:

> I want to experience, at first hand, the size of the rooms, the amenities provided, the time it takes to obtain a lift, the amount of wind whirling around the tower and any problems which might arise from my designs so that I can correct them in the future.[9]

9.3
Ernö interviewed while living in Balfron Tower

This quite reasonable strategy stirred one reader to write to the letters page of the *Guardian*. It wasn't that he thought an empirical approach wrong, it was just that he thought Goldfinger naive in believing that he could achieve his aim in so short a stay:

> Whom is he trying to fool – himself or us? Does he really think anything of sociological value can be gained in a few weeks? It would take an energetic child that time to get over the novelty of looking down on the world from 200 feet up before he realised that he would be physically separated from it.
>
> Does the GLC really have to build this block to find out how long a person will wait for a lift, the effects of the wind, or the layout of the rooms? I do not think so.[10]

This angry letter-writer went on to suggest that it would be more effective to ask residents of existing high-rise blocks what their lives are like:

> Does Mr Goldfinger really think that his perception of living is so much finer that a few weeks for him can sum up a lifetime for others?[11]

Ernö nearly always replied to letters whether sent privately or published in newspapers and journals. In this case he made it very clear that architects *did* need to have a finer perception of living than other people:

> May I assure Mr Alan K. Fox that I do not intend to fool him and his friends, the public at large or myself. I simply try to check, pragmatically, if the solution of my brief has, in fact, been successful. The architect's job is to implement the sociologist's brief. He builds the houses in which not one but several generations of people will spend a lifetime. He obviously has to have 'a perception of living' equal to his job.
>
> As to Mr Fox's question if the GLC has 'to build . . . to find out about wind, layout etc.' – this is simply putting the cart before the horse. His remarks about the power of perception of children are very unjust to children. To reassure himself, he should talk to the people who live in dwellings I have designed and not just theorise in vacuo.[12]

In fact Ernö's empiricism paid off, both as promotion for high-rise living and as experimental testing of his design. One of the more frustrating features of Balfron, and not one that could easily be remedied within that building, was that there were only two lifts. This was scarcely adequate in normal circumstances, but whenever anyone was moving into or out of the block, needing to take furniture and other belongings up or down, this resulted in long delays for anyone leaving or returning to their flat. Despite the financial implications, Ernö quickly recognised this and made sure that three lifts were provided when he came to design Balfron's sister block, Trellick Tower.[13] In a study based on nearly one thousand interviews with tenants of 168 multi-storey blocks, problems with lifts emerged as the commonest source of dissatisfaction.[14] When designing to a tight budget there is no simple solution to this potentially frustrating aspect of high-rise living. Goldfinger also adapted window fittings as a result of discovering that the ones he used on the upper levels of Balfron made trumpeting noises in high winds. A further discovery was the inadequacy of some of the heating vents. Some shortcomings, however, Ernö was not responsible for, and was powerless to alter. The council only provided door knockers, and as a result many new tenants put in their own doorbells, spoiling the clean lines of their entrance halls with botched DIY wiring. Most of the complaints in the first weeks stemmed directly from the council's oversight in not providing any information about how the heating and hot water system worked, or advice about how best to clean the windows.

For the Goldfingers there was no question of simply living in the building and observing its functioning in a non-interactive way. They had a mission to facilitate the social intermingling of the tenants, 'my tenants' as Goldfinger grandly referred to them, though the phrase carried with it not just an arrogance (they were after all the GLC's tenants), but also connotations of fatherly concern. This was social housing, not just housing. Goldfinger was well aware that for this project to work effectively, the people living within it had to relate appropriately to each other:

> The success of any scheme depends on the human factor – the relationships of people to each other and the frame of their daily life which the building provides.[15]

The building was the shell within which these relationships evolved, though obviously its design and upkeep could facilitate or hinder their interactions.

In the case of Balfron, many of the tenants already knew each other because most of them had been rehoused street by street from the surrounding neighbourhood. Of the first 160 families housed in Balfron, only two were from outside Tower Hamlets. Wherever possible, former neighbours were rehoused in flats sharing a common access gallery.[16] The Goldfingers engaged in some gentle and well-lubricated social engineering by organising a series of parties. Floor by floor they invited the tenants up to their flat for champagne (a second fridge had to be installed to keep supplies well-chilled) and a chance to meet their neighbours as well as the architect. After a string of these parties, Ernö – who was never a heavy drinker – began to feel the effects.

Despite the parties, and the transferred communities, some locals believed that council blocks like Balfron were destroying the traditional East End way of life. How could the community spirit flourish when the sense of neighbourhood that streets encouraged was replaced with the apparent anonymity of high-rise living? Goldfinger, predictably, had a robust response:

> I have created here nine separate streets, on nine different levels, all with their own rows of front doors. The people living here can sit on their doorsteps and chat to the people next door if they want to. A community spirit is still possible even in these tall blocks, and any criticism that it isn't is just rubbish.[17]

This optimism about streets in the sky did not prove entirely justified. And if he'd wanted people to sit on doorsteps, he should have provided the steps. Goldfinger's design is far superior to many others in organising access to flats around a limited number of 'streets' – nine for the twenty-six floors, thus giving the 'streets' their own identity, and a higher chance of meeting one's neighbours. But the long corridors, despite their spectacular views, did not encourage the sorts of interactions typical of an East End street. Perhaps inadvertently, the poor lift provision may have done as much to facilitate interaction as the corridor/street idea, with tenants talking to each other as they waited for a lift to arrive.

The Goldfingers enjoyed living in Balfron, with its spectacular sunsets and views over the Thames. Ursula kept detailed notes on such matters as how long it took her to clean the windows, conversations in the lifts, tenants' comments to her about their apartments, little boys knocking on the door to get the Goldfingers' autographs, and so on. She even suggested that East India Dock might be turned into a boating club with a swimming pool at one end, so that the older youths living in the estate would have more social facilities. This, she thought, should be run with the minimum of adult interference, and avoid the problems caused by 'the old sourpusses that one sees in control at GLC swimming pools who mostly hate the young'.[18]

The Goldfingers' genuine desire for the project to be a success, together with their approachability, were greatly appreciated. Those who met Ernö did not doubt his sincerity: 'he was really considerate' one declared, 'He kept coming back after he had left to see how we were getting on.'[19] Ursula transcribed into her notebook how another woman expressed her enthusiasm: 'Mrs Goldfinger you should stay longer! You are ACCEPTED! I know all the tenants and I'm telling the truth. You are ACCEPTED!'[20] Ursula would chat to neighbours in the lifts about their new homes or visit them, giving them the chance to point to flaws in the design of the buildings. She never heard anybody express the slightest regret about having left their old East End terraced houses, though they did have worries about the difficulty of cleaning windows, draughts, heating services not working properly, and the trumpeting noises in high winds. Many of the tenants, though, were exuberant about their new homes: 'I wouldn't change it for Buckingham Palace' one declared.

Shortly after the Goldfingers had moved back to Hampstead, early in the morning of 16 May 1968, the Ronan Point disaster wiped out most of the positive publicity for high-rise living that they had generated. At 5.50 a.m. Miss Ivy Lodge, who lived on the eighteenth floor of the Ronan Point tower block in Canning Town, got up and put on a kettle to make her early morning tea. This innocent action triggered a small gas explosion that ended up destroying much of the 23-storey block, and resulted in the deaths of five people and millions of pounds worth of damage. The block had been built from prefabricated concrete units, using the so-called 'industrial method' by Taylor Woodrow-Anglian. The construction method used prefabricated concrete pieces slotted together; the design of the building had resulted in stresses on relatively weak sections of the block so that a small jolt to the structure could topple the entire building. Wide press reporting of the disaster and its aftermath helped to turn the public further against architects who advocated streets in the sky. It wasn't just the social dislocation of buildings upwards that was worrying; now there were fears for safety.

Ernö, who went to examine the building himself and took his own photographs, was convinced that the Ronan Point's frailty stemmed from its method of construction: 'I do not hold with any heavy prefabricated system. Poured concrete is three times better,' he declared.[21] The clear subtext here is that his own buildings were far less vulnerable to this sort of accident. The subsequent investigation showed that he was right, in as much as the building's engineer was to blame for the block's weaknesses. Despite the explanation of how Ronan Point came to be so fragile, and the obvious success of high-rise living in cities in the United States, many Londoners had had their worst fears confirmed about the dangers of tower blocks. Public opinion was turning away from the high-rise as a solution for the problem of creating high-quality housing at a low price.

Meanwhile, Goldfinger had the opportunity to implement what he had learnt from building Balfron. In April 1966, he was given the brief to build what became the Cheltenham Estate in Kensal, north London.[22] This, like the Brownfield Estate, was a major GLC investment in social housing, designed as a combination of high- and low-rise buildings, together with shops, nursery and other amenities. The site close to the elevated section of the A40 coming into

9.4
Ernö's own photograph of the Ronan Point disaster

London, and to the rail lines into Paddington Station, was part of an eleven-acre site earmarked for redevelopment between Bosworth Road and the Great Western Road adjoining the Grand Union canal. Four acres of this were eventually given over to what is now known as 'Meanwhile Community Gardens'.

Much of the site had been occupied by slum housing that had been declared unfit for human habitation. Here again was a chance for him to have a profound effect on the quality of life of a large number of people. His solution was to create the thirty-one storey block Trellick Tower – four storeys taller than Balfron, linked to a seven-storey block, known as 'Block B'. Ernö always maintained that Le Corbusier had made a mistake in locating the shops

9.5
Trellick Tower, drawing

in his Marseilles Unité d'Habitation half way up the building since not everyone would normally pass through that level with the result that some tenants would have to make a special journey up the building. Consequently he located his shops at street level as part of Block B.

Trellick is at first glance very similar to Balfron Tower – equally uncompromising. As with Balfron, there is a separate service tower joined at every third floor by the walkways that give these buildings their distinctive silhouettes. This produces a number of 'streets' – corridors with in most cases eighteen flats leading off the corridor. The inclusion of a number of larger maisonette flats means that on the twenty-fourth floor there are only thirteen doors in the 'street', and this is also true of floors three and six of Block B. Again like Balfron, the boiler room bulges out from the service tower like some kind of observation post. Having the boilers at such a high level eliminated the need for a 300 foot flue, and allowed each of the four boilers to have its own flue – a cheaper and more efficient solution than having a single long chimney.[23] The main external difference is that the service tower at Trellick has been turned through ninety degrees compared with Balfron, so that when viewed from the Notting Hill side, it presents a slimmer profile than that of Balfron's service tower. The extra four storeys of Trellick make the building more elegant than its chunkier East End sibling. When standing on the flat roof of Trellick Tower it is surprising to see how small an area the main slab of the building occupies – a tribute to the economy of his design and his attention to the ratio of enclosed space to useable space. He gave every flat windows on at least two sides of the building. With smaller flats he achieved this by placing one window next to the front door, overlooking the corridor. Directly opposite this window, there was an external window, thus allowing substantial natural light to penetrate.

The block is remarkable not just for its distinctive silhouette, which has turned it into something of a cultural icon but, more importantly from its tenants' point of view, for its large rooms, excellent soundproofing between residences and stunning views. Goldfinger's characteristic attention to detail is apparent throughout, from the built-in cupboards, through to the neat architrave light switches and windows that swivel into the room to allow for easy and safe cleaning.

When completed in April 1972, Trellick was the tallest social housing in Europe. Its large windows and cedar-clad balconies provided its inhabitants with spectacular views over London and beyond. Many tenants were delighted to move into this clean-lined apartment block, with its generously proportioned rooms filled with light. Lee and Columb Boland, who have lived in Trellick Tower since it was first built, were initially overwhelmed by the scale of Trellick from outside. Once inside, they were enchanted by it:

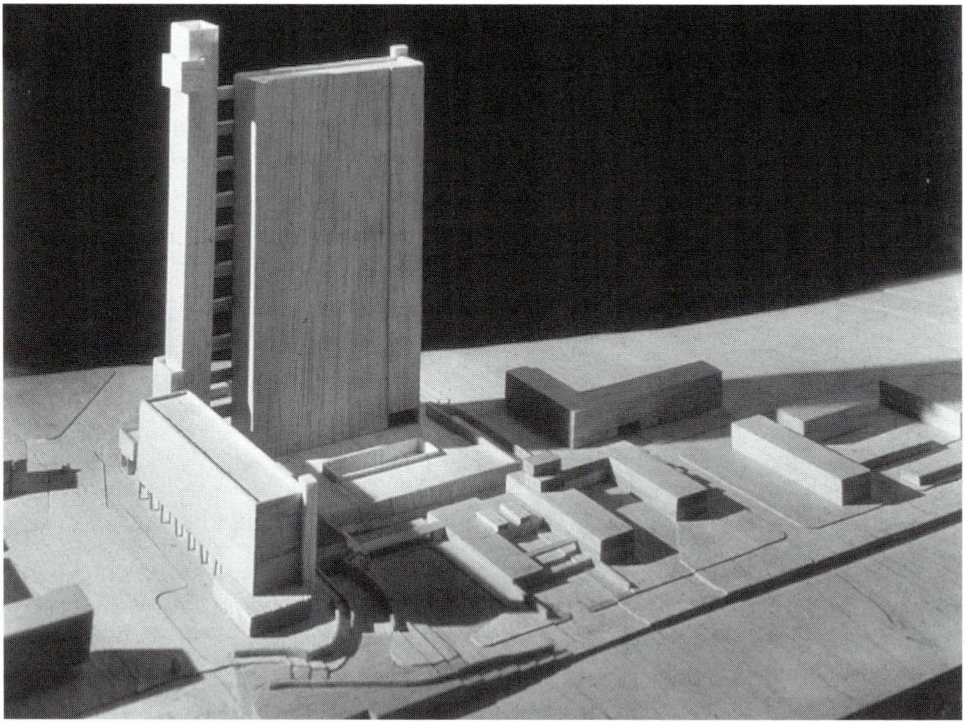

9.6
Model of Trellick Tower

> . . . the building began to cast its spell. The interior was in pristine condition. The marble-clad entrance lobby. The stained glass wall. My flat – truly remarkable, the views breathtaking. No contest. We moved in.[24]

Goldfinger seemed to have thought of everything, providing hobby rooms, a nursery school, and even well-equipped communal drying rooms as a deterrent to residents hanging out their washing on lines on their balconies and thereby spoiling the look of the building. Unfortunately the drying rooms were vandalised before the first tenants moved in, and never functioned effectively. Wall tiles on the different floors were colour coded so that when the lift doors opened tenants could tell instantly whether this was their level, an idea which might have been inspired by the colour coding used on the trains in Budapest. The eighteenth floor, for example, was tiled in yellow. Goldfinger used to joke that the coding would help prevent someone staggering home drunk from getting out at the wrong floor. As with Balfron, there was no sense of his creating the building and simply moving on or abandoning it. He moved his own architectural office into part of Block B at 19 Golborne Road in 1972, and so was a daily visitor until his retirement in 1977. He was often to be seen talking to 'his tenants' or deterring some wayward children from defacing 'his

9.7
Trellick Tower

estate'. Lee Boland shared a lift with him one day, and he asked her how she liked the flat: 'It's fine', she said, 'but there's no broom cupboard.' His response, with a twinkle in his eye, 'You bloody women are never satisfied.' It was only later that she realised that he was the architect of the building. Sadly, during the 1970s Ernö was to witness the social deterioration of the estate, something which affected him deeply. The impact of vandalism and crime on the lives of its tenants lead to Trellick being nicknamed 'The Tower of Terror'.

Those prone to the fallacy of architectural omnipotence blamed Goldfinger for much of what happened in what tenants now refer to as the 'Dark Days' of Trellick. In retrospect, though, it is clear that most of the social problems originated in the council's unwillingness to provide a concierge system or other security measures that would restrict access to the staircases, corridors, lifts, chute rooms and other communal areas. Goldfinger had tried to persuade the GLC that a concierge system was necessary for the building, and had even allowed space for it in his design.[25] But the GLC was not prepared to contemplate this.

The cost of allowing free access to the building soon became apparent. Just before Christmas in 1972, vandals opened a fire hydrant on the twelfth-floor landing, releasing many thousands of gallons of water into the lift shafts. This resulted in a power failure that left the whole block without the basic facilities of water, heat and electrical power over the holiday period. As Columb Boland put it, 'This was the Christmas from Hell for those who can remember it.'[26] Similar, though less severe, incidents of vandalism to water hydrants had occurred at least five time before this catastrophe. The council nevertheless had failed to take any preventative measures. The risk of recurrence was easily solved by locking hydrants and giving keys to the fire brigade and caretaker.

More personally threatening than vandalism, though, was the risk of violence in the lifts, chute rooms, staircases and corridors. There were several vicious sexual attacks in the building. With free access day and night, Trellick Tower became a centre for drug-dealing, drug-taking and prostitution. It was also a favourite shelter for those sleeping rough. Goldfinger had thoughtfully devised a heating system that kept the corridors warm, but that only made them more attractive for the homeless. Lee Boland recalls stepping over a man asleep in the chute room one winter morning as she attempted to take out her rubbish. She hadn't the heart to call the police because it was so cold,[27] but in many circumstances encounters with drunk or drugged rough sleepers could be a threatening and dangerous aspect of life in Trellick. Muggings were common and fear of violence was disruptive and debilitating in itself. Some older tenants felt that they had become prisoners in their own flats. There were several spates of break-ins, some of the culprits were tenants of the building itself, while others came in from outside. As Trellick's reputation spread, the more articulate council tenants would argue their way out of getting located there. It seemed to those who remained in Trellick that there was a deliberate policy of placing large numbers of 'problem families' in the building: drug addicts, alcoholics and people with severe psychiatric problems.

Opposition to tower block living in the 1960s and 70s did not just stem from concerns over safety. As services in tower blocks and council estates began to fail, largely through poor maintenance and inadequate funding, and little was done to turn the open spaces surrounding them into usable amenities for local inhabitants, opposition focused on the alleged soullessness of the concrete jungle, and on the breaking up of working-class communities which had centred on street life. The buildings themselves were scapegoated as the cause of anti-social behaviour. George Tremlett, head of GLC housing policy, was typical in his denigration of tower blocks and in his assumption of architects' omnipotence. In a speech at the RIBA's annual meeting in Liverpool in 1978, he spoke of 80,000 Londoners trapped in 'misery homes', and laid the blame with architects:

> The architects design them, and their basements have become haunts for thieves, drunks and dossers. If you doubt it, tiptoe through the mess beneath Balfron Towers and see the legacy your profession has left.[28]

The underground car parks and storage areas in both Balfron and Trellick conspicuously failed to meet the needs of the tenants, who became afraid to use them. Goldfinger was probably in this respect overly optimistic about their security. But at least some of the responsibility for this was the council's apparent belief that large-scale housing projects like this would more or less run themselves without the need for special security arrangements. Tremlett, however, went on to link the social deterioration in tower blocks with the whole concept of high-rise living. Here he was on far shakier ground: 'Has it never occurred to you' he asked his audience of architects, 'how miserable it must be never to hear the song of a bird or the waving of leaves on a tree because there, twenty storeys high, no birds sing and no trees reach?'[29] First, Tremlett seems not to have noticed that many inhabitants of any tower block will, necessarily, live well below the twentieth floor. But even at the highest levels, there is no shortage of birdlife. Herons regularly fly from the Thames close by the top floors of Balfron, pigeons visit balconies, and kestrels nest on the service tower of Trellick. Unlike the inhabitants of small-windowed Victorian terraces, those who live high up in tower blocks get spectacular and inspirational views over the city, and witness the beauty of sunsets that are invisible to those who live at street level. A survey conducted in 1986 showed that eighty-six per cent of 450 inhabitants on the Cheltenham Estate liked their flats.[30]

Those like Tremlett, who disparaged tower blocks on the grounds that they caused social deterioration, often nurtured a nostalgic vision of Victorian two-up two-down terraced housing that conveniently omitted facts about lack of heating, privacy or adequate sanitation. Much of the talk of lost community spirit was inspired by memories of the special conditions of the Blitz. Most critics also failed to appreciate that some of those being housed in tower blocks were already hardened criminals. Furthermore, as in the case of the Balfron and Trellick towers, the sites for council blocks were usually already areas of social deprivation with high levels of unemployment and relatively high crime rates.

For some conservative critics of tower blocks, architects' utopianism was the major source of misery. Architects were well-meaning meddlers who destroyed people's lives on their drawing boards. Roger Scruton, an outspoken opponent of tower blocks, wrote of:

> the desolation that is felt at the realisation of the maddest of all utopian schemes, the open-planned housing complex, where streets are replaced by empty spaces from which towers arise, towers bearing neither the mark of a communal order, nor any visible record of the individual house, and demonstrating in their every aspect the triumph of that collective individualism from which both community and individual are abolished.[31]

It is ironic that Scruton should have chosen the word 'desolation' to describe, albeit metaphorically, the experience of the tower block dwellers, since whatever else they lacked, access to sunlight and open vistas was not usually missing. Perhaps Scruton has never been inside a tower block. Goldfinger in particular had tested models of both Balfron and Trellick for insolation using his heliometer. Large windows, open spaces and, for those living on the higher floors at least, lack of overshadowing, made tower blocks anything but 'desolated' in the literal sense. The charge was that, in the wake of Le Corbusier and Mies van der Rohe, architects had rejected the accumulated tacit wisdom of generations of tradition in building for a centrally planned modernism that inadvertently neglected the basic necessities of communal human life.

The idea that tower blocks had detrimental effects on their inhabitants was expressed forcefully by Alice Coleman in her book *Utopia on Trial*, although she did not make specific reference to Goldfinger's buildings. Like Scruton she saw modern architecture as the result of idealistic zeal, and lack of attention to the features of traditional housing that promoted good citizenship and community:

> . . . it is the utopian design imposed upon post-war Britain that appears to be the chief factor in many aspects of social decline in new or redeveloped areas.[32]

This utopia, expressed most visibly in the high-rise council housing built in the 1960s and early 70s:

> was conceived in compassion but has been born and bred in authoritarianism, profligacy and frustration. It aimed to liberate people from the slums but has come to represent an even worse form of bondage. It aspired to beautify the urban environment, but has been transmogrified into the epitome of ugliness.[33]

Coleman set out to provide evidence for the destructive power of certain sorts of modern social housing, and to give guidelines for avoiding its worst effects. Like Oscar Newman – whose study of New York housing, *Defensible Space* (1972), provided a model for her work – she identified three main factors which made crime easy and tempting to commit in high-rises:

1 anonymity
2 lack of surveillance
3 alternative escape routes.

Anonymity was supposedly a consequence of living in large impersonal buildings with numerous inhabitants and few occasions for social interaction. Goldfinger had clearly anticipated this, and his inclusion of 'streets' and his conscious attempts to introduce tenants to each other at Balfron testify to the importance of this aspect of his buildings for him. Lack of surveillance was another consequence of high-rise architecture: tower blocks provide corridors, staircases, chute rooms, and so on, which are not overlooked. In a typical street, in contrast, it is hard to act unobserved. Goldfinger's long straight corridors are better than many in this respect in that anyone within the corridor can see anyone else, but there are, nevertheless, numerous hiding places in his blocks, most notably the staircases and chute rooms. Large estates also provide a range of alternative escape routes for anyone committing a crime. Fire regulations obliged Goldfinger to provide alternative exits for tenants, so this was an unavoidable aspect of the design of both Balfron and Trellick.

The combination of these three factors, together with further factors that Coleman identified in the course of her research, produced, she claimed, a greater likelihood of crimes being committed in modern high-rise housing estates than in more traditional low-rise developments:

> Living in a high-rise block does not force all its inhabitants to become criminals, but by creating anonymity, lack of surveillance and escape routes, it puts temptation in their way and makes it probable that some of the weaker brethren will succumb. By the same token it increases the probability that others will be victimised.[34]

Unlike Scruton's claim, Coleman's conclusions were based on substantial empirical research into a range of measures including crime rates, tenants' experiences, and even taking in analysis of the number of faeces (both animal and human) found in public and semi-public areas of buildings. She attempted to eliminate potentially conflating factors such as the fact that some councils have tended to put a number of problem families into high-rise buildings, creating 'sink' estates, the failures of councils to provide adequate caretaking provision, and so on. Even when these factors are allowed for, she claimed, high-rise blocks were the source of many social problems rather than their solution. Absent from her account is discussion of any of the ways in which high-rise living is superior to low-rise. It is as if there were no positive aspect of living in such buildings whatsoever.

Coleman's preferred answer to housing problems was to return to low-rise buildings designed in ways that promoted a sense of pride in one's residence, and included well-placed windows that would allow a clear view of those in public and semi-public areas around the housing. A direct consequence of this, if put into practice, would be a return to the suburban sprawl that Goldfinger railed against in *The County of London Plan Explained*.

Residents of Trellick in its dark ages would no doubt agree with Coleman that the design and running of the building led directly to high levels of crime within it. The interesting question is to what degree crime was a consequence of irreparable aspects of high-rise design for which the architect was ultimately responsible, or the result of other faults. Goldfinger was always adamant that the councils responsible for the security and management of both Balfron and Trellick had shirked their duties. The emergence of Trellick from its dark ages to a position in which the rate of crime is not significantly higher than in other types of social housing is testament to the fact that he was at least partly right.

Most of the subsequent measures taken by residents and the local council to reduce crime in both Balfron and Trellick have been based on addressing one or more of the three factors mentioned above. So, for example, the combination of a concierge system and closed circuit television cameras, by providing surveillance, reduced crime in public areas of the estate. It also restricted exit routes from the main buildings. The institution of a flourishing residents' association in Trellick was significant not just in campaigning for better upkeep, respect for, and surveillance of the building, but also in reducing anonymity for some residents.

While working on large-scale projects in the 1960s, Goldfinger also continued building one-off houses. These include the Player house in Coombe Hill, Surrey, (completed in 1962) the Motz House in Oxford (completed in 1964) and the Perry House in Windlesham (1967), also in Surrey. The Player House was a five-bedroomed house built within the wall of the garden of an old house. Its south side incorporated ten large frameless plate glass sliding windows screened with white Venetian blinds. This was a substantial house, incorporating a double garage. In contrast, the Motz House is far smaller, though more interesting in its structure. Professor Hans Motz, a physicist, and his wife Lotte, an Icelandic scholar, had approached Arne Jacobsen, who was then working on St Catherine's College, as a possible architect for his house,

9.8
The Player House, Coombe Hill, Surrey

but when Jacobsen turned them down, their friends John and Anya Berger had recommended Goldfinger. This two-bedroomed house, built on a very tight budget, combined a mono-pitch roof, reminiscent of Goldfinger's first project at the Outlook, Le Touquet, with a first-level walkway joining two parts of the house, which could be an allusion to the walkways at Balfron and Trellick. Within, the first-floor living room, reached by a spiral staircase, overlooks what was an open meadow, but is now a school playing field. The windows on three sides of this room make it seem much larger than it actually is. The main part of the house should have been a perfect square, but Goldfinger had to modify the designs slightly to cope with the demands on space of a centrally placed boiler for hot water and heating.

The Perry House used timber construction with large windows. This single-floored building snakes over a densely-wooded site. It was his personal favourite among the houses he built. Its wooden construction is reminiscent of Scandinavian design. Despite apparent dissimilarities with Goldfinger's other houses, as James Dunnett has explained, there is a structural continuity:

> The colonnade as finally evolved has a weight and gravity of which timber is rarely thought capable. In a simple way it summarises the central expressive element in Goldfinger's architecture – the structure of post and beam.[35]

9.9
The Motz House, Oxford

The Perry House, with this change of medium for Goldfinger, suggests a new direction that his domestic architecture might have taken had he received further commissions in later years. In 1999 it was listed at Grade II* in recognition of its status as 'an outstanding and rare example of his work'.[36]

Trellick, though, was to be the last of his major projects. In the 1970s, tower blocks were no longer a popular solution for social housing. The combination of the Ronan Point disaster, and conspicuous examples of crime-ridden blocks such as Trellick meant that architects like Goldfinger who still wanted to build upwards were out of favour. At the same time, Ernö's past involvement with large-scale projects in London had brought him into new circles of the establishment. On 13 November 1969, for instance, he lunched with the Queen at Buckingham Palace, sitting next to the philosopher A.J. Ayer. He was charmed when she invited him to see her Canalettos, and returned from the event full of praise for the royal family – a turnaround for a lifelong Marxist and something unimaginable a decade earlier, but he was, perhaps with some justification, hoping for a knighthood. 'They're alright, my dear' he told Iris Strachan.[37] Five years later Ernö, Ursula and their daughter Liz attended a garden party at Buckingham Palace. But Ernö never received a knighthood, or indeed an OBE. In 1975, Ernö was elected as a Royal Academician, an honour that he appreciated, not least for the parking opportunities it gave him in central London. Some of his friends suspected that he was on the brink of becoming a Tory in later life, though he still openly

9.10
The Perry House, Windlesham, Surrey

espoused a Marxist account of history. Others referred to him as a 'Gucci Socialist', though probably not to his face.

If at times his political stance appeared to have mellowed, in his later years Ernö maintained his unwavering enthusiasm for modern design and particularly for his own buildings. He was generous in showing anyone interested in architecture around his home, though young female students were usually advised to bring a chaperone. One day he phoned up his former employee and friend John Winter asking him to come over to Willow Road immediately to look at a problem he had with the house. Winter was extremely busy at the time, and reluctant to come, but Goldfinger insisted. On arrival, he showed Winter up to the flat roof. Winter examined it closely but could find nothing wrong. When he eventually descended to tell Ernö this,

Ernö's response was 'Of course you couldn't!' When Winter enquired why, in that case Ernö had dragged him over to Hampstead, his reply was 'I've been reading in the architectural journals that flat roofs don't work!'[38]

Convinced of his architectural importance, and with no large-scale projects in prospect, Goldfinger began the process of transferring most of his drawings, models and paperwork to the Royal Institute of British Architects, where it currently forms one of their largest collections associated with an individual architect. In later years he and Ursula would make regular visits to help sort the mass of plans and models, sometimes adding his signature to an unsigned sketch or drawing.

9.11
Ernö and Ursula on the Willow Road balcony

In 1982, five years after his retirement, he celebrated his eightieth birthday at the RIBA, surrounded by friends, family and colleagues. Among them was the photographer Kertész whom he'd known since the 1920s, and who took photographs of the occasion. On an earlier visit to Willow Road in 1980, Kertész had taken a photograph of Ernö's shadow cast above the mantelpiece on which is propped Goldfinger's print of Kertész's famous photograph of Mondrian's glasses and pipe. The shadow on the wall was perhaps a recognition that neither of these old friends was immortal. The Architectural Association exhibition of his work in 1983, co-ordinated by James Dunnett, indicated a resurgence of his reputation after the vilification of tower blocks in the 1970s. But this recognition came rather later in his life than he would have liked.

In the mid-1980s, Ernö was diagnosed with pancreatic cancer. His attitude to his condition and to death generally was stoical. It is summed up in a comment he made in a letter on hearing of his brother Paul's death:

> Well, as you know, we are all born with a deadly disease called 'life' and are condemned from the start of this adventure.[39]

He concealed the severity of his illness from his children, explaining away short stays in the Royal Free Hospital – five minutes walk from Willow Road

9.12
'My friend Ernö', 1980
Photo André Kertész
© Ministère de la Culture/France

– as to investigate some pimples on his back. As his health declined, he was nursed at home, with family and friends visiting regularly. In the later stages, when the cancer was particularly painful, he was heavily sedated with morphine. Offered the chance of a luxurious room in a private hospital, he flatly refused on political grounds. To the last he was committed to the welfare state and opposed to private health care – in this respect he had not given up his socialist ideals.[40] He died in his bedroom in Willow Road, on 15 November 1987. He was eighty-five and had lived for nearly fifty years in the house that he had built for his family. His body was cremated at a small private secular service in Golders Green crematorium. He has no memorial plaque or gravestone.

Notes

1 Described by Jacob Blacker on F8948.

2 Described by John Winter at the Centenary Conference, Architectural Association, London, 28/9/02.

3 Ernö Goldfinger, letter to the *Guardian*, 21/2/68, in GolEr 393/12.

4 Both quotations from 'The Skyscrapers Over London', *Sunday Times*, 10/7/1960, in GolEr 390/1.

5 Quoted in Tom Pocock, 'Escape to Hampstead Part ll', *Evening Standard*, 21/4/1964, in GolEr 390/1.

6 GLC Press Release no. 82, 12/2/68, in GolEr 171.

7 James Dunnett, 'A Terrible Beauty . . .' in James Dunnett and Gavin Stamp (eds), *Ernö Goldfinger: Works 1*, London: Architectural Association, 1983 p.7.

8 Ernö Goldfinger, quoted in the *Daily Express*, 23/2/68, in GolEr 390/1.

9 Quoted in Leonard Vigors, 'Room at the Top for Top-Job Goldfinger', *The Evening News*, 13/2/68.

10 Alan K. Fox, letter to the *Guardian*, 17/2/68, in GolEr 391/1.

11 Alan K. Fox, letter to the *Guardian*, 17/2/68, in GolEr 391/1.

12 Ernö Goldfinger, letter to the *Guardian*, 21/2/68, in GolEr 391/1.

13 See 'Sampling his Handiwork', *The Times*, 25/3/68, in GolEr 391/1.

14 Research by Pearl Jephcott and Hilary Robinson published as *Homes in High Flats*, 1971 cited by Alice Coleman 1990, p.11.

15 Ernö Goldfinger, 'Balfron Tower', *East London Papers*, vol. 12, no.1, summer 1969, p.37.

16 See Ernö Goldfinger, 'Balfron Tower', *East London Papers*, vol. 12, no.1, summer 1969, pp.33–42.

17 Ernö Goldfinger, quoted in *East London Advertiser*, 1/3/68, in GolEr 391/1.

18 Ursula Goldfinger in her notebook, March 1968, in GolEr170/7.

19 Mrs Peter Wallis, reported in 'Heady Joys of Life in a Tower Block', *Evening Standard*, 14/7/78, in GolEr 394/23.

20 Notebook, in GolEr 170/7.

21 Ernö Goldfinger, quoted in *Sydenham Gazette*, 23/5/68, in GolEr 391/1.

22 This was first known as the Edenham Estate, subsequently renamed the Cheltenham Estate by the GLC.

23 This is Goldfinger's explanation in a letter to Tony Freeman on the effect of services on architectural design, 30/12/74, in GoLEr 270/1.

24 Lee and Columb Boland, 'Ernö Goldfinger's Trellick Tower and its Environs', 1999, unpublished manuscript, introduction.

25 Recalled by James Dunnett, personal correspondence, 25/4/03.

26 Lee and Columb Boland, 'Ernö Goldfinger's Trellick Tower and its Environs', 1999, unpublished manuscript, p.14.

27 Recounted in conversation, Trellick Tower, 9/12/02.

28 Quoted in *Evening Standard*, 14/7/78, in GolEr 394/23.

29 Quoted in *Evening Standard*, 14/7/78, in GolEr 394/23.

30 Survey results quoted in 'The Joys of Living in a Tower Block', *The Times*, 3/11/93.

31 Roger Scruton, *Utopia on Trial: Vision and Reality in Planned Housing*, revised edn, London: Hilary Shipman, 1979, p.250.

32 Alice Coleman, 1990, p.173.

33 Coleman, 1990, p.182.

34 Coleman, 1990, p.22. I hope that 'bretheren' is not being used in a racist way in this quotation. I suspect that it is just an innocent and unfortunate choice of words on Coleman's part.

35 James Dunnett, in Dunnett and Stamp, p.84.

36 DCMS Press Release, 3/99, 11 January 1999. The quotation is from Alan Howarth, Arts Minister.

37 Iris Strachan, interviewed for National Sound Archive Architects' Lives, F8943.

38 John Winter at Ernö Goldfinger Centenary Conference, Architectural Association, 27/9/02.

39 Letter to Claude Bernheim in response to being told of his brother Paul's death, 17 April 1970, in GolEr 267/2. The notion that death is a disease was famously alluded to in Socrates' last words when he called for a sacrifice to Asclepius before drinking hemlock.

40 Mentioned by Mary Banham in NSA Architects' Lives, F11239A.

Chapter 10

Afterlife

In a hundred years no one will know whether I was a good architect or not because all my buildings will have been destroyed.

At his eightieth birthday celebrations, Ernö had remarked that his buildings would last longer than he was likely to, and that it would be for the next generation to look after them. This is not quite what has happened. Some of his buildings have been completely destroyed. These include the *Daily Worker* and Communist Party buildings and, sadly, two major buildings, the Player House at Coombe Hill in Surrey and the Odeon cinema at Elephant and Castle.

The bulldozing of Goldfinger's cinema at Elephant and Castle, less than a year after his death, had symbolic signficance. It was a powerful expression of a rejection of the doctrines of Perret and the aesthetics of undisguised concrete building. The building's demise was almost inevitable since the shuttered concrete exterior relied on an aesthetic that was not widely shared. In 1988 (the year after Goldfinger's death) the property developers Imry hung a 'closed for refurbishment' sign outside the cinema, despite there being no planning application for this. Southwark Council wanted to issue a Building Preservation Notice so that the building might remain intact long enough for the listing committee to meet and decide whether or not to save it for posterity. But the council, fearing the financial penalty of having to compensate the developers for incurred costs if they issued a notice and no listing of the building resulted, a cost which they would have had to bear personally, backed down.

A photographer from English Heritage perhaps unwittingly triggered Imry's fears that the building was about to be listed. One Friday afternoon, only days after the cinema had officially closed, and before any listing could take place, Imry 'Let a little light into the building' as one of its demolishers put it.[1] Andrew Saint, a research historian for English Heritage, described the building as 'one of the most important, if not the most important, of freestanding post-war cinemas'.[2] In contrast Bryan Martin, spokesman for Imry, revealed his dislike for it: 'I find this mania for buildings nobody wants standing round beyond my understanding', he declared, 'it could have been designed by the people who designed Hitler's concrete bunker'.[3] This last comment is revealing. Even in the late years of the twentieth century, for many in Britain the connotations of exposed concrete were of the bunker, the pillbox, the tank trap and the gun implacement, if not the grimy multi-storey car park and the graffiti-covered walkways of poorly-constructed shopping centres and tenement blocks. Such associations have coloured the public reception of numerous modernist buildings. For those who see concrete in this light, there is little hope of understanding Goldfinger's enthusiasm for the medium, his pleasure in juxtaposing different textures and patterns of bush-hammering. For such people the use of exposed concrete may be a temporary if oppressive necessity, like breeze blocks, but ultimately something to be eradicated wherever possible.

For purists, though, the complete destruction of the building may have been a better fate than its partial reconstruction – the sort of distortion by modification reserved for the rest of Goldfinger's Elephant and Castle complex. Much of the exterior of Alexander Fleming House has been so disguised that it is scarcely recognisable as a Goldfinger design. Goldfinger's friend the architect James Cadbury-Brown indicated that euthanasia might be the best fate for such buildings: 'There are times when it would be better to throw them away entirely rather than deform them like Chinese women's feet.'[4]

In some architects' eyes the fate of Alexander Fleming House, parts of which have been converted into apartments, is a straightforward insult to Goldfinger's architectural intelligence. James Dunnett, who has championed Goldfinger's architecture and done more than anyone else to preserve his reputation, has, for example, described the conversions as 'ham-fisted'.[5] Yet, on the other side, Virginia Bottomley as junior environment minister, rejected pleas that the building should be listed:

> We are listing only the most outstanding modern buildings where there is a broad consensus about their quality. Few think that Alexander Fleming House has proved a satisfactory building either to look at or to work in.

Certainly Alexander Fleming House is not a popular building, except among architects. Brian Sewell, writing in the *Evening Standard* in 1993 under the heading 'Let's Kill Off Ernö's Sad Eyesore', savaged the buildings:

> Of all the ugly office blocks imposed on post-war London, Alexander Fleming House at the Elephant and Castle has a formi-

> dable claim to be not only the ugliest, but the least suited to its purpose, the most shoddily constructed and the most dilapidated.

For Sewell, Goldfinger's office complex was a monument to architectural folly:

> . . . its fabric embraces the worst possible combination of post-war penny-pinching, post Festival of Britain flimsiness, and post-Corbusier notions that the working classes must live and work in cubic ant heaps.

The fact that English Heritage wanted to preserve such buildings was a mark of the decline of our society:

> A sane and reasonable society would allow the wretched block to be demolished without demur.

There was no reason whatsoever for preserving it:

> As for the perpetual preservation of this particular and particularly misbegotten block, let the panjandrums of English Heritage for once convince us of their sanity and condemn the hideous heap as of not the slightest aesthetic interest or historical significance.[6]

10.1
Dining room, 2 Willow Road

Goldfinger's supporters stressed that the condition of the exterior of the building was good, and that all that was needed was appropriate cleaning. As to the inadequacies of the building as a place to work, most of these stemmed directly from the low budget within which Goldfinger had to build. In the *Architects Journal*, Astragal was typical in praising the building's exterior:

> There are very, very few buildings built in this country since the Second World War that can claim to be architecture in the highest formal sense – a composition of rhythm, proportion and texture with a strength of commitment that amounts to a work of art: Ernö Goldfinger's Alexander Fleming House at the Elephant and Castle, London, is one. Its value is irrespective of period. With its bays and balconies and vibrant surface, it forcibly illustrates Goldfinger's feeling that 'when contemplating a façade you look at the "rhythmically modulated" membrane of the enclosure.'[7]

This echoed Philip Johnson's declaration spurred by the possibility that the building would be re-clad:

> Britain has all too few [Modern Movement] monuments of which Alexander Fleming House is a great example. It would be a cultural

10.2
The studio with Ernö's desk, 2 Willow Road

> mistake of the first order to allow this building to be altered. I am sure the architects of America would join me in urging a stop to this desecration.[8]

The building escaped total re-cladding, but its value as architectural geometry has been seriously compromised. This is probably no longer the building by which Goldfinger would have wanted to be judged by posterity.

Yet Goldfinger has achieved posthumous recognition as well as insult. In some respects his reputation is growing. On 22 December 1998, at the request of English Heritage, Trellick Tower was listed as a ll* building. This has ensured it a place on the London skyline. Its silhouette, though, is not as Goldfinger built it, since the GLC removed the parapet cornice at the top of the main block for safety reasons and never replaced it. There are plans to replace it in the near future, though, sadly, bids to the National Lottery to renovate both Balfron and Trellick failed. The insitution of a concierge system in 1987 – something Goldfinger himself always advocated, and which was refused by the GLC on the spurious grounds that it smacked of 'Big Brother' – has reduced crime within the building, as has the twenty-four hour security arrangements. The GLC had also smashed the coloured glass from the decorative window in the marble-clad entrance lobby of the building, on the grounds that it did not let in enough light. Thanks to the then chair of the Trellick Tower Resident's Association, Lee Boland, the coloured glass was eventually reinstated.

In the 1970s, when it was still known as 'The Tower of Terror', Trellick was reputed to be the model for J. G. Ballard's dystopian novel, *High-Rise* (1975). Since the 1990s, however, it has been portrayed as a design icon, a London landmark and a highly desirable place to live. During Architecture Week in London, hundreds of eager visitors queue to visit this landmark building. It features in songs by Blur and a photograph by Nick Waplington that was subsequently used as a book cover for Nick Cohn's *Yes We Have No*. It has been the backdrop for numerous television serials, advertisements, and several pop videos. The radiused corners were even an influence on the furniture designers Barber Osgerby, former tenants of the building, whose loop table echoes this form. It has become the best-known tower block in Britain, and a symbol of urban living and Notting Hill chic.

This new media image is in some ways misleading. Readers of the colour supplements and style magazines could well believe that Trellick is a trendy private sector block of flats, when in fact it still is ninety per cent social housing run by the Royal Borough of Kensington and Chelsea council. The right-to-buy policies instigated in the Thatcher years have allowed some tenants to purchase their flats, and when these have been sold on recently they have been advertised for as much as £250,000 for a two-bedroomed flat,

10.3
Works by Eduardo Paolozzi, Henry Moore and Man Ray, among others, living room, 2 Willow Road

and £325,000 for a three-bedroomed one.[9] Listing, improved security and partial yuppification provide no guarantee that Trellick's structure will be preserved appropriately. James Dunnett has described it recently as: 'a mismanaged, underfunded and progressively ruined building'.[10] Yet there are grounds for cautious optimism that many of the more obvious mistakes of management and upkeep will be avoided and even reversed.

Goldfinger's reputation as a furniture designer is in excellent hands. His work has been collected by the Victoria and Albert museum and detailed research carried out by the curator Rebecca Milner. Ernö's grandson, Nick Goldfinger, is in business in London making superbly-crafted furniture to his grandfather's designs.

If Goldfinger's reputation as an architect must ultimately rest on the preservation of his buildings, he still has some hope of achieving posthumous longevity. In James Dunnett, he has an eloquent, knowledgeable and passionate defender who, through his writing, energy and enthusiasm, has prevented several irreversible alterations being made to major buildings. Furthermore, the National Trust has assured Goldfinger's afterlife by buying his house at Willow Road together with most of its contents, and opening them to the public. If the Trust lives up to its motto of 'Forever, for everyone', then

10.4
Ernö's Study today, Willow Road

his reputation will fare better than that of most of his contemporaries. The Goldfinger family offered the house and most of its contents to the National Trust in lieu of tax, in autumn 1992 following Ursula's death in 1991.[11] The sum needed for the house and contents and endowment fund for future maintenance was £784,000. This was met partly by the National Heritage Memorial Fund, partly from the National Trust's legacy fund, and partly as the result of a public appeal for donations. Buying the house was a daring move for the Trust. This was the first significant modern building in its portfolio, and inevitably caused consternation among the more conservative Trust members. The architectural critic Colin Amery expressed strong reservations about the trust's decision on the BBC's *Late Show*, describing the house as 'a very ordinary brick box with a flat roof' and comparing the dining room to the sort of bleak classroom typical of 1950s primary schools. In the same programme Gavin Stamp, in his role as chair of the Twentieth Century Society, argued the other side, maintaining that the Goldfinger house was a change from the endless Georgian houses that the National Trust usually acquires just to pander to snobbishness.[12] Since opening as a museum, the house has acquired cult status among architecture and design students. It was even used as the location for a photo shoot for a Habitat catalogue in 2000 in which a fictional family, lodger and friends posed on Habitat furniture, including a Robin Day sofa, in place of Ernö's own designs. It is hard to imagine any other National Trust property serving this purpose. The Willow Road house remains the principal modernist building with its contents accessible to the wider public.

Ernö Goldfinger has no grave. His house at Willow Road embodies his ideas and personality and forms a fitting monument to what he valued. His children have ensured his continuing support to young Hungarian architects by setting up a Goldfinger Fellowship which provides them with the opportunity of studying in England.

Goldfinger never achieved the status of Le Corbusier, or Mies van der Rohe, had fewer commissions in later years than he would have liked, and indeed has been in danger of being written out of the history of architecture altogether. Yet, through this own house, and the landmarks of Balfron and Trellick towers, his architecture looks set to exert an influence well into the present century, and probably beyond – the only kind of afterlife an atheist might want.

Shortly after his death, Ursula asked John Winter's wife whether she believed in an afterlife. Her response was: 'Actually, yes I do.' 'I do so hope you are wrong', sighed Ursula, 'Ernö will never forgive me for the handles on his coffin!'.[13]

Notes

1 For details see 'Astragal, *Architects' Journal*, 1900, in RIBA biographical file.
2 Quoted in Deborah Thorp, 'Cinema Rescue Bid Beaten by Speedy Demolition Work', *Building Design*, 19 August 1988.
3 See Thorp, 1988. Also quoted in R. Elwall, *Ernö Goldfinger*, RIBA Drawings Monographs no. 3, London: Academy Editions, p.89.
4 James Cadbury-Brown interviewed for NSA Architects' Lives series, C467/16/06 (F5684).
5 James Dunnett at DOCOMOMO Goldfinger centenary conference, the Architectural Association, London, 28/9/02.
6 Brian Sewell, 'Let's Kill Off Ernö's Sad Eyesore', *Evening Standard*, 20/9/93. Copy in RIBA Goldfinger biographical file.
7 Astragal, *Architects' Journal*, 22/6/88, in RIBA biographical file.
8 Quoted by James Dunnett and Peter Tabori, letter to *The Times*, 30/3/89.
9 These were prices given by Leslie Marsh and Co., estate agents, Ladbroke Grove in 2001 and 2002.
10 DOCOMOMO conference, the Architectural Association, London, 28/9/02.
11 Ursula died on 16/1/91.
12 *Late Show*, video in NSA, no. V1537/03.
13 Recounted by John Winter at DOCOMOMO Goldfinger Centenary conference, the Arrchitectural Association, London, 28/9/02.

Bibliography

Abrams, Joseph, *Les Premières Élèves d'Auguste Perret*, Nancy: École d'Architecture de Nancy, SRA, 1985.

Andrews, Geoff, Fishman, Nina and Morgan, Kevin (eds), *Opening the Books*, London: Pluto Press, 1995.

Benton, Charlotte, *A Different World: Emigré Architects in Britain 1928–1958*, London: RIBA publications, 1995.

Boland, Colomb and Boland, Lee, 'Ernö Goldfinger's Trellick Tower and its Environs', [unpublished manuscript], 1999.

Britton, Karla, *Auguste Perret*, London: Phaidon, 2001.

Bryce, Ivar, *You Only Live Once: Memories of Ian Fleming*, London: Weidenfeld & Nicolson, revised edn, 1984.

Calvocoressi, Richard, *Lee Miller: Portraits from a Life*, London: Thames and Hudson, 2002.

Carter E. J., and Goldfinger, E. *The County of London Plan Explained*, London: Penguin, 1945.

Chadwick, Whitney, *Women Artists and the Surrealist Movement*, London: Thames and Hudson, 1985.

Coe, Peter and Reading, Malcolm, *Lubetkin and Tecton: Architecture and Social Commitment*, London: Arts Council of Great Britain, 1981.

Cohn, Laura, *The Door to a Secret Room: A Portrait of Wells Coates*, Aldershot: Scolar, 1999.

Cogn, Nik, *Yes We Have No*, London: Vintage, 2000.

Coleman, Alice, *Utopia on Trial: Vision and Reality in Planned Housing*, revised edn, London: Hilary Shipman, 1990.

Collings, Jane with the assistance of Andrea Meyer Ludowisz, 'The Ernö Goldfinger Papers: A Descriptive List', unpublished catalogue, the British Architectural Library, Royal Institute of British Architects, 1997.

Collins, Peter, 'Auguste Perret' in Dennis Sharp, *The Rationalists*, London: Architectural Press, 1978, pp.16–25.

Dean, David, *The Thirties: Recalling the English Architectural Scene*, London: Trefoil Books, RIBA drawings series, 1983.

Dunnett, James and Stamp, Gavin, *Ernö Goldfinger: Works 1*, London: Architectural Association, 1983.

Dunnett, James and Hiscock, Nigel, 'To this Measure of Man: Proportional Design in the work of Ernö Goldfinger' in Louise Campbell (ed.), *Twentieth-Century Architecture and its Histories*, London: Society of Architectural Historians of Great Britain, 2000, pp.87–124.

Dunnett, James, 'Conversations with Ernö Goldfinger', [unpublished manuscript].

Elwall, Robert, *Ernö Goldfinger*, RIBA Drawings Monographs no. 3, London: Academy Editions, 1996.

Fleming, Ian, *Goldfinger*, London: Coronet, 1989 [first published 1959].

Ginsburger, Roger, *Junge Französische Architectur*, Verlag 'Meister der Baukunst' Akt.-Ges in Genf, 1930.

Glendinning, Miles and Muthesius, Stefan, *Tower Block: Modern Public Housing in England, Scotland, Wales and Northern Ireland*, New Haven: Yale University Press, 1994.

Gold, John R., *The Experience of Modernism: Modern Architects and the Future City 1928–1953*, London: E & FN Spon, 1997.

Kehoe, Louise, *In This Dark House: A Memoir*, London: Penguin, 1995.

Klüver, Billy and Martin, Julie, *Kiki's Paris: Artists and Lovers 1900–1930*, New York: Harry N. Abrams, 1994.

Le Corbusier, *Essential Le Corbusier L'Esprit Nouveau Articles* [includes *Towards a New Architecture*, trans. by Frederick Etchells; *The City of Tomorrow*, trans. by Frederick Etchells; and *The Decorative Art of Today*, trans. by James Dunnett], Oxford: Architectural Press, 1998.

Lycett, Andrew, *Ian Fleming*, London: Phoenix, 1995.

MacEwen, Malcolm, *The Greening of a Red*, London: Pluto Press, 1991.

Madsen, Axel, *John Huston*, London: Robson Books, 1979.

Manasseh, Leonard and Cuncliffe, Roger, *Office Buildings*, London: B.T. Batsford, 1962.

Máté, Major, *Goldfinger Ernö*, Budapest: Akadémia Kiadó, 1973 [in Hungarian].

Milner, Rebecca, 'Ernö Goldfinger: The Architect as Furniture Designer' in Edwin Heathcote (ed.), *Furniture and Architecture*, London: John Wiley and Sons, 2002, special edition of *Architectural Design*, vol. 72, no. 4, July 2002, pp.7–13.

Morgan, Kevin, 'The Communist Party and the *Daily Worker* 1930–1956' in Andrews, Fishman and Morgan (eds), 1995, *Opening the Books*, London: Pluto Press, pp.142–159.

Mumford, Eric, *The CIAM Discourse on Urbanism, 1928–1960*, Cambridge, Mass.: MIT Press, 2000.

Naylor, Gillian, 'Modernism and Memory: Leaving Traces' in Marius Kwint, Christopher Breward and Jeremy Aynsley (eds), *Material Memories*, Oxford and New York: Berg, 1999, pp.91–106.

Penrose, Antony, *The Lives of Lee Miller*, London: Thames and Hudson, 1985.

Peter, John, *The Oral History of Modern Architecture*, New York: Harry N. Abrams, 1994.

Pezzini, Barbara, 'For an appreciation of art and architecture: The Goldfinger Collection at 2 Willow Road', *Apollo*, vol. CIlll, no. 470, April 2001, pp.55–59.

Pezzini, Barbara, 'Aid to Russia, a wartime modern art exhibition in a modernist setting', *British Art Journal*, forthcoming Spring 2004.

Powers, Alan, *2 Willow Road Hampstead* [pamphlet], London: The National Trust, 1996.

Powers, Alan, *Serge Chermayeff: Designer, Architect, Teacher*, London: RIBA Publications, 2001.

Remy, Michel, *Surrealism in Britain*, Aldershot: Lund Humphries, 2001.

Rogers, Ben, *A.J. Ayer: A Life*, London: Vintage, 1999.

Sharp, Dennis, (ed.), *The Rationalists*, London: Architectural Press, 1978.

Snowman, Daniel, *The Hitler Emigrés: The Cultural Impact on Britain of Refugees from Nazism*, London: Chatto & Windus, 2002.

Stamp, Gavin, 'A Conversation with Ernö Goldfinger', *Thirties Society Journal*, no. 2, 1982.

Trevelyan, Julian, *Indigo Days*, London: Macgibbon and Kee, 1957.

Vellay, Marc and Frampton, Kenneth, *Pierre Charreau*, London: Thames and Hudson, 1985.

Willey, Simon, 'Housework Made Easiwork: Easiwork Limited: The Ideal Modern Kitchen 1919–1939' [unpublished undergraduate thesis], Department of History of Art, Edinburgh University, 1989.

Yorke, F.R.S., *The Modern House in England*, Surrey: The Architectural Press, 2nd edn, 1944.

Ziegler, Philip, *London at War 1939–1945*, London: Pimlico, 2002.

Index

Page references for illustrations are in *italics*; those for notes are followed by n
All buildings and writings are by Goldfinger unless otherwise attributed